Wonder and Ed

On the Educational Importance of Contemplative Wonder

Anders Schinkel

BLOOMSBURY ACADEMIC
LONDON • NEW YORK • OXFORD • NEW DELHI • SYDNEY

BLOOMSBURY ACADEMIC
Bloomsbury Publishing Plc
50 Bedford Square, London, WC1B 3DP, UK
1385 Broadway, New York, NY 10018, USA
29 Earlsfort Terrace, Dublin 2, Ireland

BLOOMSBURY, BLOOMSBURY ACADEMIC and the Diana logo
are trademarks of Bloomsbury Publishing Plc

First published in Great Britain 2021
This paperback edition published in 2022

Series design by Clare Turner

A catalogue record for this book is available from the British Library.

Library of Congress Cataloging-in-Publication Data
Names: Schinkel, Anders, author.
Title: Wonder and education : on the educational importance of contemplative
wonder / Anders Schinkel.
Description: London, UK ; New York, NY : Bloomsbury Academic, 2020. |
Series: Bloomsbury philosophy of education | Includes bibliographical references and index.
Identifiers: LCCN 2020029961 | ISBN 9781350071896 (hardback) | ISBN 9781350071902
(ebook) | ISBN 9781350071919 (epub)
Subjects: LCSH: Education–Aims and objectives. | Wonder (Philosophy) | Experiential
learning. | Education–Moral and ethical aspects. | Education–Political aspects.
Classification: LCC LB41 .S3455 2020 | DDC 370.11/4–dc23
LC record available at https://lccn.loc.gov/2020029961

ISBN: HB: 978-1-3500-7189-6
PB: 978-1-3502-1372-2
ePDF: 978-1-3500-7190-2
eBook: 978-1-3500-7191-9

Series: Bloomsbury Philosophy of Education

Typeset by Integra Software Services Pvt. Ltd.

To find out more about our authors and books visit www.bloomsbury.com
and sign up for our newsletters.

Wonder and Education

Bloomsbury Philosophy of Education

Series Editor: Michael Hand

Bloomsbury Philosophy of Education is an international research series dedicated to the examination of conceptual and normative questions raised by the practice of education. There is a particular focus on philosophical dimensions of current policy debates, though work of a less applied nature will also have a place.

Also available in the series:

Cherishing and the Good Life of Learning, Ruth Cigman

A Critique of Pure Teaching Methods and the Case of Synthetic Phonics, Andrew Davis

Children, Religion and the Ethics of Influence, John Tillson

Every view of things that is not wonderful is false.
CAROLINE WALKER BYNUM[1]

[1] Caroline Walker Bynum, 'Presidential Address: Wonder', *American Historical Review* 102, no. 1 (1997): 1–26 (i.c. 26), doi:10.1086/ahr/102.1.1. Reprinted with permission of Oxford University Press on behalf of the American Historical Association.

Contents

Preface

This book is the fruit of some four years of thinking and reading about wonder, and of course of many more years of experiencing it. As is often the case, thinking began before reading; reading then informed and changed thinking. What increasingly became clear to me as I came across more and more of other people's often excellent writings about wonder is that more or less everything I had thought of had been thought of before by someone – though of course not everything by the same person. That means that, when it comes to wonder, there is little in this book that is original in the ordinary sense of the term; a bit more conventional originality may be found in my 'application' of wonder to education. But actually none of this matters – it was merely to be expected. What does matter, especially in a book about wonder, is whether the writing is original in another, much more important, sense of the word – namely whether I have been able to 'make contact' with the experience of wonder both as a source of inspiration and as the origin of all relevant thinking about wonder. It is easy enough, with any philosophical subject, to get stuck in too soon and start analysing concepts and arguments. What gets forgotten, what recedes out of view, are the experiences that gave rise to the activity of thought in the first place. That is always disastrous, but in the case of wonder – 'the beginning of philosophy' – it would be entirely unforgivable. So I hope that you will find this book original in this sense of the word, and that it will evoke the same originality in you as a reader and, no doubt, a wonderer.

On a more practical note: this book offers a philosophical argument for the educational importance of wonder. It is not intended to be relevant in the educational context of the UK alone, or that of any other specific country. That said, the book is written against the background of 'Western' educational systems, that in many countries have seen similar changes due to developments in educational policy (such as those related to the rise of neoliberalism). It will therefore be particularly relevant in the context of educational systems in which increasing significance is being attributed to standardized tests, particular types of accountability and 'evidence-based' education. That may well cover most education systems in industrialized (or post-industrial) countries in the world.

Acknowledgements

This book has been written as part of a larger (and apart from this book largely empirical) research project, 'Wonder, Education, and Human Flourishing', generously funded by the John Templeton Foundation; I am grateful for their support, in particular for their willingness to fund a project on such a seemingly 'useless' thing as wonder. My first papers, that formed the basis of much of the present book, were written with a Large Grant from the PESGB, for which I would also once more like to express my gratitude.

I wish to thank Michael Hand, series editor of the Bloomsbury Philosophy of Education book series, for inviting me to submit a book proposal (and thereby give me the nudge I needed to write my first book since my dissertation), and Mark Richardson at Bloomsbury for his support for the manuscript. Thanks are also due to Michael Hand and an anonymous reviewer for their reviews of the first version of the manuscript.

I would further like to thank John Wiley & Sons as publisher of *Educational Theory* and Springer Nature as publisher of Marianna Papastephanou, ed., *Philosophical Perspectives on Compulsory Education* (Dordrecht: Springer, 2014) for permission to publish revised versions of (sections of) earlier articles in this book. Oxford University Press kindly gave permission on behalf of the American Historical Association to use the quotation from Caroline Walker Bynum as the motto for this book.

Many people helped me to develop my thinking on wonder and education. I would in particular like to thank Mario di Paolantonio for an inspiring conversation over dinner at the 2016 PESGB Conference in Oxford, Paul Standish for our conversation after a 2016 PESGB London Branch Seminar for which he had kindly invited me, and Michael Hand for his thoughtful and thought-provoking response to my article 'Wonder and moral education'. Thanks are also due to many other people who helped me through conversations or comments on unpublished manuscripts or published articles, or by their support of the whole project. These include audiences at the aforementioned seminar, at the Winterschool of 'De Activiteit' in 2016 and 2018, at the VFVO (Organisation for Philosophy teachers in secondary education) Conference in 2018, at Lumion secondary school in Amsterdam in 2019, at a section meeting in my own department in 2019, at a 2019 seminar at Wageningen University, and at the conference Wonder, Education, and Human Flourishing held in Amsterdam on 5–6 April 2019. They also include students who wrote or are writing their bachelor or master thesis on wonder and education. I will list the many other individuals to whom I wish to owe my gratitude in alphabetical order, hoping against all odds that I will not forget anyone: Lucija Andre, Thirza Brand, Gerdien Bertram-Troost, Evelien Broekhof, Doret de Ruyter (I am going to place her both at the 'd' and the 'r'), Marjolein Dobber, Johannes Drerup, Kevin Flint, Bob Fuller, Yannis Hadzigeorgiou, Finn Hansen, Nick Hebbink, Jonas Hoppe, Mariëtte Huizinga, Linde van Ittersum, Rob Jansen, Femke Keeren, Kristján Kristjánsson, Guido Leerdam, Dick van Lente, Genevieve Lloyd, Ismail Maghnouji, Marleen de Moor, Bert van Oers, Laura D'Olimpio, Jan B.W. Pedersen, Sander van Perlo, Bea Pompert, Willeke Rietdijk, Eline Rusman, Doret de Ruyter, Kees Schinkel, Willem Schinkel, Lewis Stockwell, Judith Suissa, Bob Timmer, Sophia Vasalou, Chiel van der Veen, John White and Lynne Wolbert.

Much gratitude and love go to my wife, Eva Moraal, for conversations about wonder, supporting me when writing was hard work, and especially for being such a wonderful person.

Series Editor's Foreword

Bloomsbury Philosophy of Education is an international research series dedicated to the examination of conceptual and normative questions raised by the practice of education.

Philosophy of education is a branch of philosophy rooted in and attentive to the practical business of educating people. Those working in the field are often based in departments of education rather than departments of philosophy; many have experience of teaching in primary or secondary schools; and all seek to contribute in some way to the improvement of educational interactions, institutions or ideals. Like philosophers of other stripes, philosophers of education are prone to speculative flight, and the altitudes they reach are occasionally dizzying; but their inquiries begin and end on the ground of educational practice, with matters of immediate concern to teachers, parents, administrators and policy-makers.

Two kinds of question are central to the discipline. *Conceptual* questions have to do with the language we use to formulate educational aims and describe educational processes. At least some of the problems we encounter in our efforts to educate arise from conceptual confusion or corruption – from what Wittgenstein called 'the bewitchment of our intelligence by means of language'. Disciplined attention is needed to such specifically educational concepts as learning and teaching, schooling and socialising, training and indoctrinating, but also to the wider conceptual terrain in which educational discourse sits: what is it to be a person, or to have a mind, or to know or think or flourish, or to be rational, intelligent, autonomous or virtuous? *Normative* questions have to do with the justification of educational norms, aims and policies. What educators do is guided and constrained by principles, goals, imperatives and protocols that may or may not be ethically defensible or appropriate to the task in hand. Philosophers of education interrogate the normative infrastructure of educational practice, with a view to exposing its deficiencies and infirmities and drawing up blueprints for its repair or reconstruction. Frequently, of course, the two kinds of question overlap: inappropriate aims sometimes rest on conceptual muddles, and our understanding of educational concepts is liable to distortion by ill-founded pedagogical norms.

In terms of scholarly output, philosophy of education is in rude health. The field supports half a dozen major international journals, numerous learned societies and a busy annual calendar of national and international conferences. At present, however, too little of this scholarly output finds a wider audience, and too few of the important ideas introduced in journal articles are expanded into fully developed theories. The aim of this book series is to identify the best new work in the field and encourage its authors to develop, defend and work out the implications of their ideas, in a way that is accessible to a broad readership.

It is hoped that volumes in the series will be of interest not only to scholars and students of philosophy of education and neighbouring branches of philosophy, but also to the wider community of educational researchers, practitioners and policy-makers. All volumes are written for an international audience: while some authors begin with the way an educational problem has been framed in a particular national context, it is the problem itself, not the local framing of it, on which the ensuing arguments bear.

Michael Hand

Introduction

The Waning of Wonder

According to the cliché young children are naturally prone to wonder, but, unfortunately, our sense of wonder wanes as we grow older.[1] The cliché is not wrong, of course, but not exactly right either – I will return to that.

I suspect it would be hard to find a teacher, at any level of formal education, who does not acknowledge the importance of wonder in education. Whenever I discuss the subject with primary school teachers, for instance, it is immediately clear that they see children's wonder as something that lies, or should lie, at the heart of education. They see it as their task not just to keep alive but also to nurture and stimulate their pupils' sense of wonder. And it was often their own sense of wonder – about the world or some aspect of it, or about children, or both – that led them to become a teacher.

Insofar as the cliché is right, then, something odd is going on. Despite the efforts and intentions of teachers who recognize the value of wonder, children gradually lose (much of) their natural inclination to view things with wonder and to wonder about the why, how, or what of things. Common sense, or common experience, says that it is indeed the case that the older children get, the less likely they are to be excited by things that are not by adult standards extraordinary. Teenagers are not known for being suddenly struck by how

1 Russel Stannard, for instance, writes: 'I use the word "wonder" in the first place to refer to that childlike emotional reaction to something awesome and mysterious – a response that can lead to worship. Secondly, it refers to the way we are led to enquire, to wonder, what it all means. In this connection, one is reminded of the child's endless stream of questions beginning "Why?" Wonder, in the sense of curiosity, is when we move beyond pure emotion to where the intellect is engaged. Both types of wonder become submerged in the early teens'. Russell Stannard, *Science and Wonders: Conversations about Science and Belief* (London/Boston: Faber Books, 1996), 199.

special or remarkable something ordinary like a blackberry (the fruit) or a BlackBerry (the smartphone, incidentally the first thing that comes up when I google 'blackberry') actually is. A sunset would have to be really spectacular to make many a teenager look up from their smartphone. The 'been there, seen that, done that' attitude is much more common among adolescents than among pre-teens, and when I do notice it in a younger child, it always saddens me.

The question is to what extent the waning of wonder is a 'natural' phenomenon, something that will occur no matter what teachers do or what kind of education children enjoy (or are subjected to). There is no extant literature that I am aware of that offers a straightforward answer to this empirical question, but it stands to reason that increasing familiarity with the world will almost inevitably be accompanied by a decreasing inclination to wonder, and that in that sense we have to row against the tide. As the names and explanations of more and more phenomena become known, less and less remains (at first sight at least) to wonder about or to wonder at. A need to deal efficiently with incoming information undoubtedly plays a role here: things that are familiar are only worth pausing at if they are either potentially very good or very bad for us, and for the rest it is only when things are unfamiliar that they arrest our attention. As Alexandra Horowitz writes: 'One way to solve the problem of the "blooming, buzzing confusion" an infant confronts on entering the world is to tune much of it out.'[2] So it seems plausible that there is a 'natural' aspect to the waning of wonder. Horowitz concurs: 'Part of normal human development is learning to notice less than we are able to.'[3]

That does not absolve the education system, however, nor does it mean that teachers can only stand by and watch as children lose (touch with) their sense of wonder. Eleanor Duckworth writes: 'What happens to children's curiosity and resourcefulness later in their childhood? Why do so few continue to have their own wonderful ideas?' She proposes that 'part of the answer is that intellectual breakthroughs come to be less and less valued. Either they are dismissed as being trivial (…) or else they are discouraged as being unacceptable – like discovering how it feels to wear shoes on the wrong feet, or asking questions that are socially embarrassing, or destroying something to see what it's like inside.'[4] These

[2] Alexandra Horowitz, *On Looking: Eleven Walks with Expert Eyes* (New York: Scribner, 2013), 11. The term 'blooming, buzzing confusion' comes from William James.

[3] Ibid., 26.

[4] Eleanor Duckworth, '*The Having of Wonderful Ideas' and Other Essays on Teaching and Learning*, 2nd ed. (New York: Teachers College Press, 1996), 6.

examples are so recognizable that they alone make a good case for a partly social cause for the waning of wonder.[5]

The school system may also play its part here. I remember being in primary school – aged eight or nine or so – and receiving the assignment to collect leaves from trees and stick them in an exercise book. We were supposed to collect leaves from as many different trees as possible, draw their outlines, I think, identify them, and I cannot remember what else. I only remember it because I hated the assignment, thinking it incredibly childish and stupid – picking up leaves and gluing them on paper, come on! Surely there were better things we could do with our time! Reflecting on this now I see it as a clear case of a missed opportunity, on my own part, but especially on the part of the teacher, to engage my sense of wonder. Leaves and trees are wonderful in many ways. Let some light shine through a leaf and its intricate and perfect structure becomes immediately apparent, and all manner of questions readily arise. But for me it was just an assignment with no reason or rhyme to it. Another point about this example is more important, however, one that relates to the system, not the teacher. Primary school, for me, was mainly about the cognitive stuff: spelling, arithmetic, geography, things for which we received tests that earned you grades. Perhaps this was because this came quite easily to me and I liked being 'the best' (who doesn't?), but I think it was the school system that provoked and encouraged that kind of attitude. Children easily pick up on what adults find important, and everything about our school system says that how you do on tests (in comparison to others) is the main thing.

Current critiques of education bear this out. Gert Biesta has shown how a culture of measurement has come to pervade education at all levels.[6] 'Evidence-based' educational research focuses on what it *can* measure – like how schools do from year to year in terms of students' test scores – at the cost of thinking about what we *should* be trying to measure (or judge). Because for schools (and countries) much depends on league tables and rankings – you want to be able

5 Howard Parsons has argued for a social cause for the waning of wonder on a *cultural* level, so not in individuals' development towards adulthood, but in the historical development of Western societies. He argues that, partly due to the rise of natural science, people today are less capable of or less prone to wonder than in the (premodern) past. There may be some truth in this, but I will not evaluate this claim here. For the purposes of this book it suffices to note that the sense of wonder has not been *lost*; people in (post)modern societies are still capable of experiencing wonder. See Howard Parsons, 'A Philosophy of Wonder', *Philosophy and Phenomenological Research* 30, no. 1 (1969).

6 Gert Biesta, 'Good Education in an Age of Measurement: On the Need to Reconnect with the Question of Purpose in Education', *Educational Assessment, Evaluation, and Accountability* 21, no. 1 (2009); and Gert Biesta, *Good Education in an Age of Measurement* (Boulder, CO: Paradigm Publishers, 2010).

to say you offer a quality education, leading to good life prospects for your students – raising test scores becomes all important. In a 2001 article Andrew Davis and John White quote William Taylor, who noted in 1978 that 'discussions of Accountability are peculiarly subject to technical regression; arguments about values become arguments about techniques. The weakest link in the goals–objectives–assessment–feedback–improvement model of accountability is its first'.[7] It should not come as a surprise, then, that (despite efforts of ardent critics like Alfie Kohn) 'teaching to the test' is still so widespread that it has its own Wikipedia page.[8]

Even though schooling in many countries in the world – certainly in Western Europe and the United States – is still strongly centred on how students perform on standardized tests in a limited number of subjects, and on how well schools prepare children for their participation (as flexible innovators or whatever) in a globally competitive economy, some space has at least been opened for public discussion of different views on what education should be about. Against this background, this book argues for a renewed appreciation of the educational importance of wonder. Three things make me think this is not a lost cause. Firstly, wonder inevitably arises in classrooms even today, not least due to inspired and committed teachers who (fortunately) refuse to surrender to the perverse pressures of certain systems of accountability. Secondly, although there is probably a natural aspect to the waning of wonder in the course of childhood, it is certainly not an inevitable fact, beyond the influence of educators. Thirdly, and this is where the cliché is least insightful, it is by no means the case that the sense of wonder 'peaks' in (early) childhood, never to be recovered to the same intensity in later life. In fact, I would argue that, although their wonder will never have the exact same quality as young children's wonder, adults are at least as capable of experiencing wonder as their younger selves were. (As Genevieve Lloyd observed, the difference between adults and children is that 'a wondering child has not yet learned *not* to wonder'.[9]) Moreover, 'mature' wonder has a depth

7 William Taylor, 'Values and Accountability', in *Accountability in Education*, eds. Tony Becher and Stuart Maclure (Windsor: NFER-Nelson, 1978), 26, cited in Andrew Davis and John White, 'Accountability and School Inspection: In Defence of Audited Self-Review', *Journal of Philosophy of Education* 35, no. 4 (2001).

8 Alfie Kohn, *The Case against Standardized Testing: Raising the Scores, Ruining the Schools* (Portsmouth, NH: Heinemann, 2000); https://en.wikipedia.org/wiki/Teaching_to_the_test.

9 She writes: 'Wonder comes naturally to children. What Spinoza added to that was the stronger claim that it is inherent in a mind's effort to persist in being; and hence that it belongs in adult life as much as in childhood. The important insight here is that a wondering child has not yet learned *not* to wonder'. Genevieve Lloyd, 'Wonder and Education: Some Lessons from Spinoza', in *Wonder, Education, and Human Flourishing*, ed. Anders Schinkel (Amsterdam: VU University Press, 2020)

that young children's wonder cannot have. There are good reasons, therefore, to take a closer look both at the educational importance of wonder, and at education's potential importance for our sense of wonder.

The (Mutual) Importance of Wonder and Education

Many people – whether educators or not – will agree that an education that draws no inspiration from wonder is dead, an education that does not inspire wonder barren. That wonder has educational importance will strike many as obvious, because wonder is commonly perceived as akin to curiosity, as stimulating inquiry, and as something that enhances pleasure in learning. But many experiences of wonder are rather different, and do not have an obvious place in education: wonder at the bare fact of existence, for instance (the fact that there is something rather than nothing); or being struck by wonder at a magnificent sunset, or at the magical swirling murmurations of a million starlings. Such experiences (more akin to, but still distinct from, awe – though it is of course also possible to be awestruck by these things) are likely to leave us lost for words; they are a silent response to mystery, and as such seem rather anti-educational. Neither of these experiences, at any rate, is clearly connected with the things we usually associate with education: getting to know and understand things, learning new concepts, furthering one's analytic and communicative abilities, et cetera.

Yet as I argue in this book, this type of wonder – that I call 'deep' or 'contemplative' wonder as distinct from the 'active' or 'inquisitive' wonder that is more akin to curiosity – is (also) of fundamental educational importance. It makes us vividly aware of the limits of our knowledge and understanding, of the known and the knowable. It pierces frameworks of understanding that are taken for granted and perceived as natural, draws our attention to the world behind our constructions, and it may spark or deepen our interest in the world as something worth attending to for its own sake rather than for our purposes. Deep wonder opens up space for the consideration of (radical) alternatives wherever it occurs, and in many cases is linked with deep experiences of value; therefore, it is not just important for education in general, but also, more specifically, for moral and political education.

You will have noticed that I do not argue for the educational importance of deep wonder in terms of how it might contribute to children's *religious* or spiritual education – even though this might seem an obvious route to take.

The reasons for this are, firstly, that I am more interested in emphasizing what might be called a 'spiritual' dimension in *all* of education – that is, in the role of wonder and especially contemplative wonder in all forms of education – than in 'compartmentalized' spiritual and religious education (such as the subject RE in schools). Some good papers on wonder and religious education exist,[10] and undoubtedly wonder will often receive attention in more general work on religious education and religious pedagogy. It is not my intention to contribute to that literature (and if I did I would be moving outside of my field of expertise). Secondly, and relatedly, I find it more interesting to draw more specific attention to the importance of wonder in educational domains where one would be less inclined – perhaps even surprised – to see it mentioned, as I think is true for moral education and even more strongly for political education.

This book argues for the educational importance of contemplative (or deep) wonder.[11] But as my plan for the book ripened I came to realize that at the very same time the book argues for the importance of education to our sense of wonder. The reason is quite simple, that in educational practice – in the classroom, in educational activities outside the classroom, in the interaction between teachers and students – only mutual importance is conceivable. If we acknowledge that wonder is educationally important – meaning that if we allow it to surface in education it will enhance students' understanding and appreciation of the world and support the 'transmission of what is worthwhile' – then we will be committed to making space for wonder in our schools.[12] This includes making room for wonder-inspired teaching, providing time and opportunities for children to wonder about and at things, and actively stimulating or provoking experiences of wonder. But if we do these things, we also nurture and cultivate children's sense of wonder and convey the message that wonder matters. Furthermore, wonder depends in various ways on knowledge and understanding; what we wonder about and wonder at, as well as the tone or quality of our wonder,

[10] For instance: Anabel Proffitt, 'The Importance of Wonder in Educational Ministry', *Religious Education: The Official Journal of the Religious Education Association* 93, no. 1 (1998); and Sturla Sagberg, 'Wonder and the Question of Truth in Religious Education', *Sewanee Theological Review* 48, no. 4 (2005).

[11] Other texts on wonder and education tend to focus on the educational importance of active (or inquisitive) wonder. An excellent collection is Kieran Egan, Annabella Cant, and Gillian Judson, eds., *Wonder-full Education: The Centrality of Wonder in Teaching and Learning across the Curriculum* (New York: Routledge, 2014). Some of the contributions to this volume, especially Laura Piersol's 'Our Hearts Leap Up: Awakening Wonder within the Classroom', 3–21, and Yannis Hadzigeorgiou's 'Reclaiming the Value of Wonder in Science Education', 40–65, also pay explicit attention to (what I call) deep or contemplative wonder.

[12] Richard Peters described education as the transmission of what is worthwhile in Richard S. Peters, *Ethics & Education* (London: George Allen and Unwin Ltd., 1970), 45.

depend on frameworks of understanding and emotional and moral dispositions that are partly shaped by education. More about this will follow; what matters for now is that this book should not be read narrowly, as an argument for the instrumental significance of wonder for the realization of educational ends, but rather as a book about the value of education, the value of wonder, and their mutual importance.

It is also worth noting, in connection with what I said earlier about adults' capacity for wonder, that although the primary context of my inquiry is the education of children, the book will not only feature examples of children's wonder or things children (of a particular age) may wonder at or about. Like Philo Hove in his beautiful meditation on the subject, I do not limit my inquiry to children. As he rightly says, 'at a deep level wonder seems to reveal, or put into question, certain fundamental features of human experience: among other things, wonder can expose our vulnerability. Before teachers – adults – can appreciate the subtlety and delicacy of wonder more fully in the living experience of children, we need to become attuned to, and reflect more deeply upon, wonder in our own lives'.[13]

Before I turn to an overview of the book a few more words on 'education': in writing this book I have constantly had its relevance to educational practice as it goes on in schools in the back of my mind, but I do not use the term 'education' merely as shorthand for 'formal education', i.e. as a synonym for schooling. In line with Peters' view, briefly alluded to above, I see education as something that *can* happen in schools and ideally *should* happen in schools, but that in practice does not always happen, perhaps does not happen enough, and can and does also happen *outside of* schools, and not only at home either. That is, I employ a *normative* conception of education according to which someone may learn a whole lot of things without thereby becoming educated, and another person may receive little formal education and become educated by life experience and her own efforts to deepen and widen her understanding. The difference was famously expressed by Alfred North Whitehead in terms of education as the imparting of 'inert ideas', 'ideas that are merely received into the mind without being utilised, or tested, or thrown into fresh combinations', and education as 'the acquisition of the art of the utilisation of knowledge'. And 'utilisation' should not be understood narrowly here – utilising an idea means 'relating it to that stream, compounded of sense perceptions, feelings, hopes, desires, and

[13] Philo Hove, 'The Face of Wonder', *Journal of Curriculum Studies* 28, no. 4 (1996): 437–8.

of mental activities adjusting thought to thought, which forms our life'.[14] As I will show in Chapter 3, there is an intimate connection between wonder and education, understood in this way, but insight into this connection is highly relevant to educational practice as well.

Outline of the Book

The book consists of six chapters. The first two deal with wonder as such – what it is and how it is different from other types of experience with which it does have elements in common, such as curiosity and awe, and what it 'tells us' about the world (if anything), or, more broadly, how it relates (us) to the world. The latter discussion will also include a comparison of wonder with (more obviously) 'functional' or evolutionarily adaptive emotions. Chapters 3, 4, and 5 are devoted to the relations between wonder and education, and Chapter 6 discusses the upshot of the previous chapters for educational practice and policy. The outline of the book per chapter is as follows.

The purpose of *Chapter 1* is to provide clarity about the experience and concept of wonder. I explain the similarities and differences between wonder on the one hand and curiosity and awe on the other hand, as well as the distinction between active/inquisitive wonder and deep/contemplative wonder. The former is more akin to curiosity, entails an urge to explore and investigate, and is therefore the more obvious 'ally' of the teacher. In deep or contemplative wonder the receptive element dominates; it is a 'silent' response to mystery. It is closer to awe, but still importantly different from it. My concern in this chapter is to stay as true as I can to the *experience* of wonder – better: to the different types of experience of wonder – and how these experiences differ in quality from what it is like to be curious about something. I say a bit more about this below, under the heading 'Approach'. Chapter 1 concludes with a section on the development of wonder and potential differences between (young) children's wonder and adults' wonder.

14 Alfred North Whitehead, 'The Aims of Education', in *The Aims of Education and Other Essays* (London: Ernest Benn Limited, 1962), 1–2, 6, 4. In another essay, 'The Rhythmic Claims of Freedom and Discipline', Whitehead repeats his view of education in slightly different terms: 'Education is the guidance of the individual towards a comprehension of the art of life; and by the art of life I mean the most complete achievement of varied activity expressing the potentialities of that living creature in the face of its actual environment. (…) Each individual embodies an adventure of existence. The art of life is the guidance of this adventure'. Alfred North Whitehead, 'The Rhythmic Claims of Freedom and Discipline', in *The Aims of Education and Other Essays* (London: Ernest Benn Limited, 1962), 61.

Chapter 2 deals with the ways in which wonder relates (us) to the world.[15] I argue for an inclusive and, I think, intuitive conception of 'the world', at the heart of which lies the notion of 'out-there-ness'. I will discuss how wonder continually draws our attention to – and draws us into relation with – the world 'out there', which is also the world beyond our constructions of the world. An important thread that runs through this chapter is that of the thorny question of what wonder 'tells us'. Experiences of wonder are often, though not always, strongly suggestive of importance, of value – something not just worth attending to but something worthwhile, *period*; in short, experiences of wonder often suggest that the world *is* wonderful. But does this suggestion withstand critical scrutiny? I first approach this question by comparing wonder with emotions that do seem to tell us something about the world, that are therefore functional, and that have been selected for this in evolution, e.g. the emotion of fear. The discussion of a possible evolutionary background for wonder tends to lead to either of two positions, neither of which I find fully convincing: either wonder is seen as a useless by-product of our (generally useful) cognitive–affective systems, or wonder is seen as an adaptive emotion. Instead, I foreground the idea of wonder as a phenomenon of the limit: wonder occurs at the limits of our understanding; it reveals those limits, and in so doing it reveals that there is something beyond them. So although naive claims that in wonder we 'see things as they are' must be rejected, there is still something about the idea of wonder as 'revelatory' that we should hold on to – something that will prove important, too, in moral and political education.

The general aim of education, I have argued elsewhere, is to provide 'access to the world', to open up the world to children.[16] This is in fact what biology teachers, maths teachers, history teachers, et cetera, (try to) *do*: they enable children to see and understand the world through the lens (the concepts, the instruments) of their particular field, thus enlarging the world that children can 'move about' in; and at the same time that they introduce children to the world *through* their subject (and this becomes more important in higher education) they introduce children *to* the world *of* their subject – the world of biology, biologists, and laboratories; of history, historians, and archives. In *Chapter 3* I intend to show that there is a deep intrinsic connection between this

15 After Chapter 1 'wonder' always means 'deep/contemplative wonder', unless otherwise stated.

16 Anders Schinkel, 'On the Justification of Compulsory Schooling', in *Philosophical Perspectives on Compulsory Education*, ed. Marianna Papastephanou (Dordrecht: Springer, 2014). My view is in some respects similar to, but also different from, Biesta's Arendtian perspective on this (Biesta, 'Good Education in an Age of Measurement'; and Biesta, *Good Education in an Age of Measurement*).

general aim of education and wonder – not simply because wonder provides a motivational force to explore the world (and the worlds of the various disciplines), but because wonder shares with education a 'revelatory' intent; it orients us towards the world, arrests our gaze, and demands that we stop and look (or listen). Although there is no such thing as 'the objective world' available to us – and exactly because this is so – it is crucial in education that we are never satisfied with any contingent representation of it. Thus it must always move with wonder, breaking out of accepted frameworks, towards the world beyond them.

Many authors have suggested that wonder is closely linked with certain moral emotions, attitudes, and virtues, such as respect, care, and humility. Kathleen Moore, for instance, says that wonder implies a motivation to protect the object of wonder, and that wonder closes the gap between is and ought.[17] If these claims hold up, wonder could have an important role to play in moral education. In *Chapter 4* I ask whether we do indeed have reason to stimulate the sense of wonder, and provoke experiences of wonder, in education, with a view to its *moral* effects or importance. My answer is cautiously positive: wonder is often accompanied by the aforementioned moral emotions and attitudes, and generally speaking coheres more easily with them than with their opposites; but much depends on how we interpret our wonder and how we make sense of the object of our wonder. Wonder *as such*, if it is not already a morally charged kind of wonder, does not have the magical power to call forth moral emotions and dispositions. Approaching the relation from the other end, however, I would argue that moral education should, ideally, include an element of wonder; that at the heart of moral education should lie the attempt to sensitize children to the experience of the other as a subject like them, a precious but fragile being, and that this experience is closely related to – and indeed hardly thinkable without – the experience of wonder.

Chapter 5 argues that wonder's crucial importance to political education lies in the fact that it defamiliarizes the familiar. What seemed natural before now appears to us as strange or mysterious, and lacking in reason or necessity. Wonder is thus inherently subversive and therefore politically important. Whereas those in power prefer to think – and prefer that other people think – that the existing political order is natural or at minimum inevitable, wonder sparks the notion that this may not be so. A challenge to be met in this chapter is the historically recurring association of wonder with passivity and otherworldliness; those who

[17] Kathleen D. Moore, 'The Truth of the Barnacles: Rachel Carson and the Moral Significance of Wonder', *Environmental Ethics* 27, no. 3 (2005).

wonder would supposedly turn away from the world, rather than towards it. Although that is indeed a possibility, this is at best a one-sided insight – for at the core of wonder is a turning *towards* the world that, although not political in *intent*, has important political implications. And this means that the cultivation of wonder (assuming it is not limited to politically 'safe' areas) can and should play an important role in political education.

In the concluding *Chapter 6* I draw out some general implications of the book's argument for educational practice and policy: should governments actively try to promote 'wonder-full' education and if so, what policy changes would this require? More specifically, to what extent would this imply a break with recent educational policy in the UK, the Netherlands, and Europe, generally? In the UK, every other primary school seems to list among the aims of its science, geography, or religious education curriculum the fostering of a 'sense of awe and wonder' (this claim is not the result of an actual count, but google 'UK curriculum awe wonder' and you will see what I mean) – does this mean that, for the UK context at least, this book is superfluous? I think not. Whenever something receives such widespread explicit affirmation there is reason to be suspicious, for it may also be a sign that something is actually missing.

Approach

Like many philosophers I do not – I cannot – have a method, if that is taken to imply a 'methodical' way of going about things, the following of a predetermined procedure in order to (reliably) attain the desired result. Perhaps the closest thing to such a method that contemporary philosophy has to offer and that would seem to lend itself to a study of wonder is conceptual analysis, which tries to discover the necessary and sufficient conditions of concepts by studying the 'correct' use of the corresponding term(s) in everyday language. It often proceeds by way of examples and counterexamples, probing the limits of the concept under investigation. For instance, if I am taken aback by a journal's rejection of a manuscript because I felt sure it would be accepted, am I experiencing wonder or not? Would that be the right word to use? It sounds unlikely, but to be sure we would need to know more about my state of mind. Less dependent on detailed knowledge about mental states (or other details of the example) would be tests of a purely linguistic nature. For example, is it possible to say: 'As Wordsworth looked out over the lake, wondering at its sheer presence and its mysterious beauty, his attention was all over the place'? I hope you will agree there is something not right here. Wonder entails that one's attention is arrested by and focused on an object ('object', not in the sense of 'thing', but as that which one perceives or contemplates), so wonder is not compatible with scattered attention. By probing our linguistic intuitions in this way, conceptual analysis can help us become aware of the central features of concepts. And this can be done in a very systematic way.

For my purpose, however, it is insufficient. Conceptual analysis is inevitably part of my approach, but it can only play a subsidiary role, because, ultimately, I am not interested in how the word 'wonder' is used or is to be used, but in the importance of particular types of *experience*. (I will return to this in Chapter 1.) These experiences are typically expressed in terms of wonder, perhaps, but not necessarily. And it may well be the case that 'our' concept of wonder – if 'we' have a single concept of wonder – does not capture all that is important and interesting about those experiences. Conceptual analysis, in so far as it limits itself to describing the meaning of concepts, is inherently (too) conservative.[18]

Furthermore, a lot of the business of philosophy is concerned with trying to make people (first ourselves, then you, the reader) *see* things in a certain way. In this book this is the case in two ways. In the first two chapters of the book I will give the best account that I can of what it is like to experience (different kinds of) wonder. To be able to come up with that account it was not enough to interrogate my linguistic intuitions and to read what others have written about wonder, but it was necessary, first and foremost, to recall experiences of wonder of my own and to 'get them into focus' as sharply as possible. In communicating these experiences to you I hope to 'test' my descriptions and interpretations of them. That is, my hope is that you will be prompted, and be brought in the right state of mind, to recall and examine experiences of wonder of your own; *and* of course that what I say about wonder will resonate with you, that you recognize it and will think: yes, wonder is like that. (If you feel that wonder is *not* as I describe it, do share your thoughts with me.)

In the chapters that follow I will argue for the educational importance of deep or contemplative wonder, which means that I will be making normative claims. Conceptual analysis cannot substantiate any normative claims other than linguistic ones. By clarifying the connections between concepts it can help

[18] There are also types of conceptual analysis that go beyond description. Vincent Brümmer, for instance, argued that conceptual analysis can and should also have a constructive and prescriptive aspect; see Vincent Brümmer, *Theology & Philosophical Inquiry: An Introduction* (London and Basingstoke: The Macmillan Press Ltd, 1981), 76–9.

to show that if you are committed to X you should logically also be committed to Y, and if X and Y are principles or claims that centrally include normative (for instance, ethical) concepts, conceptual analysis can help you to reach normative conclusions. But this is because the normative content was already there; it was assumed. No moral or political obligations follow from language or logic alone. Logic – or, better: reasoning – has an important role to play in ethics and politics, but in the end (so I believe) it comes down to *how we 'see' things* – not in the sense of what our 'views' are, but in the sense of our immediate affective–cognitive response: when you see a cow in a field, do you see future steaks and spareribs, or a creature with awareness and feelings and a life of its own? When you think of the world as a whole, do you see matter in motion or an animated, vibrant whole? And this means that to argue for a normative claim in these domains, and to try to bring people around to a certain point of view, is to try and make them see things and emotionally, even viscerally, respond to things the way you do. Rational argument alone can only succeed in this when your discussion partner already agrees with you in her basic assumptions. When this is not the case, a shift of perspective is needed, a different way of looking at things. This is where language needs to be *evocative*. What matters lies *beyond* language, but we need language to get there; it needs to propel us beyond itself to that which demands expression and evocation in language. This is why Whitehead said that 'philosophy is akin to poetry'.[19]

My approach to wonder is primarily phenomenological and hermeneutical. Phenomenology, as I understand it here, is a philosophical approach that aims to articulate the nature and meaning of prereflective, lived experience. This implies interpretation; it is therefore a hermeneutic phenomenology.[20] It constitutes both the most fitting and the most satisfying way to study wonder, because it is an approach that itself 'proceeds through wonder'.[21] Phenomenology entails a wondering stance, which means that if one studies wonder phenomenologically one gets to know one's object not just by means of, but also *in* one's manner of

[19] Alfred North Whitehead, *Modes of Thought* (New York: The Free Press, 1968), 174.

[20] Max van Manen, 'Phenomenology of Practice', *Phenomenology & Practice* 1, no. 1 (2007): 16. That I see what I am doing here as necessarily involving interpretation means that I reject a Husserlian conception of phenomenology as a purely descriptive exercise; my approach resembles Van Manen's (Heideggerian) phenomenology; for an overview of different phenomenological traditions see David Woodruff Smith, 'Phenomenology', in *The Stanford Encyclopedia of Philosophy*, ed. Edward N. Zalta, https://plato.stanford.edu/archives/sum2018/entries/phenomenology.

[21] Max van Manen, 'Phenomenology in Its Original Sense', *Qualitative Health Research* 27, no. 6 (2017): 816.

studying it. This approach is therefore particularly apt in this case. At the same time there is something paradoxical about studying wonder phenomenologically, since wonder is a state that is (self-)reflexive in nature and often triggers reflection on the object of wonder. But it is indeed no more than a paradox, since to experience wonder is not the same as reflecting on that experience or interpreting that experience, and 'prereflective wonder' is therefore not a contradiction in terms.

Because I take a phenomenological approach, examples of experiences of wonder – from my own life, but also from the philosophical literature on wonder – will play an important role in this book. By examples I do not mean mere illustrations of conceptual or empirical points that could also be made without them. They are not just there to enliven the narrative. Rather, they are the 'data' of the investigation; for as Van Manen explains, 'lived experiences are the data of phenomenological research'.[22] Of course they are not the type of data that can be processed by running them through a computer programme or unleashing some kind of statistical operation on them. They are 'experiential data that require study, investigation, probing, reflection, analysis, interrogation', in short: interpretation.[23] Phenomenology thus goes hand in hand with hermeneutics: the experiences I try to describe as faithfully as possible also require interpretation, because they do not carry their meaning on their sleeve. Moreover, in the act of describing them – and before that, in the act of selecting them for description – I cannot hope to free myself entirely from the past that gave me my pre-understanding of wonder; and if I could, I would have no idea where to look. If a phenomenology of wonder focuses on the 'appearance' here and now, a hermeneutics of wonder contextualizes this experience. Wonder is both synchronically and diachronically diverse. The wonder I experience is thus socially and historically situated; my wonder could not have been Aristotle's, and vice versa. This means that there are layers of meaning to discover in the experiences of wonder that form the 'data' for this study.

How does one 'gather' such experiential 'data'? Not the way 'phenomenological' approaches in the social sciences do this, which is by asking people to reflect on their personal experiences, for this is not phenomenology in the sense in which I am using the term here, and fails precisely to capture what (philosophical)

[22] Ibid., 814.
[23] Ibid.

phenomenology is looking for, namely prereflective experience.[24] As Finn Hansen writes, '[i]n an existential phenomenological description we are not interested in the "narrative constructionism" of the situation, that is, the meaning-making of the storyteller. (...) We want to go deeper and beyond the empirical and constructivist approaches in order to reach what I call "the lyrical realism" of the situation'.[25] The primary way to gather these 'data' that are not data in the common sense but rather in the original sense of the word is by recalling, bringing to mind again, experiences of wonder, and listening 'with a "poetic ear" or with the heart'.[26] This involves remembering and therefore reconstructing and (re-)imagining. It involves dwelling in them and exploring their different aspects like the different rooms in a house and the views their windows provide. This is a very personal exercise, even where one draws on other people's examples of experiences of wonder, because one can only make sense of them and use them if one succeeds in 'making them one's own'. This means that one must imaginatively transpose oneself into the situation of the 'wonderer' in the example and come to understand and share their wonder. All this is quite difficult and therefore not always successful. For that reason there is ultimately no real substitute for one's own experiences of wonder. This results in the awkward situation that what is the best starting point of this study for *me* is by definition a suboptimal starting point for *you*, the reader. You are therefore once again encouraged to recall and reflect on your own experiences of wonder as you are reading the chapters that follow. I hope that in that way we will find common ground.

[24] See Max van Manen, 'But Is It Phenomenology?' *Qualitative Health Research* 27, no. 6 (2017). As Van Manen explains, an approach like Interpretive Phenomenological Analysis focuses on 'the "person" and on the personal experience of a participant and on his or her views and understandings, rather than on the phenomenon itself'; ibid., 778. Note that to call an experience 'prereflective' is not to deny that it may at the same time be 'postreflective' in the sense that past reflection may be one of its shaping influences.

[25] Finn Thorbjørn Hansen, 'The Call and Practices of Wonder: How to Evoke a Socratic Community of Wonder in Professional Settings', in *The Socratic Handbook: Dialogue Methods for Philosophical Practice*, ed. Michael Noah Weiss (Münster: LIT Verlag, 2015), 221–2.

[26] Ibid., 222.

1

What Is (It Like to Experience) Wonder?

A primary school teacher begins a fourth-grade science class with the announcement that she drives a solar-powered car. Incredulous, many children turn towards the window to see if there is anything unusual parked in the street. Many of them know what solar-powered cars look like – low, long racing cars covered in solar panels – and they are pretty sure there is nothing like that out there. Nonetheless, their curiosity is piqued. Some begin to ask questions, others to protest that they don't believe her, that she is leading them on. And she is, in a way. She admits that she does indeed own a very ordinary car, but insists that it is still solar powered. Before the children's curiosity gives way to impatience she explains what she means: her car runs on petrol, and this is a product derived from petroleum, a fossil fuel formed naturally when dead (micro-) organisms (plankton, algae, plants) get buried and are subjected to intense heat and pressure for millions of years. In life, those organisms captured energy from the sun through photosynthesis. Thus, the energy stored in fossil fuels is solar energy. And that means that, in this roundabout way, a car that runs on petrol is solar powered. (Indeed, *any* car is, because all types of energy we can tap except nuclear energy derive from the sun.)

No doubt some students would feel duped in a situation like the above (that I made up). But it also seems likely that some children's interest would rather be *heightened* by the teacher's explanation. Unlike in the beginning, however, when they were just curious to see what the teacher's car looked like, their interest could take different forms. Curiosity is still an option, of course; perhaps some students would have become really curious about how fossil fuels are formed or about what energy is and how you can get it out of something. But other students might experience something subtly or even quite strongly different. They might feel impressed and at the same time intellectually shaken, having registered – on some level – a shock to their understanding of the world. Perhaps in their minds solar power had been fundamentally different from the power generated from fossil fuels – just two entirely different types of energy – and now this turned out not to be true. If they also experience a desire or a need to look into this further, to acquire a new, more adequate understanding, their experience might be one of 'inquisitive wonder'. This would be subtly but significantly different from curiosity. Another possibility, even further removed from curiosity, is that students would feel impressed, intellectually shaken, but *not* immediately inclined to '(dis)solve' their wonder. They might just let what the teacher explained sink in and wonder at it: millions of years ago, the sun shone on the earth as it does today. Some of its energy was captured by plants and microorganisms. These got buried, only to be pumped up out of the earth as oil today, to be fed into cars, and to make these run. However much of this one might be able to understand, it is mind-boggling – and both strange and beautiful, in a way – or one or the other, depending on one's mood.

If you are with me so far you will have an intuitive sense of how wonder, in both forms, differs from curiosity (and, by the way, from the everyday I-wonder-what's-for-dinner type of wondering). The purpose of this chapter is, firstly, to arrive at a fuller description of the phenomenology of wonder, of what it is like to experience wonder, and secondly, to provide a summary statement of this phenomenology that may serve as a definition or at least a more precise delineation of the concept of wonder used in this book (in fact, of two concepts, namely inquisitive and contemplative wonder, the latter of which is the focus of this book). For these purposes it helps to contrast wonder with curiosity; but to see how wonder differs from curiosity is also important because this helps us to see that wonder's potential educational importance is an issue that deserves attention in its own right. All too often in educational writing as well as school mission statements and the like wonder is mentioned in one breath with either curiosity or awe, and in both cases wonder appears to be superfluous, just another way to say the same thing. But wonder – and this goes for both types of wonder that I distinguish in this book – is importantly different from curiosity, as well as from awe, and it is important for education for only partly similar reasons.

The remainder of this chapter is divided into three main sections and a conclusion: the first section deals with the phenomenology of wonder and how this differs from curiosity and awe, and the second presents my conceptualization of wonder. In the third section I return to a topic briefly touched upon in the introduction: the development of wonder from early childhood into adulthood.

The main reason to discuss that here is that it is important to know whether the description of wonder that I present in this chapter applies to adults and children alike. But anything we might be able to say about the development of wonder is also bound to have educational implications; these will be briefly indicated, to be developed more fully in Chapter 3. In the conclusion I briefly summarize the findings of this chapter and indicate connections with the chapters that follow.

The Phenomenology of Wonder, Curiosity and Awe

As I explained in the introduction, experiences of wonder – my own and other people's – form the primary 'data' of this study. But my interpretation of these experiences is informed by a great number of philosophical books and articles on wonder, in particular (in alphabetical order) the work of Robert Fuller, Yannis Hadzigeorgiou, Ronald Hepburn, Philo Hove, Paul Martin Opdal, Howard Parsons, Jan Pedersen, Dennis Quinn, Mary-Jane Rubenstein and Sophia Vasalou.[1] Whatever I say about wonder, similar things can be found in the work of these authors, and it is impossible for me to distinguish what I 'discovered' on my own from that which I have taken from others. So I mention these authors here both to acknowledge my indebtedness to their work and for the practical reason that I can then keep references to a minimum; it would simply be impossible to reference their work at every turn.

I will start below with an initial analysis of some personal experiences of wonder and supplement these later with some examples taken from the literature. It is important to realize from the outset that there is no such thing as *the* experience of wonder. Wonder manifests itself more or less differently in each of these examples – and even that way of putting it is tricky, since it suggests a stable thing called 'wonder' that appears now in this guise, then in that. The diversity or plurality of wonder comes into view even more strongly when we look at its history, where we find the linguistic predecessors of wonder associated

[1] Robert C. Fuller, *Wonder: From Emotion to Spirituality* (Chapel Hill: The University of North Carolina Press, 2006); Hadzigeorgiou, 'Reclaiming'; Ronald W. Hepburn, 'The Inaugural Address: Wonder', *The Aristotelian Society*, Supplementary Volume LIV (1980); Hove, 'The Face of Wonder'; Paul Martin Opdal, 'Curiosity, Wonder and Education Seen as Perspective Development', *Studies in Philosophy and Education* 20 (2001); Parsons, 'A Philosophy of Wonder'; Jan B. W. Pedersen, *Balanced Wonder: Experiential Sources of Imagination, Virtues and Human Flourishing* (Lanham: Lexington Books, 2019); Dennis Quinn, *Iris Exiled: A Synoptic History of Wonder* (Lanham: University Press of America, 2002); Mary-Jane Rubenstein, *Strange Wonder: The Closure of Metaphysics and the Opening of Awe* (New York: Columbia University Press, 2011); Sophia Vasalou, *Wonder: A Grammar* (Albany: State University of New York Press, 2015).

with both joy and fear, and where we see shifting and alternating evaluations of wonder and curiosity.[2] I do believe that, for instance, Socrates' or Plato's wonder, Thomas Aquinas' wonder, Adam Smith's wonder, and so on are recognizable to us because they share important elements with experiences of wonder that we might have today. I also believe that this is the case because despite socially inherited differences in our make-up we still belong to the same animal species. Nevertheless, not to complicate the discussion too much at this stage, I will limit my analysis to more or less contemporary experiences. (Historical comparisons *will* play a role in the subsection on 'the meaning of wonder'.)

Some Personal Experiences of Wonder: An Initial Analysis

I don't know whether it is peculiar to the Dutch, but in the Netherlands people organize themselves around the most obscure topics of interest. For example, I am a member of the 'Working-group Pleistocene Mammals', a society for people that share an interest in mammals of the Pleistocene age, such as the extinct woolly mammoth and woolly rhinoceros, the cave lion, cave bear, and cave hyena, the giant deer, the aurochs, and of course many smaller mammals, as well as birds, fish, and reptiles.[3] (We are not particular.) This means that I also like to go to the beach – to some particular beaches, that is, namely those beaches that were suppleted with sand sucked up from the bottom of the North Sea in places rich in fossil remains of Pleistocene and early Holocene animals. Those remains can now be found on those beaches when they are exposed by the tides and the wind, so I go there regularly to search for them. Hence, among my most frequent experiences of wonder are those induced by holding in my hand the fossil remains (a tooth, a bone) of a once-living creature from a long-gone age. Some knowledge and more imagination enter into such experiences. One has

[2] For the history of wonder see Quinn, *Iris Exiled* and Vasalou, *Wonder*; also Lorraine Daston and Katharine Park, *Wonders and the Order of Nature, 1150–1750* (New York: Zone Books, 1998) and Ekkehard Martens, *Vom Staunen oder Die Rückkehr der Neugier* (Leipzig: Reclam, 2003).

[3] The Pleistocene, the geological epoch that lasted from about 2.6 million years ago to about 11,700 years ago, is more commonly known as 'The Ice Age'. It was a relatively cold epoch characterized by ice sheets around the earth's poles and frequent glaciations. Such geological epochs are called 'ice ages'; the Pleistocene was by no means the only ice age, it was merely the last one. Things are made more confusing by the fact that people sometimes speak of 'the last Ice Age' when they mean the last glacial period within the Pleistocene (called the Wisconsinan in the United States, the Devensian in the UK and the Weichselian in parts of Europe, and lasting from *c.* 116,000 to 11,700 years ago). The Pleistocene is followed in the geological time scale by the Holocene, our current epoch. (This may change, however, because the idea that we have entered a new era that might be called the 'Anthropocene' is now hotly debated. This might follow the Holocene, but it could also replace it, if it is acknowledged, as some argue, that the naming of the Holocene was inconsistent with the standard criteria for naming geological epochs.)

to know what one has found – that it is the molar of a baby woolly mammoth, for instance, or a vertebra that once supported the neck muscles of a wolf – but more important even is that one's imagination builds up, if only in broad strokes, a picture of the creature and its context around the fossil – putting flesh to the bones, if you'll forgive the obvious pun.

I once found a bone tool fashioned out of an aurochs bone by Mesolithic hunter-gatherers. When I imagine some prehistoric man or woman, some five or ten thousand years ago, handling this object that I am holding now, using it to soften leather perhaps; and when I realize how unthinkable it would be for him or her, how unimaginable, that this tool would end up in a drawer in my study in this modern world, I am filled with wonder. (*Often*, at any rate, since if I deliberately engage in such an imaginative exercise – if it does not simply happen to me – I do not always attain a state of wonder. This depends on conditions I will get back to.)

A similar experience of wonder may be evoked by contrasts of space rather than time. For me, a desolate lamplit bus stop late at night can do this very powerfully. It suddenly appears to me not as a familiar object in its familiar context, but as something extremely unlikely in a far-flung corner of the universe. Imagining myself at 'the other end' of the universe and still knowing that down here there would be this bus stop for line 126, or whatever its number, makes it in some sense inconceivable, an unfathomable mystery.

For a third and, for now, last example I return to the beach. On a late summer day last year I noticed something odd: a small, dark bump on the otherwise smooth surface of the sand close to the waterline. The odd thing was that it seemed to be moving, but from the distance from which I'd spotted it I couldn't be sure, so I walked towards it. As I came close enough to identify it I found it hard to believe my eyes: it was a toad, and it seemed slowly but surely to be headed for the sea! I know now that there are places in the world where toads on beaches are not at all uncommon, and that they are occasionally spotted on Dutch beaches as well, but at that time I'd never seen or heard of anything like it. How did it get there? What was it doing there? The picture it presented was quite surreal, as if I'd walked into a fairy tale. So I was baffled, really taken aback by this (to me) utterly incongruent and surreal scene. Would it actually walk into the water – the *salt* water? It did not. After taking a few more steps towards the edge of the sea, at just a few metres from the waterline, the toad stopped. A few seconds later a decision had emerged; the toad turned 180 degrees and began, with equal determination, its long and slow way towards the dunes.

In each of these examples my *attention is arrested* and held captive, as it were, by something that appears to me as *other* in some way. It is other than I expected on the basis of what I thought I knew about the world, or other in a more profound sense, implying a mystery that defies complete assimilation into any of our categories, any framework of interpretation. I am holding a Mesolithic tool, I *know* what it is, I can imagine how it was used and by whom, as well as, very roughly, the succession of prehistorical and historical eras that span the distance between then and now – and yet I cannot wrap my head around it. Despite what I know, and despite not having any specific question in mind, I am filled with (a) question. A kind of *puzzlement* is therefore part of any experience of wonder, a feeling that there is a question there, even if in a literal sense there is not. In some cases, as in my third example, this puzzlement may take the form of a feeling of disorientation or dislocation – which is one reason why wonder is not necessarily a pleasant state to be in, though in this case it was not unpleasant either.

Because wonder is a response to 'otherness' the *imagination* plays an important role in it. In some cases we need imagination to evoke the otherness that evokes wonder – as in my first example. In other cases it is wonder that stirs the imagination. And sometimes they are intertwined from the start and there is no telling which came first or 'caused' the other. In the toad example I found my imagination challenged by something I could not have imagined; it felt rather as if I had walked into a fairy tale (would the toad transform into a prince if it touched the sea?). Even where the role of the imagination is more modest wonder is still a 'seeing *as*' rather than just a 'seeing *that*' – the object of wonder is perceived as remarkable, worthy of attention, in some way. I did not merely see a toad on a beach, I saw something remarkable: an animal 'out of place' (or so I thought).

The arrest of attention that characterizes wonder is also (experienced as) an arrest of time. Wonder has a *different temporality* from our 'ordinary' experience of the world; in wonder we seem to step outside of the flow of time into an extended present in which we are alone with the object of wonder. The bus stop, standing apart from everything and being lit up in the night, takes me into a gap in time; everything else recedes. Yet I do not lose myself entirely; on some level I remain aware of my own presence in relation to the 'other' that confronts me. There is in experiences of wonder a *sense of being an observer*, of witnessing something, that is not normally present in our everyday experience of things. And with this comes a sense of *reflective distance* to the object of wonder that is expressed well by Parsons where he observes that '[w]onder retains an element of detachment or ideation, a minimal curiosity, a control of emotion that gives psychic distance to the event and permits at least in small degree the play of imagination'.[4] Because of this 'psychic distance' to the object wonder is never an *entirely* overwhelming experience; one is not entirely overcome by emotion, however strongly one may be moved. Furthermore, this distance to the object also distinguishes wonder from mystical experiences, in which subject and object merge into a unified, boundless whole, in which the distinction between subject and object is lost.[5]

One thing wonder does have in common with mystical experiences is that it involves a temporary *'forgetting'* or falling away of everything apart from the object of wonder. This is, firstly, because wonder cannot be experienced other than with complete, undivided attention, and secondly, because the object of wonder dominates the experience (though the aggressive connotations of 'dominates' are unfortunate here), meaning that one's 'self' is temporarily bracketed in wonder. Hence Hepburn observes that 'wonder is essentially *other-acknowledging*', 'not shut up in self-concern'.[6] And Nussbaum writes that wonder 'responds to the pull of the object, and one might say that in it the subject is maximally aware of the value of the object, and only minimally aware, if at all, of its relationship to her own plans'.[7]

These two aspects – the sense of distance and awareness of being an observer on the one hand, and the 'self-forgetting' on the other hand – may seem contradictory, but they are not. The first is a self-reflexive aspect that belongs to the *quality* of the experience; it is not something that is itself an *object* of experience, that is to say it does not become articulated in an *explicit* (verbalized) awareness that 'I am witnessing something', let alone 'I am experiencing wonder'. The second aspect entails not only a lack of an explicit awareness of one's self or anything about oneself, but also a complete absence (in the experience) of wanting anything from the object, or of any other purpose, volition or affect that would foreground one's self.[8] Pride, fear, and contentment, to give a few random

4 Parsons, 'A Philosophy of Wonder', 87.

5 Michael Argyle, *Psychology and Religion: An Introduction* (London and New York: Routledge, 2005), 48. Robert Fuller rightly points out that there are strong similarities between what William James called 'mystical states of consciousness' and experiences of wonder; but mystical experiences, for James, were not necessarily experiences in which the distinction between subject and object dissolved. See Fuller, *Wonder*, 133–4, and the chapter on mysticism (lectures XVI and XVII) in William James, *The Varieties of Religious Experience: A Study in Human Nature* (New York, London, and Bombay: Longmans, Green, and Co., 1902).

6 Hepburn, 'Wonder', 14.

7 Martha C. Nussbaum, *Upheavals of Thought: The Intelligence of Emotions* (Cambridge: Cambridge University Press, 2001), 54. Also cited in Vasalou, *Wonder*, 15.

8 On this point see also Cornelis Verhoeven, *Inleiding tot de Verwondering* (Bilthoven: Amboboeken, 1971), 32.

examples, are cognitive–affective states that *do* foreground or draw attention to one's self in one way or another. Wonder, Nussbaum notes, is a peculiarly 'non-eudaimonistic emotion', since whereas other emotions tend to involve a judgement on the value of an object (of perception or contemplation) that – in some way – makes reference to our flourishing, wonder foregrounds the value of the object as such, regardless of its connection with our well-being, our plans, desires, and commitments.[9] (Note, however, that this is not to say that wonder itself cannot contribute to one's flourishing!)

Although the terminology used by Hepburn ('other-*acknowledging*') and Nussbaum ('the *value of the object*') goes somewhat beyond a phenomenological description of wonder it does indicate another central aspect of experiences of wonder, namely the sense of *importance* that it includes. Whether it was the unlikeliness of our existence in our tiny corner of the universe, the contingency of evolution and history, or the surreal appearance of a toad by the sea, each was 'important' in my experience in the literal sense of contributing the main 'ingredient' of the experience and arresting my attention. And each impressed itself upon me as – for whatever reason – worth attending to for its own sake. This is not the same as saying that the object of wonder *is* important or valuable, nor even that it is *perceived* as valuable (as Kevin Tobia suggests), for that something is deemed worth attending to does not mean or imply the judgement that it is valuable, only that it *might* be valuable – or problematic, or important in some other way.[10] Whitehead suggested that wonder is one manifestation of the sense of value or importance.[11] I would qualify this by saying that wonder *is* a way in which the world is important in our experience; it does not necessarily *reveal* the world to be important or valuable in a more objective (subject-independent) sense. The former, at least, is in my view a legitimate interpretation of the phenomenology of wonder; the latter is a judgement I would not be prepared to make for all experiences of wonder. (I will return to the question of the 'revelatory' quality of wonder below, in the subsection on wonder's relationship with meaning, as well as in Chapters 2 and 4.)

9 Ibid.
10 Kevin P. Tobia, 'Wonder and Value', *Res Philosophica* 92, no. 4 (2015).
11 Whitehead, 'Rhythmic Claims', 63.

A Further Interpretation of Wonder

The Object of Wonder

We typically wonder *about* something or *at* something.[12] This 'intentionality', wonder's 'having an object' is in fact central to the experience of wonder, as we have seen. Yet it is worth asking, before we look more closely at the object(s) of wonder, whether wonder *necessarily* has an object. Nussbaum answers this question in the affirmative; she cannot conceive of objectless, free-floating wonder.[13] For single, isolated experiences of wonder I wholeheartedly agree. But it seems to me that there can be such a thing as *dispositional* wonder, and not just in the sense that someone is inclined to experience wonder every time certain conditions prevail, but also in the sense of wonder as a permanent tone in the background, something that influences the hue of our perception of the world, even when we do not actively wonder about or at something. Such wonder does not have a particular object, because its 'object' is indistinguishable from the whole, undifferentiated content of a person's consciousness; this wonder is more like a *mood*, but without its connotation of arbitrariness (moods depend on how some invisible wind blows), and with more permanence. It becomes wonder *about* or wonder *at* something only when something triggers this. Nussbaum doubts whether 'background wonder' exists, not only because she is inclined to think that wonder 'always involves a focused awareness on some object', but also because 'what is especially likely to persist in the background is a structure of personal goals and plans'.[14] I am not convinced. Firstly, I do not think we are dealing with the same 'backgrounds' here; the experiential background formed by a dispositional wonder is not the same as the motivational 'background' – our unconscious motives, desires, intentions – that underlies everything we do. Secondly, some forms of religion or spirituality aim at the cultivation of a disposition of (contemplative) wonder or something close to it, precisely as a way of *detaching* ourselves from our personal desires, goals, and plans – and, though difficult, this does not seem to be impossible.[15]

[12] These are the terms used in Alan Goodwin, 'Wonder in Science Teaching and Learning: An Update', *School Science Review* 83, no. 302 (2001). I return to the distinction in the subsection on contemplative wonder and inquisitive wonder.

[13] Nussbaum, *Upheavals of Thought*, 73.

[14] Ibid.

[15] A good example is the secular version of Buddhism advocated in Stephen Batchelor, *After Buddhism: Rethinking the Dharma for a Secular Age* (New Haven and London: Yale University Press, 2015).

Trigger and Object of Wonder

The trigger of a particular experience of wonder is that which evokes wonder. It sparks the experience; it throws one into this particular experiential state or 'mode of consciousness', as I will call it further on. This trigger is not to be confused with the object of wonder. Sometimes object and trigger coincide, but just as often they do not; quite often the wonder moves on from the trigger to a different or wider object. In my first example, for instance, wonder is triggered by a prehistoric artefact – or, to be more precise, by the activation of certain knowledge about what I am holding – but it becomes wonder about human life and its evolution, about existence on this planet as such. There is no clear boundary between the perception that triggers wonder and the wondering perception; it seems to be a spiralling process, involving a positive feedback loop. Wonder – even if it is not the 'active wondering' of someone in search of explanations (something I will come back to) – is a dynamic state. It involves 'intensified cognitive focus',[16] but its object is not sharply *in* focus and may shift and expand or contract. What began as wonder about the unlikely presence of a toad by the sea developed also into wonder about my own presence there and here, on earth – perhaps triggered by the appearance of this animal 'contemplating' the sea (and, by metaphorical implication, life).

The contrast between the initial object of observation, the perception of which for some reason triggers wonder, and the 'object' of wonder can be quite stark; sometimes the former is (or seems) entirely unremarkable – a pound coin, maybe, or a grain of sand. Then some imaginative leap, some realization, plunges you into the depths – or heights – of wonder. It is often unclear what triggers this event, why it is that perceiving this object, at this moment, gives rise to wonder. But when it happens you are struck by the magical power of the coin to buy something, perhaps, and your awareness is flooded with a sense of the history of trade between people and ways of making a living in this world. Or you imaginatively retrace the grain of sand to the mountain it eroded from and the mountain to the earth's interior that gave birth to it. Part of what it is like to experience wonder is to be cognitively overwhelmed (and this in turn has affective consequences, which however do not go so far as to engulf us with emotion); we experience something like an imaginative equivalent of the 'aboriginal sense of muchness' that according to William James characterizes

[16] Pedersen, *Balanced Wonder*, 18.

infants' initial experience of the world.[17] Wonder is perceived at – or is a way in which we perceive – the limits of our understanding; but the sense of the world being too much is the 'positive' side to this experience.

The Ultimate Object of Wonder

Wonder may be evoked by observing something that conflicts with our expectations: a child may believe that metal objects must necessarily sink, simply because they are made of metal and metal is heavy. Confronted with a metal ship they must revise their theories about how the world works, and once they are familiar with this phenomenon – whether or not they understand precisely why a metal ship does not sink – they will cease to wonder about this. This is how it goes with many experiences of wonder, so the question naturally arises whether all wonder could in principle be (dis)solved by new knowledge or more adequate explanations. Hepburn discusses this question extensively and argues for a compatibilist view of the relation between wonder and causal explanation; i.e. wonder and causal explanation can exist side by side. He proposes that there are various forms of wonder that are immune to dissolution by causal explanation: 'the persistence of the "fragile", living beings (…), on the thin habitable zone of the earth's surface, surrounded by enormous airless spaces', for instance, may evoke wonder; and while this may partly be dissolved by causal explanations that reduce the 'surprise-element' of wonder, what remains is 'the contrast for perception and imagination between living beings and their cosmic environment, between their sensitivity, sentience, internal complexity, vulnerability and the indifferent and mindless regions around them. This contrast, and the wonder it can evoke, survive the acceptance of a causal account'.[18] He continues to suggest that there is a 'finally secure object of wonder', which is 'the *totality* of laws and entities, the world as a whole'. 'Explanation runs *towards* the totality, but there absolutely ends.'[19] The world just *is*, and its being is an utterly contingent fact, which we cannot explain and which evokes a wonder that cannot be undermined by reasoning or causal explanations.

Now, this should not be taken to mean that *only* wonder at the world as a whole, or at existence as such, is 'secure', because wonder at something in particular – the intricate symmetrical pattern of a snowflake, DNA as an information carrier,

[17] William James, *Some Problems of Philosophy: A Beginning of an Introduction to Philosophy* (New York: Longmans, Green, and Co., 1916), 50, cited in Horowitz, *On Looking*, 26.

[18] Hepburn, 'Wonder', 7–8.

[19] Ibid., 9.

the possibility of being understood by another person – often stems from the unlikeliness or contingency of these phenomena, and ultimately receives its 'charge' from 'the wonder appropriate to the whole'.[20] This explains why the object of wonder often shifts from something particular to something more general – it is then pushed back towards its ultimate object. At any rate wonder at a particular thing receives much of its phenomenological character from the mystery of existence or being as such; that is to say that wonder's ultimate object is also always its 'latent' object – without, however, displacing the particular object of wonder that in that occasion embodies being.[21] When you wonder at a particular phenomenon, whether physical or not – a flower perhaps, or photosynthesis, or an act of violence (for such things, too, may be objects of wonder) – you perceive them not analytically but as wholes, but since we cannot grasp wholes conceptually (but only abstracted aspects of wholes), they are 'too much' for us, and become carriers of mystery.

Wonder and Meaning

Further analysis of experiences of wonder reveals that wonder has a strange, two-sided relationship with meaning.[22] On the one hand, the advent of wonder indicates the breakdown of meaning. In Opdal's words: 'Wonder is the state of mind that signals we have reached the limits of our present understanding, and that things may be different from how they look'.[23] Our frames of interpretation either fall short (and are shattered) or fail to perform their normal function. Hence we experience puzzlement, even disorientation perhaps. Wonder can therefore be unsettling. In a (matter-of-factly) way it always is, but sometimes this is experienced as delightful; at other times it can be emotionally, even existentially unsettling, too. Verhoeven writes that 'wonder is a crisis and comes with the dangers of a crisis'.[24] To experience wonder is to experience the dissolution of the ordinary meaning of things; we are lifted out of the world of meaning we

[20] Ibid., 10. See also Thomas Green, *The Activities of Teaching* (New York: McGraw-Hill Book Company, 1971), 195ff., where he explains that the contingency of the world is 'the clue to wonder'.

[21] The same point is expressed in Jeff Malpas, 'Beginning in Wonder', n.d. https://www.academia.edu/3982911/Beginning_in_Wonder: 'It is not the world in general that preoccupies us, but the world in its specificity; and, similarly, it is not the world in general that immediately evokes wonder, but some part or aspect of the world. It is, however, through the part – through the particular thing or event – that the whole is brought to light; it is through the particular encounter or appearance that the fact of encounter or appearance as such is brought into view.'

[22] This section contains material from, and developed more fully in, Anders Schinkel, 'Wonder, Mystery, and Meaning', *Philosophical Papers* (online first, November 2018): 1–28, https://doi.org/10.1080/05568641.2018.1462667.

[23] Opdal, 'Curiosity, Wonder, and Education', 332.

[24] Verhoeven, *Inleiding tot de Verwondering*, 33 (my translation).

normally inhabit and stand aside from it.[25] There is a 'revelatory' aspect to this: by stripping things of their everyday meaning wonder *reveals* that they had this meaning; and this may count as a revelation because of the 'meaninglessness', the taken-for-grantedness, of everyday meaning – that everything always has some meaning for us tends to go unnoticed until this meaning is suspended.

I remember lying awake early one morning – though the sun was already up and the room was quite light – in a state of wondering estrangement (or estranged wonderment): there we were, my wife and I, two individuals of a sexually dimorphic species, lying in a structure called a 'bed' contained within a structure called a 'room', a space with decorated walls within a house made up of such spaces – et cetera. Not only was meaning – in almost every sense of the word – far away, the fact that we are symbolic animals, as Cassirer called it, had itself become the object of wonder.

On the other hand (to return to wonder's two-sided relationship with meaning), wonder also contains the suggestion, often even the promise, of a new, deeper or more encompassing meaning; sometimes it even seems pregnant with meaning.[26] This connects with the sense of 'muchness' referred to earlier as the positive side to the experience of having reached the limits of one's understanding. Parsons writes: 'What attracts and holds the wondering imagination is the mystery of quality and meaning, dramatically or silently challenging man [*sic*], waiting to be unraveled'.[27] It seems plausible that the (probably uniquely) human propensity to wonder is intimately connected with our need for meaning.[28] In light of the fact that wonder can be unsettling because it deprives us (or confronts us with our being deprived) of the comfort of everyday meaning it might seem that wonder's connection with the need for meaning is simply a case of homesickness: we are lost and want to find our way back home. But I think both the phenomenology of wonder and the action wonder inspires suggest otherwise. Whether illusory or not, in wonder – especially in contemplative wonder – one feels the pull of a deeper meaning, not of the comfort of everyday meaning.

[25] This is one of the things that makes wonder so central to philosophy. Pieper stresses their essential connection, writing that '[t]o philosophize means to withdraw – not from the things of everyday life – but from the currently accepted meaning attached to them'; see Josef Pieper, *Leisure: The Basis of Culture* (New York: Mentor Omega/Random House, 1963), 98.

[26] Empirical research also suggests that 'a mind-set of wonder' helps people discover meaning in life; see Jacky van de Goor, Anneke M. Sools, Gerben J. Westerhof, and Ernst Bohlmeijer, 'Wonderful Life: Exploring Wonder in Meaningful Moments', *Journal of Humanistic Psychology* (2017), https://doi.org/10.1177%2F0022167817696837.

[27] Parsons, 'A Philosophy of Wonder', 87.

[28] See Fuller, *Wonder*, and, for the idea of a 'need for meaning', Roy Baumeister, *Meanings of Life* (New York: Guilford Press, 1991).

An example offered by Hove brings out this aspect of wonder quite clearly:

> When I was a student in Strasbourg I had to walk across a bridge on the Rhine every day to get to the university. On this particular day, I lingered awhile in the middle to look out over the city and for some reason all of a sudden became profoundly affected by all the old buildings, and the parks, and the people. There was a touching, timeless beauty to the whole scene. A powerful appreciation welled up in that moment as it dawned on me that for centuries people had lived and died here, and had stood there right where I was standing: all those human beings. And instead of being the reference point for everything in my life I was suddenly taken outside of myself. I was deeply appreciative – just to be living, just to be alive to experience all of this.[29]

In *The Edge of the Sea* Rachel Carson wrote:

> Underlying the beauty of the spectacle there is meaning and significance. It is the elusiveness of that meaning that haunts us, that sends us again and again into the natural world where the key to the riddle is hidden. It sends us back to the edge of the sea (…) where the spectacle of living creatures faced by the cosmic realities of their world is crystal clear.[30]

Hove's example shows that it does not have to be the natural world; a similar sense of depth can be experienced in the human world. Carson did not mean to suggest there is a key that will actually unlock the mystery: the meaning 'haunts and ever eludes us, and in its very pursuit we approach the ultimate mystery of Life itself'.[31] Similarly, in Hove's example we do not find an articulate meaning; instead, he experienced the world as suffused with value and meaning. In a case like this, instead of describing this as a breakdown of meaning or of one's interpretative frameworks it might be more apt to speak of an overflowing of those frameworks, and thus of a surplus of meaning (that still, however, eludes adequate articulation).

The aspect of appreciation that is so central to Hove's example is often – though by no means always – part of experiences of wonder. In wonder one always experiences the object of wonder as interesting and as important at least in the sense that it is worth *attending to* for its own sake; but quite often the object of wonder is also experienced as inherently valuable and worthy of respect – evoking feelings and attitudes of appreciation, respect, and reverence

[29] Hove, 'The Face of Wonder', 454.

[30] Rachel Carson, *The Edge of the Sea* (Boston: Houghton Mifflin, 1955), 250, cited in Fuller, *Wonder*, 106.

[31] Ibid.

that colour one's wonder.[32] A certain 'admiring' type of wonder at the intricate web of dependencies in ecosystems like the Amazon rainforest or the Great Barrier Reef, for instance, is likely to be associated with a desire to protect such places.[33] It can readily be seen, with this type of wonder in mind, how wonder can be described as 'our love of the land', and as lying at the core of an ecocentric education.[34] Nevertheless, it is important not to overgeneralize, because not all experiences of wonder result in a positive sense of meaning; I will return to this in Chapter 4.

The Meaning of Wonder

Before I continue to explore the phenomenology of wonder, this seems a good moment to note that this phenomenology – how we experience wonder – is influenced by how we think about wonder. Wonder not only breaks down or reveals meaning, it also *has* a meaning that is culturally and historically contingent. Exploring a few aspects of the meaning of wonder will help us understand its phenomenology. So whereas the previous subsection concerned what wonder does with our frameworks of interpretation and our experience of meaning, this one focuses on what the frameworks of interpretation that are available to us do with our experience and interpretation of wonder.

Histories of wonder like those offered by Quinn, Martens and Daston and Park show the alternating evaluations of curiosity and wonder.[35] For Plato and Aristotle wonder was the 'beginning' or (moving) principle of philosophy (though for each in different ways), and as such a good thing; and in early Christian times and during the Middle Ages a 'converted' wonder was perceived as a state of mind that focussed our attention on God. 'The very purpose of wonder,' Quinn observes, 'was now seen to be changed from the obtaining of knowledge for self-satisfaction or "happiness" or rendering the world order secure and just, to the quest for eternal life.'[36] Curiosity, on the other hand, was by Christian authors like Augustine and Thomas Aquinas condemned as a vice: to be curious was to try to get to know things that were none of your business,

[32] Cf. Moore, 'The Truth of the Barnacles', also Anders Schinkel, 'Wonder and Moral Education', *Educational Theory* 68, no. 1 (2018), revised and expanded into chapter 4 of this book.

[33] 'Admiring' wonder is a type of wonder distinguished by Hannah Arendt; see Mario Di Paolantonio, 'Wonder, Guarding against Thoughtlessness in Education', *Studies in Philosophy and Education* 38 (2019).

[34] Haydn Washington, 'Education for Wonder', *Education Sciences* 8, no. 3, art. no. 125 (2018), https://doi.org/10.3390/educsci8030125.

[35] Quinn, *Iris Exiled*; Martens, *Vom Staunen*; Daston and Park, *Wonders*.

[36] Quinn, *Iris Exiled*, 118–99.

or to seek immoral knowledge, and to be insufficiently humble.[37] This changed dramatically in the early modern period. Wonder came to be associated with 'enthusiasm' and (religious) sentimentalism, and to be regarded as something that stood in the way of clear-headed thinking and scientific inquiry. Curiosity, on the other hand, came to be seen as a virtue, an indispensable instrument of scientific (and, therefore, general) progress. Thus, at the same time that wonder became 'marginalized' and 'distrusted', curiosity was in the ascendant.[38] Curiosity, in the (early) modern view, is the spur to science and discovery, wonder is at best useless and at worst a positive hindrance to the progress of knowledge and civilization.

Wonder, although it had started out (in Plato's dialogues) as closely linked to the pursuit of knowledge and wisdom, became dissociated from these things in the sixteenth and seventeenth century. Unlike curiosity, wonder was sentimental. It is not entirely surprising, therefore, that in the eighteenth century wonder became a 'romantic' sentiment, closely linked with the feeling of the sublime, that curious mixture of 'delightful horror' and 'terrible joy', as experienced especially in nature.[39] 'In this discovery of the sublime in nature,' Vasalou writes, 'the changing experience of mountains (…) formed a linchpin.'[40] Robert Macfarlane summarizes this change in mentality succinctly: 'The qualities for which mountains were once reviled – steepness, desolation, perilousness – came to be numbered among their most prized aspects.'[41] In his classic *Man and the Natural World* Keith Thomas explains how the strongly utilitarian bent of English thinking led people to see 'unproductive mountains' as 'physically unattractive', compared to cultivated lands, which with their order were seen as beautiful.[42] Furthermore, mountains were perceived as 'the home of uncivilized people',[43] and as dangerous.[44] But all this changed radically in the course of the eighteenth century. In reaction to the prevailing rational, utilitarian aesthetic

[37] Quinn, *Iris Exiled*, 26; Martens, *Vom Staunen*, 51–61.

[38] Vasalou, *Wonder*, 39, 42; this reversal is at the centre of Daston and Park's *Wonders*, and is also discussed (in more normative terms) by Quinn, who speaks of the 'tendency to confuse wonder and curiosity' and of the 'trivialization of wonder and its reduction to curiosity' by seventeenth-century thinkers (Quinn, *Iris Exiled*, 194).

[39] Vasalou, *Wonder*, 79. See this work for extensive discussion of the sublime in relation to wonder, as well as Genevieve Lloyd, *Reclaiming Wonder: After the Sublime* (Edinburgh: Edinburgh University Press, 2018), chapter 4.

[40] Ibid. Vasalou's source is Marjorie H. Nicolson, *Mountain Gloom and Mountain Glory: The Development of the Aesthetics of the Infinite* (Ithaca: Cornell University Press, 1959).

[41] Robert Macfarlane, *Mountains of the Mind: A History of a Fascination* (London: Granta Books, 2008), 18.

[42] Keith Thomas, *Man and the Natural World: Changing Attitudes in England, 1500–1800* (Harmondsworth: Penguin Books, 1987), 258.

[43] Ibid.

[44] Macfarlane, *Mountains*, 15.

ideals an appreciation of wilderness appeared in which wild nature was viewed as beautiful and spiritually and morally healing.[45] It is as a result of this cultural transformation that Macfarlane can write:

> Ultimately and most importantly, mountains quicken our sense of wonder. (...) Being in the mountains reignites our astonishment at the simplest transactions of the physical world: a snowflake a millionth of an ounce in weight falling on to one's outstretched palm, water patiently carving a runnel in a face of granite, the apparently motiveless shift of a stone in a scree-filled gully. (...) Mountains return to us the priceless capacity for wonder which can so insensibly be leached away by modern existence, and they urge us to apply that wonder to our own everyday lives.[46]

No single factor can explain why this transformation occurred; it was the result of a combination of partly contradictory tendencies. When wild nature was everywhere, it was easier to overlook; only when it was increasingly and increasingly visibly transformed did it become bounded and thereby an object of observation and did it become remarkable. Only when 'civilization' was everywhere could nature become a place of refuge. Connected with this was an experience of loss (of wild nature, of animal species, of open space). Thomas offers a number of reasons for the 'growing concern to preserve uncultivated nature as an indispensable spiritual resource':

> [A]n aesthetic reaction against the regularity and uniformity of English agriculture; a dislike for the artificialities of the garden movement; a feeling that wilderness, by its very contrast with cultivation, was necessary to give meaning and definition to the human enterprise; a preoccupation with the freedom of open space as a symbol of human freedom (...); and an element of alienation or lack of sympathy for the dominant trends of the age.[47]

The romantic reaction to modern civilization, while provoked by it and opposed to it, was at the same time made possible by it. To quote Thomas once more: 'If weeds now had their friends, the same was true of the wild animals and birds against whom earlier generations had battled in their struggle for subsistence.

45 Thomas, *Man and the Natural World*, 260.

46 Macfarlane, *Mountains*, 275–6. Another wonderful book that would probably not have been written without this cultural transformation is Nan Shepherd, *The Living Mountain* (n.p.: Canongate, 2019), a meditation on walking through the Cairngorms (Scotland) written in the last years of the Second World War, first published in 1977.

47 Thomas, *Man and the Natural World*, 267–8.

Here, too, new security was the essential precondition for greater tolerance'.[48] Control over nature enabled people to overcome their fear, or to experience it as a form of pleasure (as in the sublime).

The transformation of cultural perceptions of nature in Western Europe not only gave wonder a new role in the aesthetic appreciation of nature, but also reconfigured wonder's emotional signature. Having been associated with *fear* (of God or of ignorance) by Augustine and medieval philosophers, wonder could now become a source of intrinsic pleasure (or, of course, a pleasurable combination of fear and delight).[49] I suspect that many people today will be surprised to read that people once associated wonder with fear, and will readily associate wonder with pleasure. The predominance of an aesthetic sense of wonder is a Romantic inheritance that is still with us, and apart from fear and other 'darker' aspects of wonder this has also subdued epistemic aspects of the phenomenology of wonder, and thus its link with inquiry and with education.[50]

What does this (extremely) brief foray into the history of wonder tell us about the meaning of wonder? Firstly, that, in general terms, wonder has a different meaning and a different value for people in, say, the UK or the Netherlands today than it did for people three or four centuries ago, or for Aristotle, Augustine, or Aquinas. Secondly, that it is dangerous to speak about wonder in general terms; wonder is, in a sense, more a name for an experiential *potential* that is plural, than for a particular type of experience. And yet, continuous threads connect conceptions of wonder at various points in our history, and despite the differences and the plurality it would be too hasty to conclude that people were talking about 'different things'. Thirdly, that both what we wonder at or about and how we wonder at that or about that is shaped in important ways by our cultural history. In his cultural history of mountains and mountaineering Macfarlane speaks of 'mountains of the mind' because we '*read* landscapes,

[48] Ibid., 273.

[49] Vasalou, *Wonder*, 40. Fisher notes that for seventeenth-century philosopher Blaise Pascal wonder was also associated with fear, and that '[w]hat Descartes calls a wonder, Pascal will often call an abyss'; see Philip Fisher, *Wonder, the Rainbow, and the Aesthetics of Rare Experiences* (Cambridge and London: Harvard University Press, 1998), 50. It seems to me, therefore (and I agree with Vasalou here), that it is problematic to define wonder as 'a sudden experience of an extraordinary object that produces delight', as Fisher, *Wonder*, 55, does. As Vasalou shows, no aspect of this definition – though it captures many experiences of wonder – is unproblematic.

[50] It is for this reason that both Mary-Jane Rubenstein and Genevieve Lloyd attempt to rehabilitate wonder as a philosophically and politically important sensibility; see Rubenstein, *Strange Wonder*, and Lloyd, *Reclaiming Wonder*. My own attempt, in this book, to highlight the importance of (deep/contemplative) wonder for education stems from a similar concern; and I agree with Quinn, *Iris Exiled*, at least to the extent that if in education we speak only of curiosity and not of wonder we leave a lot that is important out of the picture.

in other words, we interpret their forms in the light of our own experience and memory, and that of our shared cultural memory'.[51] Similarly, it is because of our cultural history that certain types and experiences of wonder are now available to me (and others not). My own secular but, if you will, spiritual wonder at the mystery of existence, the apparent groundlessness of being – a wonder, also, suggestive of meaning without ever revealing it – would have been unthinkable to medieval theologians, and is shaped by Romanticism. But fourthly, the rich history of wonder also enables us to become aware of tones and shades of our experiences of wonder that we might otherwise not have noticed; and even to interpret and experience sensations and feelings as wonder that we might otherwise have interpreted differently – as fear or anxiety, for instance, or simply as joy.[52]

Contemplative Wonder and Inquisitive Wonder

The personal examples of wonder given so far, as well as the example borrowed from Hove, are all cases of what I have called 'deep wonder' or 'contemplative wonder'; such wonder is different in quality from a more active 'wondering' for which 'inquisitive wonder' might be a good name, and which is (relatively speaking) closer to curiosity.[53] It is with some hesitation that I introduce this

[51] Macfarlane, *Mountains*, 18.

[52] I will go into the complexities of the interpretation of emotions and feelings more deeply in the following chapter.

[53] This distinction (or an equivalent distinction) has been made more or less explicitly by many authors; see, for instance, Parsons, 'A Philosophy of Wonder', 88; Goodwin, 'Wonder in Science Teaching'; Hove, 'The Face of Wonder'; Proffitt, 'The Importance of Wonder', 105; Nathalie Sinclair and Anne Watson, 'Wonder, the Rainbow and the Aesthetics of Rare Experiences', *For the Learning of Mathematics* 21, no. 3 (2001); Hadzigeorgiou, 'Reclaiming'; Dov Zazkis and Rina Zazkis, 'Wondering about Wonder in Mathematics', in *Wonder-full Education: The Centrality of Wonder in Teaching and Learning across the Curriculum*, eds. Kieran Egan, Annabella Cant, and Gillian Judson (New York: Routledge, 2014), 67; James Le Fanu, *Why Us? How Science Rediscovered the Mystery of Ourselves* (London: Harper Press, 2010), 58. Other terms used are: 'passive' v. 'active' wonder and 'wonder at' and 'wonder(ing) about' or 'wonder why'; inquisitive wonder has also been called 'curiosity wonder' (Proffitt); alternative terms for contemplative wonder are 'existential wonder' (Hepburn, 'Wonder'; Hove, 'The Face of Wonder', 442) and (as I have called it elsewhere) 'deep wonder'; see Anders Schinkel, 'The Educational Importance of Deep Wonder', *Journal of Philosophy of Education* 51, no. 2 (2017)). Rubenstein makes a similar distinction in terms of Aristotelian and Socratic/Platonic wonder; see Rubenstein, *Strange Wonder*, and Mary-Jane Rubenstein, 'Heidegger's Caves: On Dwelling in Wonder', in *Practices of Wonder: Interdisciplinary Perspectives*, ed. Sophia Vasalou (Cambridge: James Clarke & Co., 2015), 144–65 and cf. Vasalou, *Wonder*, 56–69. Green, *The Activities of Teaching*, 195ff., speaks of 'wondering how' and 'wondering at', but he identifies the former with curiosity. My distinction in terms of inquisitive and contemplative wonder is closest to Hepburn's, who speaks of a 'variable relation between the element of curiosity or interrogation in wonder and a contemplative-appreciative aspect ("dwelling"), in which it is furthest from mere curiosity'; Hepburn, 'Wonder', 4.

distinction, because I am aware of how easily it can solidify into thinking that there really are, in reality, two perfectly distinct types of wonder, two 'things' picked out by the distinction between inquisitive and contemplative wonder. We must beware not to commit the 'fallacy of misplaced concreteness', and keep in mind that the distinction is an abstraction, and no more or less than a helpful way to get to grips with a more fluid and more complex reality.[54]

A way to clarify the relation between the distinction between inquisitive and contemplative wonder and the reality of wonder is to imagine a multi-dimensional experiential 'space', like a coordinate system in mathematics, in which experiences of wonder can be plotted along various axes. One axis may represent the sense of puzzlement, another desire for knowledge or understanding, and yet another a sense of aesthetic appreciation. It is easiest to imagine a three-dimensional space, but in reality it would have a much larger, perhaps indefinite number of dimensions, including also various other affective qualities wonder may have (fearful, joyful, melancholy). Experiences of wonder differ in the degree to which they share the phenomenological features represented by the various axes; the sense of puzzlement may be weaker or stronger, aesthetic appreciation may be a dominant aspect of the experience, or even entirely absent. Thus, experiences of wonder plotted (by placing a dot) in this coordinate system will occupy different positions. And in fact, it is even misleading to suggest that a single experience of wonder would occupy a single, stationary position, because experiences of wonder are dynamic, they are better pictured as fluid, shapeshifting blobs than as solid, sharply defined entities. Nevertheless, we can imagine experiences of wonder as hovering around particular positions in experiential space (with some shifting position more radically). Now, what the distinction between inquisitive and contemplative wonder (or between active and deep wonder) is meant to express is the idea that if we were to plot a large number of experiences of wonder in this coordinate system, we would find that they were not spread evenly across the coordinate system, but were grouped in clouds; one of these clouds would be inquisitive wonder, the other contemplative wonder. (It may well be possible to discern other clouds, or clouds within these two clouds, but for the purpose of this book the distinction between these two is most useful, and sufficient.)

[54] The 'fallacy of misplaced concreteness' is the name given by philosopher Alfred North Whitehead to the (widespread) error of mistaking the abstract for the concrete, our concepts for the reality they are supposed to represent; Alfred North Whitehead, *Science and the Modern World* (New York: The Free Press, 1967), 51.

To get a sense of what inquisitive wonder is like, and how it differs from contemplative wonder, it is again helpful to look at an example. Here is one from Charles Darwin's Beagle diary, 2–8 June 1834:

> The Adventure rejoined us, after having examined the East side of this part of the Straits. – The weather has during the greater part of the time been very foggy & cold; but we were in high luck in having two clear days for observations. On one of these the view of Sarmiento was most imposing: I have not ceased to wonder, in the scenery of Tierra del Fuego, at the apparent little elevation of mountains really very high. – I believe it is owing to a cause which one would be last to suspect, it is the sea washing their base & the whole mountain being in view. I recollect in Ponsonby Sound, after having seen a mountain down the Beagle Channel, I had another view of it across many ridges, one behind the other. – This immediately made one aware of its distance, & with its distance it was curious how its apparent height rose.[55]

Puzzlement is one of the foremost elements in this type of wonder, and the meaning sought is an explanation – something that explains the significance of one's observations, that makes sense of them.[56] It is worth noting that Darwin writes: 'I have not ceased to wonder'; the protracted nature of his wondering is typical of inquisitive wonder. Intense experiences of contemplative wonder tend to pass relatively quickly. That said, contemplative wonder may arguably also become a more or less permanent background state that partly determines the tone of all of one's waking life; and that Darwin for days or weeks did not cease to wonder does not mean, of course, that every minute or hour was spent wondering.[57]

Inquisitive wonder(ing) is a state that has, to a greater or lesser degree, all of the phenomenological qualities described so far, but it differs from contemplative wonder in two important interrelated respects. Firstly, whereas in contemplative wonder the mystery one responds to is experienced as beyond the limits of

[55] Charles Darwin, *Beagle Diary*, ed. Richard Darwin Keynes (Cambridge: Cambridge University Press, 2001), 241, http://darwin-online.org.uk/content/frameset?itemID=F1925&viewtype=text&pageseq=1.

[56] Darwin's wonder(ing) at and about the discrepancy between the actual height of the mountains and their appearance of modest elevation was not accidental. He was strongly influenced by Charles Lyell's *Principles of Geology* (1830–1833), which he read on his voyage with the HMS *Beagle*, and in various observations he found support for Lyell's ideas about the gradual (step-wise) elevation of mountains (and, to a great extent, for Lyell's general theoretical views); see Martin J. S. Rudwick, *The Meaning of Fossils: Episodes in the History of Paleontology* (Chicago and London: The University of Chicago Press, 1985), 188–9.

[57] As mentioned before, something like the cultivation of a disposition of contemplative wonder – so that it would become a permanent 'background state' – seems to be the aim of the secular version of Buddhism presented by Batchelor, *After Buddhism*.

human understanding – it may be 'grasped' or approached metaphorically or in some other indirect way, but cognitive control or mastery is unattainable – in inquisitive wonder this is not the case. Instead, attention is focused on a 'solvable' mystery – an explanation is out there, it just needs to be found. (I will nuance this in a moment, but for now this is close enough.) The second difference can be understood in light of the first: inquisitive wonder has an intense and focused 'searching' quality that is much more diffuse and sometimes virtually absent in contemplative wonder. What are 'silent' why and how questions in contemplative wonder are questions of a different nature in inquisitive wonder, questions one expects (in theory) to be able to answer.

But as I already suggested, this distinction is to be treated with caution. If we look closely at experiences of inquisitive wonder it becomes clear that more often than not there is no expectation of full 'closure' – on the one hand because an adequate explanation (as might be found in the case of Darwin's deceptively low-seeming mountains) does not necessarily render the object of wonder unremarkable (in Darwin's example the surprising aesthetic effect remains), and on the other hand because behind every explanation lie further questions.[58] Inquisitive wonder is interested in 'pushing back' the mystery, but it is not insensitive to mystery. Furthermore, the distinction between inquisitive and contemplative wonder is in reality not clear cut, and not to be seen as an impenetrable border; in my example of the toad on the beach my initial wonder lay close to inquisitive wonder, but it developed in the other direction. It is not difficult to imagine the one type of wonder giving way to (or leading on to) the other, or a person oscillating between the two, as some scientists probably do.[59]

Thus, to repeat, we must be careful not to reify the distinction between inquisitive and contemplative wonder, as if we were dealing with two clearly separate realities. The terms are abstractions, the use of which I believe to be justified only because they help us articulate noticeable qualitative differences. The reason I accept the risk of reification here is twofold. Firstly, in educational contexts wonder is virtually always associated with inquisitiveness, but it is important to realize that this is not the whole story. Secondly, it is at the same time important to prevent that, once the possibility of deep or contemplative wonder is acknowledged, inquisitive wonder is identified with curiosity.

A final qualifying observation: that it is useful to distinguish inquisitive from contemplative wonder does not mean that there are no differences within

[58] The aesthetic element may also explain Darwin's speaking of wonder *at* the apparent little elevation of the mountains.

[59] See, for example, the preface of Norman Davies, *The Mind of God: Science and the Search for Ultimate Meaning* (London: Penguin Books, 1993).

those categories; for instance, contemplative wonder may be of a more aesthetic, admiring kind, or of a more questioning kind ('pure', indeterminate wonder), and these differences are important with regard to the potential educational role of such experiences.

How Wonder Differs from Curiosity and Awe

In the philosophical literature it is quite common to distinguish between wonder and curiosity. In some cases no further distinction is made within wonder, so that wonder comes to be identified with what I have called contemplative wonder.[60] Others maintain that wonder can be inquisitive yet still crucially different from curiosity,[61] and some (like me) also uphold a distinction between a more 'active' or inquisitive and a more 'passive' or contemplative type of wonder.[62] The situation is rather different in psychology. For whatever reasons – for reasons I will not explore here, at any rate – there is a huge body of psychological research on (various types of) curiosity, but virtually none on wonder.[63] Moreover, wonder is not even mentioned in this literature.[64]

60 For instance, Quinn, *Iris Exiled*; Fuller, *Wonder*; Frederick F. Schmitt and Reza Lahroodi, 'The Epistemic Value of Curiosity', *Educational Theory* 58, no. 2 (2008).

61 E.g. Opdal, 'Curiosity, Wonder and Education'.

62 E.g. Hadzigeorgiou, 'Reclaiming'.

63 A recent exception is Peter Lamont, 'A Particular Kind of Wonder: The Experience of Magic Past and Present', *Review of General Psychology* 21, no. 1 (2017). This theoretical article also lists some literature in the psychology of emotion that pays some attention to wonder.

64 See, for example, Daniel E. Berlyne, 'A Theory of Human Curiosity', *British Journal of Psychology* 45, no. 3 (1954); Schulamith Kreitler, Edward Ziegler, and Hans Kreitler, 'The Nature of Curiosity in Children', *Journal of School Psychology* 13, no. 3 (1975); George Loewenstein, 'The Psychology of Curiosity: A Review and Reinterpretation', *Psychological Bulletin* 116, no. 1 (1994); Jordan A. Litman, 'Curiosity and the Pleasures of Learning: Wanting and Liking New Information', *Cognition and Emotion* 19, no. 6 (2005); Todd B. Kashdan and Paul J. Silvia, 'Curiosity and Interest: The Benefits of Thriving on Novelty and Challenge', in *The Oxford Handbook of Positive Psychology*, 2nd ed., eds. Shane J. Lopez and C. R. Snyder (Oxford: Oxford University Press: 2009); Jamie Jirout and David Klahr, 'Children's Scientific Curiosity: In Search of an Operational Definition of an Elusive Concept', *Developmental Review* 32, no. 2 (2012); Jacqueline Gottlieb et al., 'Information-seeking, Curiosity, and Attention: Computational and Neural Mechanisms', *Trends in Cognitive Sciences* 17, no. 11 (2013). The word 'wonder' only figures occasionally (but still very rarely) in the colloquial sense of 'I wonder' or 'one may wonder'. Note that I have not cherry-picked texts that fail to mention wonder, but have simply selected theoretical studies on curiosity or studies with a strong theoretical component over a range of time (beginning with Berlyne's influential work), making sure to include some of the most important authors in the field. It may not be particularly surprising that philosophers have a stronger interest in wonder than psychologists, but it is remarkable that while no philosophical study of wonder will fail to mention curiosity, the opposite seems true for psychological work on curiosity. Also remarkable is that even where Litman, 'Curiosity', 807n9, writes that 'the nature of the complex relationships between awe, aesthetic experience, and curiosity are not well understood and will be an interesting topic for future study' he still sees no need to mention wonder.

Although a wealth of conceptual work on curiosity thus exists in the field of psychology, none of it is phenomenological in nature. Philosophical studies of wonder also tend to spend relatively little time on the phenomenology of curiosity. It is at the phenomenological level, however, that it is most important to distinguish wonder and curiosity – or those (families of) experiences we may want to distinguish conceptually as wonder and curiosity – since we are dealing with experiential phenomena first, and only secondarily with concepts. If we begin with a focus on the conceptual level, we are much more likely to lose sight of what we wanted to study in the first place and why. So, without attempting to present an elaborate phenomenological description of curiosity, I will try to clarify some phenomenological differences between wonder and curiosity; and I will do the same for awe, a phenomenon and concept that is receiving increasing attention from psychologists of late.[65] The advantage of this work on awe is that, since it is a fairly young field of psychological inquiry (though of course it can and does refer to older work, such as that of William James and contemporaries), it stays somewhat closer to the experience of awe.[66]

Loewenstein begins his review article on the psychology of curiosity with a quote from philosopher Edmund Burke (1729–1797): '[C]uriosity is the most superficial of all the affections; it changes its object perpetually; it has an appetite which is very sharp, but very easily satisfied; and it has always an appearance of giddiness, restlessness and anxiety'.[67] Although exaggerated and in some respects one-sided, it is a good place to start; later philosophical descriptions of curiosity, such as Heidegger's, are not much different.[68] The type of experience Burke describes here will be instantly recognizable to anyone: you accidentally catch a few stray words from a conversation between colleagues and your name

[65] Dacher Keltner and Jonathan Haidt, 'Approaching Awe, a Moral, Spiritual, and Aesthetic Emotion', *Cognition and Emotion* 17, no. 2 (2003); Michelle N. Shiota, Dacher Keltner, and Amanda Mossman, 'The Nature of Awe: Elicitors, Appraisals, and Effects on Self-Concept'. *Cognition and Emotion* 21, no. 5 (2007); Edward T. Bonner and Harris L. Friedman, 'A Conceptual Clarification of the Experience of Awe: An Interpretative Phenomenological Analysis', *The Humanist Psychologist* 39 (2011); cf. Kristján Kristjánsson, 'Awe: An Aristotelian Analysis of a Non-Aristotelian Virtuous Emotion', *Philosophia* 45 (2017).

[66] Note, however, that although Bonner and Friedman use IPA, this is not the same as philosophical phenomenology (see Introduction); as Kristjánsson, 'Awe', 130, neatly summarizes, they 'consider individual agents to be experts on their own experience; the role of the researcher is simply to help map out the meaning of this experience by distilling common themes that emerge from the experience of a group of people and systematising those as far as possible'. This differs from attempting to articulate as precisely as possible what it is like to experience awe, and to reveal its normally unperceived meaning.

[67] Edmund Burke, *A Philosophical Enquiry into the Origin of Our Ideas of the Sublime and Beautiful* (London: Routledge & Kegan Paul, 1958), 31, cited in Loewenstein, 'The Psychology of Curiosity', 75.

[68] See Rubenstein, 'Heidegger's Caves', 146–7.

is among them, and instantly you want (or need) to know what they were saying about you; there are carefully wrapped presents under the Christmas tree, in 'curious' shapes even, perhaps, but you don't know what's in them and which are for whom (in particular: which are yours), so your curiosity battles with internal voices that say you cannot open them yet; a researcher comes across a study on her specialist topic that she wasn't aware of, and is curious (and anxious) to see what its author has to say about it.

Typical of such examples of curiosity is that one's attention is drawn involuntarily to (something that makes you aware of the fact that there is) something you do not know but want to know.[69] To experience curiosity is, on some level, to experience a lack; on this point I think a phenomenological account of curiosity must agree with 'deprivation' accounts of curiosity like Loewenstein's information gap theory.[70] But that does not mean that the sense of deprivation needs to be foremost in the experience; in fact, curiosity is often a quite pleasant state to be in (for some time, at least). Like wonder, curiosity has an intentional object (we attend *to* something), but in curiosity our relation to the object is qualitatively different; whereas in wonder the object itself takes centre stage, in curiosity it is the *desire to know* the object that is foregrounded. The difference is *not* that wonder implies an interest in the object for its own sake and curiosity an instrumental interest, for curiosity also presupposes that the desire to know is not 'practical' or instrumental; the difference is that in curiosity one's interest is in *knowing* its object (e.g. 'what's in the box with your name on it under the Christmas tree') rather than in the object itself – a knowing for the sake of knowing.[71] (Obviously, curiosity, as in this example, can go together with other types of interest; once you know what's in the box you may want to have it, play with it, et cetera – or not.) Phenomenologically, the desire to know is dominant, and it can be very intense ('burning curiosity'). This aspect comes out much more clearly in German and Dutch, where the words 'Neugier' and 'nieuwsgierigheid', respectively, both contain a term that in English would have to be translated as 'greed' or 'lust' or 'possessiveness' in the sense of a strong appetite to acquire something for oneself.[72] In the actual emotional valence of the German and Dutch terms for curiosity little of the negative charge of 'gier(igheid)' remains, but these terms still point to some important aspects of curiosity; apart from the (potential) intensity of the experience they reveal

[69] Schmitt and Lahroodi, 'The Epistemic Value of Curiosity', 128.
[70] Loewenstein, 'The Psychology of Curiosity'.
[71] Schmitt and Lahroodi, 'The Epistemic Value of Curiosity', 128n8.
[72] Cf. Hepburn, 'Wonder', 4.

something about the 'directionality' of curiosity. Curiosity is 'self-centred' and is experienced as the self moving towards an object, and this forward movement of a self seeking to satisfy an appetite distinguishes curiosity from wonder, in which the self is rather de-centred, 'emptied', waiting for the object to approach.

Someone might object and say that curiosity need not be like this, that it *can* be a desire to know something for the sake of knowing *that object*, i.e. out of a genuine interest in the object. In speaking about curiosity the way I just did ('curiosity is … ') I exposed myself to such criticism, for such convenient ways of speaking inevitably suggest that I am somehow defining, or describing the essence of, everything we may mean when we use the term 'curiosity'. And sometimes no doubt we mean something like an active, genuine interest in a particular subject matter. But my main interest is in getting at a particular type of experience and a particular way of relating to things; one that is best expressed in terms of curiosity, but need not be the *only* referent of the term as used in everyday language. At the same time, my aim here is not so modest as merely trying to capture one use of the term 'curiosity', but to get at a type of experience that arguably engendered – gave rise to the need for – a concept of curiosity as distinct from the concepts of attention, interest, wonder, et cetera. Central to that type of experience, or to that mental state, are such things as mentioned above – things that do not belong to the phenomenology of interest as such. Though its evaluation varied, curiosity as the knowledge-seeking state or trait described above has been the dominant conception since early Christianity.[73]

Several authors have also remarked that wonder entails a heightened awareness of one's own 'ignorance' – and more so than curiosity. Whereas curiosity implies there is some particular thing one does not know, or – when curiosity takes the more positive form of exploration with the purpose of encountering something interesting – simply that there are things to be known out there, wonder foregrounds the general extent of one's ignorance or lack of ability to comprehend what one is confronted with.[74] To experience curiosity is to experience a lack or an appetite, yes, but in no way is this a 'shock to the system'. The remedy is simple: when you are thirsty, drink; when you are curious, satisfy your curiosity by getting to know whatever it is you don't know yet. At no point, in typical cases of curiosity, does the experienced lack or appetite become reflexive, and does it shake your confidence in your knowledge of the world and

[73] Cf. Quinn, *Iris Exiled*.

[74] Quinn, *Iris Exiled*, 18ff.; Hadzigeorgiou, 'Reclaiming', 48; Opdal, 'Curiosity, Wonder and Education', 331–2.

your frameworks of understanding. Curiosity does not suggest that things might be entirely different than you believed, but rather that there is more knowledge to add to your existing stock; and quite often, as said, once this is done you lose interest.

The experience of wonder is always characterized by an attitude of receptivity, an openness to what shows itself or gives itself to one's experience. Wonder waits, curiosity investigates. Even inquisitive wonder keeps a certain respectful distance from its object, it entails inquiring activity permeated by stopping and waiting to see or listen. Wonder, as Fuller says, 'is typically characterized by a strong sense of the fullness of the present'.[75] This cannot be said of curiosity, which is immersed in the stream of time and has a spatio-temporally isolating focus on its object: zooming in on the object with focused attention, you may lose all sense of time, rather than experiencing it as an extended present (as in wonder).

The differences between wonder and curiosity described above may be explained in terms of a fundamental phenomenological difference. While both have an intentional object, we might say that while wonder *has* an object, curiosity *seeks* its object. Wonder contemplates its object or, in the case of inquisitive wonder, moves around it, alternately leaning in and stepping back; but curiosity has nothing to behold, its object is at the same time its goal: new knowledge, the answer to a question. Imagine seeing a video of a fertilized human ovum that divides to become two cells, then four, some time after that a recognizable foetus, and so on. This may arouse curiosity – about the biological processes behind this, about the next step in the development, or perhaps the whole reproductive system. The intentional object of that curiosity will then be, not what you are seeing, but something you *cannot* see (yet) – in that sense curiosity *seeks* its object. The object of inquisitive wonder, however, should this be evoked, would remain the same – the strange, incomprehensible spectacle you are witnessing – but you would be trying to understand it better. All the while you are investigating this 'object' from a state of inquisitive wonder, your attention remains focussed on the spectacle that is the object of your wonder. Hence curiosity is characterized by focussed, goal-oriented activity, whereas wonder is a more receptive stance, open to what unfolds before it.

Another aspect of wonder's openness, apart from its receptive quality, is that wonder is indeterminate, undecided, or at least less than fully decided about

[75] Fuller, *Wonder*, 41.

its object.[76] As long as wonder is the dominant mood we have not completely and definitively decided what our attitude towards the object should be (other than one of puzzled wonder). In this respect wonder differs most clearly from awe. Kristjánsson describes three personal experiences that, he suggests, 'had in common (...) the single emotion of awe, but targeting the different ideals of beauty, goodness, and truth, respectively'. I reproduce the first of these here:

> I first visited Hljóðaklettar – a well-known area of columnar-craters, presenting unique 'basalt roses', in a national park in the north-east of Iceland – on an early October day as a 17-year-old. All the tourists had gone, there was not a single person in sight; only the 'rosy' columns surrounded by low birch trees in autumn colours, with a mighty grey glacial river providing a stark background contrast. I experienced feelings of aesthetic ecstasy, mingled with a sense of enormity, oneness and of time standing still. I have never been fully able to recapture that feeling, there or elsewhere, although I have caught glimpses of it when listening to great pieces of music such as Tchaikovsky's Violin Concerto.[77]

Crucial to this experience, and to what makes it an experience of awe, is the perception of 'greatness', in a sense that includes a positive evaluation. The object of experience is 'great' in an evaluative sense (it is ineffably beautiful, true, or good, in Kristjánsson's analysis), and you are therefore 'small' by comparison, though somehow connected with or taken up in the larger whole you are contemplating (experienced as 'elevation'). This 'identification' of the object as 'great' makes awe different even from the type of experience I have termed deep or contemplative wonder; if there is still an element of puzzlement in awe it is connected with the problem of how to express such greatness or how such greatness can exist, not with the nature or quality of the object as such – in awe it is clear that admiration is the appropriate attitude.

This can also be expressed in terms of the reflective distance (or, in Parsons' terms, 'psychic distance') to the object that characterizes wonder. Parsons notes that this distinguishes wonder from 'almost purely emotional' experiences 'like panic or terror or awe'. 'Wonder retains an element of detachment or ideation (...), a control of emotion that (...) permits at least in some small degree the play of imagination. When detached imagination is overcome by emotion, such as great fear or terror, wonder disappears.'[78]

[76] Verhoeven, *Inleiding tot de Verwondering*, 30.
[77] Kristjánsson, 'Awe', 128–9.
[78] Parsons, 'A Philosophy of Wonder', 87.

In practice there is no clear dividing line between (contemplative) wonder and awe, though.[79] Both share a strongly aesthetic character not found in curiosity. A sense of 'vastness' (seen by Keltner and Haidt as central to awe) is often part of experiences of wonder, and the experience of 'cosmic flight' that is historically a recurring motif in descriptions of experiences of wonder involves a shift in perspective on oneself that is not altogether unlike the humbling effect of awe.[80]

A Conceptualization of Inquisitive and Contemplative Wonder

Wonder as a Mode of Consciousness

From the above phenomenological description and interpretation of wonder it will be more than clear that wonder is not easily captured in a single, comprehensive definition; and this is a point agreed upon by most, if not all, philosophers who have devoted significant attention to the matter. Still, with a view to the remainder of this book it is helpful to settle on a more precise delineation of what I mean by wonder, and what I take to be most central to those experiences commonly expressed in terms of wonder.

With Fuller I would like to emphasize (once more) that wonder is not to be reified: '[W]onder is not so much a separate "thing" as the feeling state accompanying the body's response to certain environmental situations'.[81] Somewhat similarly, Pedersen speaks of a 'state of mind'.[82] My own preferred term is 'mode of consciousness'.[83] To say that wonder is a mode of consciousness is to say that it is a particular way in which we are aware of the world. I presuppose here an understanding of consciousness as 'what it is like to be' the subject of that consciousness at that particular moment in time.[84] As Nagel

[79] See Kristjánsson, 'Awe', 133.

[80] For the 'cosmic flight' motif see Vasalou, *Wonder*, 156–9.

[81] Fuller, *Wonder*, 33.

[82] Pedersen, *Balanced Wonder*, 6.

[83] Bendik-Keymer uses the term 'mode of attention' once; Jeremy Bendik-Keymer, 'The Reasonableness of Wonder', *Journal of Human Development and Capabilities* 18, no. 3 (2017): 338. Given that consciousness can itself be seen as a mode of attention – as pointed out in Alfred North Whitehead, *Adventures of Ideas* (Cambridge: Cambridge University Press, 1964), 182, 'mode of attention' and 'mode of consciousness' are very similar terms.

[84] This understanding of consciousness was developed independently at more or less the same time by Timothy Sprigge and Thomas Nagel; see Timothy Sprigge, 'Final Causes', *Proceedings of the Aristotelian Society*, Suppl. Vol. 45 (1971); Timothy Sprigge, *The Importance of Subjectivity: Selected Essays in Metaphysics and Ethics*, ed. Leemon B. McHenry (Oxford: Oxford University Press, 2011); Thomas Nagel, 'What Is It Like to Be a Bat?' in Thomas Nagel, *Mortal Questions* (Cambridge: Cambridge University Press, 1979).

explains, 'conscious experience is a widespread phenomenon', occurring 'at many levels of animal life'.[85] 'But no matter how the form may vary, the fact that an organism has conscious experience *at all* means, basically, that there is something it is like to *be* that organism. (…) [A]n organism has mental states if and only if there is something that it is like to *be* that organism – something it is like *for* the organism.'[86] Thus, consciousness is a matter of subjective experience, it is *phenomenal*.[87] To be sure, consciousness must not be mistaken for *explicit* or second-order awareness. As Sprigge notes, a spider will have some level of consciousness, but it does not 'know the answer' to the question what it is like to be himself except 'in a very special sense in which certain realities are the knowing of themselves'. 'Experience is the only thing which has this kind of being in which being and knowing are one.'[88] For Sprigge, this is another way to define experience or consciousness. In human beings, obviously, consciousness may vary greatly in reflexivity and in its level of explicitness.

So the term 'mode of consciousness' does not refer to cognition only. Since I understand consciousness as what it is like to be the subject of that consciousness it encompasses the subject's total state of feeling and thinking – cognition, affect, and bodily sensations and background feelings.[89] The question, then, is what marks out wonder from other modes of consciousness. We should be able to derive an answer to this question from the phenomenological account of wonder presented above.

Wonder, I propose, is *a mode of consciousness in which we experience that which we perceive or are contemplating as in some way strange, beyond our understanding, yet worthy of our attention for its own sake, and in which our attention takes the form of an open, receptive stance.* This conceptualization captures, though very compactly, the central phenomenological elements of puzzlement or surprise, arrest of attention, centrality of the object, and openness and receptivity. To define *deep* or *contemplative* wonder – the main focus of this book – we need to qualify this definition slightly: contemplative wonder is *a mode of consciousness in which we experience that which we perceive or are*

[85] Nagel, 'What Is It Like', 166.

[86] Ibid.

[87] Perhaps the strongest critic of this view is Daniel Dennett; see Daniel Dennett, *Consciousness Explained* (Boston: Little, Brown, and Company, 1991), and Daniel Dennett, *From Bacteria to Bach and Back: The Evolution of Minds* (n.p.: Penguin Books, 2018).

[88] Sprigge, *The Importance of Subjectivity*, 41.

[89] A comprehensive phenomenological account of wonder should therefore attend also to the body of someone in a state of wonder, and a complete psychological account should include the bodily 'preconditions' for wonder (which might include attention to breathing, muscle relaxation, and the digestive tract).

contemplating as strange, deeply other or mysterious, fundamentally beyond the limits of our understanding, yet worthy of attention for its own sake, in which our attention takes the form of an open, receptive stance, and an attunement towards mystery.[90]

Note that I say 'worthy of our attention for its own sake' rather than 'valuable'. A number of authors make the perception of value – of the object *as valuable* – central to the definition of wonder.[91] I would prefer to be a bit more cautious in this regard. Although many experiences of wonder, as mentioned, do include a (strong) element of appreciation, and thus a sense that what one is experiencing is intrinsically valuable, this is not necessarily part of wonder. What *is* always part of wonder is that the object is 'important' in one's experience in a quite literal sense – it contributes strongly to one's experience, it is the dominant influence in it, and it arrests one's attention. There is thus a sense that the object is *worth attending to*, but the *reason* why this is so is not necessarily clear – the reason may be that the object seems valuable in some way (exceedingly good or beautiful perhaps), but it may also be its utter mysteriousness or incomprehensibility, its complete overturning of one's expectations, even its *refusal* to allow a judgement of value.

As mentioned before, Whitehead suggested that wonder is one manifestation among others of the sense of value or importance; he mentioned curiosity as another.[92] I qualified the former suggestion by saying that although I take it to be true for *some* forms of wonder, for wonder in general it would be better to say that wonder *is* a way in which the world is important in our experience than that it *reveals* the world to be 'objectively' important or valuable. As to curiosity, in light of its directionality (a self or subject reaching out to an object) it seems more fitting to see this as a species of *interest* – a term closely allied to 'importance', but with a stronger emphasis on the subjective.[93]

90 Cf. Fuller, *Wonder*, 99, who, referring to the work of Ernest Schactel, presents wonder as an 'allocentric' (as opposed to 'autocentric' or self-centred) mode of perception and cognition, 'in which people or objects are attended to in their own fullness and richness'.

91 Nussbaum, *Upheavals*, 54; Hepburn, 'Wonder', 12ff.; Vasalou, *Wonder*, 31; Tobia, 'Wonder and Value'. In Tobia's case, as mentioned before, this is indeed merely the *perception* of value: '[The concept of] wonder requires its object to *seem* valuable, but whether the object is *in fact* valuable remains an open question. Wonder enraptures us with objects that might be of true *or* merely illusory value'. (Tobia, 'Wonder and Value', 960).

92 Whitehead, 'Rhythmic Claims', 63.

93 Whitehead, *Modes of Thought*, 8. I would not go so far as to *identify* curiosity and interest, though, as Kashdan and Silvia, 'Curiosity and Interest', 367, do.

The Epistemic Element in Wonder

Curiosity is rightly seen as essentially an *epistemic* emotion or drive. Kashdan and Silvia write that '[a]ll theories of curiosity agree that curiosity is an approach-oriented motivational state associated with exploration. (…) [A]ll theories agree that curiosity's immediate function is to learn, explore, and immerse oneself in the interesting event'.[94] Berlyne even wrote that 'the drive produced in these various ways by conflict can only rightly be called "curiosity" or a "drive to know" if it is reduced by the process of knowledge-rehearsal'.[95] In other words, if information (of the right kind) does not reduce it, it cannot be curiosity.

The same may be said of inquisitive wonder, but not of contemplative wonder. Wonder always includes an epistemic element, since some form of puzzlement or surprise is a necessary part of any experience of wonder, even contemplative wonder, and even the most aesthetic kinds of wonder.[96] But in contemplative wonder this epistemic element is different in kind than in inquisitive wonder and in curiosity; the puzzlement it entails, the 'why' and 'how' questions implied in it, cannot be answered and do not expect an answer. Therefore, any information we gain, anything we learn about the object we wonder at, will not be an answer to those silent questions, and will not reduce our wonder. Inquisitive wonder, on the other hand, *is* reduced by information of the right kind. If a child is at first stumped by the fact that a metal boat floats, learning more about the physics will reduce the child's inquisitive wonder. But this reduction may easily go unnoticed, since the only thing she might in theory notice may be a subtle change in the quality of her wonder – a shift from inquisitive to contemplative (a distinction that, as said, is not to be perceived as rigid anyway) – and it may also well be that her inquisitive wonder remains unsatisfied, because explanations can always be pushed back to a deeper level, and then a level below that.

A further difference between wonder and curiosity is that the epistemic element in wonder always has to do with puzzlement or surprise, with 'violated expectations' in a broad sense at least, whereas in the case of curiosity this

[94] Kashdan and Silvia, 'Curiosity and Interest', 368.

[95] Berlyne, 'A Theory of Human Curiosity', 187. He wrote this about 'epistemic' curiosity. He distinguished between 'perceptual' and 'epistemic' curiosity (ibid., 180), the former being 'a drive which is aroused by novel stimuli and reduced by continued exposure to these stimuli'; Berlyne used the former term to refer to 'the curiosity drive that has been studied in lower animals'. He did note that the two types of curiosity may well be closely related. I would also note that 'perceptual' curiosity is still epistemic in a less narrow sense of the term: it is still a matter of exploring, information-seeking, et cetera.

[96] Green, *The Activities of Teaching*, 199–200, also argues that wonder necessarily contains an element of curiosity, of puzzlement, a confession of ignorance, because 'to marvel at something always involves the confrontation with a mystery'.

is just one source of the perceived 'knowledge gap' or the appetite for new information that is central to the phenomenon.[97] And a third difference related to the epistemic element in wonder and curiosity has already been discussed: in wonder the scope and depth of one's awareness of one's own ignorance is much larger than in curiosity.

Awe, bluntly put, is *not* an epistemic phenomenon; although it may be tinged by puzzlement or amazement that such greatness as perceived exists and uncertainty about how to express it, the important thing in awe is that the greatness of the object is clearly and strongly perceived, and awe is therefore not a questioning, perplexed or bemused attitude.

Characteristic Elements of Wonder

If I distil all I have said so far about what it is like to experience wonder, and what is typical of and important in the type(s) of experience that concern us in this book, I arrive at the following list of characteristics:

1. Wonder is a mode of consciousness, thus not an isolated feeling but a total state of thinking and feeling.
2. It entails an epistemic element in the form of surprise, puzzlement, perplexity or yet another form; in contemplative wonder this takes the form of an experience of mystery (the object of wonder being beyond one's powers of comprehension).
3. To experience wonder is therefore to experience a 'meaning gap'. In most cases it will also contain the suggestion or promise of a new, deeper or more comprehensive, meaning, but this is not always the case; and where it is, this meaning is also elusive, thus also sensed in its absence.
4. Wonder is object-centred.
5. One's attention is 'arrested' by the object.
6. The object of wonder is perceived as worth attending to for its own sake.
7. There is a strong receptive element to wonder, and contemplative or deep wonder is (phenomenologically) wholly receptive.
8. Wonder entails an intensification of the present; the experience is fuller and more vivid than ordinary experience.

97 Loewenstein, 'The Psychology of Curiosity', 93.

9. Wonder has an 'open', to some extent indeterminate, character, in the sense that the attitude to take towards the object of wonder (other than one of wonder), or how to respond to it, is not fully and definitively decided.
10. It entails a certain 'psychic distance' from the object, a sense of being an observer, without being overwhelmed by emotion.
11. Wonder involves a stirring of the imagination, which may range from a delicate probing to a wandering, restlessly searching attempt to 'get one's head around' something, and again to an active 'play' of the imagination.

When I speak of wonder in this book, I have in mind a type of experience with these characteristics. It would be a mistake, however, to set this or any other such list in stone. The above list represents an attempt to capture and formalize something that ultimately resists being pinned down with precision. We should not expect to be able to come up with a single definition of wonder that captures all types of wonder and only wonder, nor to be able to identify a clear and impermeable boundary between inquisitive and contemplative wonder. We have to be satisfied with less – a less, however, that is also more, since wonder (like anything else, really, if you attend to it in wonder) spills over any definition that tries to contain it. As Bergson wrote: 'In vain we force the living into this or that one of our molds. All the molds crack.'[98] In the chapters that follow, then, when I speak of wonder I intend a mode of consciousness as described above; and more specifically, unless otherwise stated, I mean deep or contemplative wonder, thus a type of wonder that is experienced as wholly receptive and that involves a sense of mystery. But when you read on it remains more important to breathe life into whatever is said about wonder by bringing to mind your own experiences of wonder than to leaf back to these pages to remind yourself of the exact definition of wonder used here.

The Development of Wonder from Childhood to Adulthood

The phenomenological exploration of wonder presented above is an exploration of 'adult' wonder, which in a book about wonder and education is potentially a problem, of course, for we cannot simply assume that children's

[98] Henri Bergson, *Creative Evolution* (Mineola: Dover Publications, 1998), x. The original French runs: 'En vein nous poussons le vivant dans tel ou tel de nos cadres. Tous les cadres craquent'. See for the original Henri Bergson, *L'Évolution Créatrice*, Édition Électronique (ePub, PDF) v.: 1.0, Les Echos de Maquis, https://philosophie.cegeptr.qc.ca/wp-content/documents/L%C3%A9volution-cr%C3%A9atrice.pdf.

wonder is exactly the same as adults' wonder (or more 'mature' or 'developed' forms of wonder more commonly experienced by adults). Unfortunately, the development of wonder in children has received very little attention from both empirical researchers and theorists.[99] On the basis of the latter's speculative work, in combination with studies of the development of curiosity (that often encompass more than curiosity in the strict sense), it is possible to make a few general points about children's wonder with a fair degree of plausibility.

Babies may not be able to be curious in the full sense of the word, since this presupposes a level of (self-)awareness that they do not yet possess – they lack the concept of knowledge, so they cannot be aware of a 'knowledge gap' – but they do have 'an effective equivalent of curiosity: an innate disposition to handle and examine novel objects in their environment'.[100] Wonder, too, may be seen as part of human beings' innate directedness towards the world. Quinn suggests that because young children still need to get 'a grip on' reality their 'first sensible knowledge is of being *as* mystery'.[101] Self and world are not yet separated in the child's experience; but once they are, any object they encounter – being unfamiliar – may evoke a form of wonder in a child. In this regard it is telling that, insofar as wonder can be said to have a physical expression, it is the wide-eyed, open-mouthed face that we associate with young children taking in some mysterious or fascinating aspect of their surroundings.[102]

It seems unlikely that in the earliest stages of a child's life it is possible to distinguish between inquisitive and contemplative wonder, since the world must be an overwhelmingly mysterious place. But as soon as some familiarity arises, as soon as conceptual frames arise, and thus *expectations* arise with regard to the world, room is created for the appearance of both types of wonder.[103] It seems likely, though – also from a functionalist perspective – that inquisitive wonder

[99] The question as to the development *of* wonder in individuals is to be distinguished from the question as to the developmental role of wonder, i.e. wonder's role in children's cognitive and emotional development. The latter question has also not received much attention, but is treated in Fuller, *Wonder*, ch. 6. Fuller also discusses the evolutionary development of the capacity for wonder; I look into this in the next chapter.

[100] See Schmitt and Lahroodi, 'The Epistemic Value of Curiosity', 141, on John Dewey's 'organic level' of curiosity, in *How We Think: A Restatement of the Relation of Reflective Thinking to the Educative Process* (1910 and 1931; repr. Chicago: Henry Regnery, 1971), 38.

[101] Quinn, *Iris Exiled*, 32.

[102] See Nico Frijda, *The Emotions* (Cambridge and New York: Cambridge University Press/Paris: Édition de la Maison des Sciences de l'Homme, 1986), cited in Vasalou, *Wonder*, 24.

[103] Cf. Fuller, *Wonder*, 81: '[Wonder] presupposes a discrepancy between previous cognitive expectations and some new event. This discrepancy produces the "astonishment mingled with perplexity or bewildered curiosity" that defines wonder'.

is the dominant form of wonder at least in children's primary school years.[104] Contrary to how philosophers are wont to think about wonder, wonder's *first* 'function' might be said to help children become *familiar* with the world.[105] This still operates through an experience of 'strangeness': something surprises, because it does not match one's expectations. Take the following example:

> ONE DAY John Edgar (four years), who had often seen airplanes take off, rise, and gradually disappear into the distance, took his first plane ride. When the plane stopped ascending and the seat-belt sign went out, John Edgar turned to his father and said in a rather relieved, but still puzzled, tone of voice, 'Things don't really get smaller up here.'[106]

Thus in Piagetian terms a 'need for accommodation' arises: the child's mental schemes need to be adjusted in such a way that the object of experience can be made sense of. Inquisitive wonder always contains this thrust towards 'refamiliarization' or restoration (on a deeper or more encompassing level) of one's ability to make sense of the world – which is not to say that it can be entirely satisfied or resolved the way curiosity can, however. There is irony here: it is a cliché that curiosity and wonder wane as children grow older, and it seems plausible that this has to do with the increased familiarity of the world; but curiosity and wonder probably play an important role in establishing that familiarity.[107]

If indeed inquisitive wonder is the dominant type of wonder in primary school-aged children, this by no means implies that they are incapable of contemplative wonder. Both everyday experience with children and observations by proponents of philosophy for children strongly suggest they are; Opdal cites his son Martin, aged 6: 'Look, Daddy. This is a mug, and even if there are lots of mugs in the world, there couldn't be any exactly like this one.'[108] He also quotes Gareth Matthews, who observed that 'what philosophers do (in rather

[104] That wonder can also be seen as being 'functional' or 'adaptive' in human development is persuasively argued for from an evolutionary perspective by Fuller, *Wonder*. He suggests that both surprise, curiosity, and wonder 'originate as reactions to unexpected events, mobilizing efforts to change cognitive structures in ways that will ensure our overall well-being' (ibid., 83) – I would note, however, that the link with well-being is highly indirect (at best; cf. Nussbaum's 'non-eudaimonistic emotion'), that *contemplative* wonder has no necessary immediate connection with the mobilization of such efforts, and that such connections as are there are more subtle than in the case of inquisitive wonder. See further Chapter 2.

[105] Willmott even calls '*de*familiarization' wonder's 'central knowledge effect'; Glenn Willmot, *Reading for Wonder: Ecology, Ethics, Enchantment* (Chaim: Palgrave Macmillan, 2018), 24.

[106] Gareth B. Matthews, *Philosophy & the Young Child* (Cambridge, MA and London: Harvard University Press, 1980), 4.

[107] Formal education may also have something to do with it, though (see Susan Engel, 'Children's Need to Know: Curiosity in Schools', *Harvard Educational Review* 81, no. 4 (2011): 633).

[108] Opdal, 'Curiosity, Wonder and Education', 334.

disciplined and sustained ways) is much closer than is usually appreciated to what at least some children rather naturally do'.[109] As children grow older and their worldview solidifies the *second* 'function' of wonder – *defamiliarizing* the world – arguably becomes educationally more important; this asks for the cultivation of contemplative wonder. But I dare not venture a guess as to the relative importance of inquisitive and contemplative wonder in adolescents' actual experience.

At any rate, although infants' wonder will be phenomenologically quite different from adults' wonder, I see no reason to think that the phenomenology of wonder in children from primary school onwards is crucially different. It will be triggered in the same way, and it may contain all of the elements described above (puzzlement, a sense of mystery, a sense of importance, and so on). Wonder presupposes an epistemic background, in Opdal's terms 'the existence of frames', but as he argues, 'even small children are able to conceive of some order in their life, and (…) this impl[ies] the existence of frames'.[110] Any differences in the *quality* of wonder are likely matters of nuance, to do with the level of self-awareness (the degree of reflexivity of the experience) and the many ways in which life experience (for better or worse) influences the affective tone of wonder. Differences in the *triggers* and *objects* of wonder, however, are likely to be much more important, precisely because wonder presupposes a certain epistemic background. This includes knowledge and expectations about the world, interpretative frameworks, and a 'vocabulary' for the experience to draw upon – someone familiar with the question 'why there is something rather than nothing' may well experience wonder at the bare fact of existence somewhat differently than someone unfamiliar with that expression, even if in the former it never reaches the level of explicit thought in the moment itself. Such potential differences between adults and children in what triggers wonder and what they wonder at or about are obviously important to bear in mind in an educational context.

Conclusion

Wonder is first and foremost a type of experience, and therefore it is best approached phenomenologically. If we wish to understand the educational

[109] Gareth B. Matthews, 'Philosophy and Children's Literature', in *Philosophy for Children*, Special Issue of *Metaphilosophy*, eds. Terrell Ward Bynum and Matthew Lipman (Oxford: Basil Blackwell, 1976), 14–15, cited in Opdal, 'Curiosity, Wonder and Education', 334.

[110] Opdal, 'Curiosity, Wonder and Education', 333.

importance of wonder, it is crucial to know what it is like to experience wonder, or to experience the world in wonder. There is no single thing 'it is like' to experience wonder – and in different cultural–historical circumstances it has had different shapes and meanings – but we are justified in saying that the experiences we tend to express in terms of wonder share a particular phenomenology. I have also argued, however, that experiences of wonder 'cluster' in at least two types of wonder, which I have called *inquisitive* wonder and *contemplative* or *deep* wonder. Inquisitive wonder lies somewhat closer to curiosity, sharing with curiosity a drive to explain the (as yet) inexplicable object of one's wonder, whereas contemplative wonder – the type of wonder I will be concerned with in the remainder of this book – is a 'silent' response to mystery, not immediately accompanied by an active search for answers; and at any rate there are no answers here, nothing that will dissolve the mystery or the wonder. I have distilled the phenomenological characteristics of experiences of wonder into a general concept of wonder as a mode of consciousness in which we experience that which we perceive or are contemplating as in some way strange, beyond our understanding, yet worthy of our attention for its own sake, and in which our attention takes the form of an open, receptive stance. And I have defined *contemplative* wonder more specifically as *a mode of consciousness in which we experience that which we perceive or are contemplating as strange, deeply other or mysterious, fundamentally beyond the limits of our understanding, yet worthy of attention for its own sake, in which our attention takes the form of an open, receptive stance, and an attunement towards mystery*. This mode of consciousness differs from our 'ordinary', everyday mode of experiencing the world in many important – and educationally important – respects. Among other things, it is 'object-centred' – we forget ourselves and perceive the world as worth attending to for its own sake, rather than for what we might want from it – and 'unsettling', in that it shakes our taken-for-granted understanding of the world. At the same time, in many cases, it is a type of experience in which we sense a hint of a deeper or more comprehensive meaning. Because it confronts us with mystery it stirs the imagination. And it is an open, receptive mode of attention, rather than our ordinary, active and goal-oriented mode of consciousness. The next chapter explores what this means for wonder's relation to the world, or for how we relate to the world in wonder; and the chapters that follow build on this and the next chapter to argue for wonder's educational importance.

2

Wonder and the World

In the previous chapter I have offered a description and interpretation of experiences of wonder, of what it is like to be in a state of wonder, and on that basis I have explained in some detail what I mean by 'wonder'. Now it is time to go beyond phenomenology and conceptualization to ask how wonder relates to the world – or how we relate to the world in wonder, and what way(s) of relating to the world are made possible by wonder. (N.B. I realize that from certain, e.g. Heideggerian, phenomenological perspectives, the term 'relating' will suggest a distance between ourselves and the world that needs to be overcome, and thus a denial of our always already 'being-in-the-world'. Let me just ask readers to whom this applies to bear with me, and not to read too much – especially in terms of a supposedly implied metaphysics – into my use of the word 'relate'.)

I cannot ask about the relation between wonder and the world without also addressing the thorny issue of whether wonder 'tells us' something about the world. This may sound odd to you: how could a 'mode of consciousness' tell us something about the world? If this does indeed sound odd to you, it may be for purely linguistic reasons, and we could solve it by rephrasing the question: in the mode of consciousness we call 'wonder', is anything revealed to us about the world and our place in it? But perhaps the difficulty goes deeper; perhaps the problem is that 'wonder' and 'mode of consciousness' (despite my efforts to prevent this) still sound like purely subjective states to you, 'subjective' in the sense that they characterize a subject (a centre of experience) at a particular moment *and* tell us something *only* about that subject at that moment. This is an important issue, and to get to grips with it I will (firstly) make a comparison between wonder and various emotions, adopting an evolutionary perspective. It is not difficult to see why this can be helpful: many authors speak of wonder as an emotion, and although I do not think it can be called an emotion, they are certainly right in that wonder has a strong affective component; furthermore, emotions are generally seen as functional or adaptive, from an evolutionary perspective, and some are so because of their tendency to 'tell us' something about the world. Fear, for instance, is often informative. Had this been a book about fear, and had I started with a phenomenological description followed by a conceptualization of fear, all that work would have been far less interesting if fear could not be shown to be functional due to its informational value. Emotions may also be functional for other reasons than that they tell us something about the world, and this might also be true for wonder, but because wonder (like fear) *feels like* it says something about the world it is this implicit 'claim' that I wish to investigate – wonder would be *disappointing*, if it could in no way make good on its implicit 'promise' of revealing something about the world, and not just something, but something important. We will see that this approach is ultimately less than satisfactory, however, and therefore I will (secondly) approach the issue anew from a phenomenological perspective, a perspective that foregrounds the world-as-experienced – though not one that rejects the idea of a world that exists independently of our experience altogether.

But before I continue I need to say something about what I mean by 'the world'. This is one of those concepts of which we all 'know what it means', but which proves to be extremely tricky once you attempt to define it. For instance: are ideas part of the world, or only 'material' things (assuming ideas are not material things)? Are possibilities part of the world? It is not strange to say that a situation 'holds' possibilities, and surely 'situations' are part of the world, or are they not? Another problem is that by 'the world' we sometimes mean the human world only – as when we speak of a 'world war' or say that the world is in crisis, or that the eyes of the world are on someone (e.g. an astronaut 'spacewalking' to repair a space station), and at other times much more – often everything that exists or happens on our planet (and sometimes this is unclear: compare 'my dad is the greatest dad in the world' with 'Mount Everest is the highest mountain in the world'). And some uses of 'world' are probably even wider, transcending the limits of our planet (though we might often switch to 'universe' in those cases). And beyond this lies an even bigger question: is the world an objective reality, or is the world we (can) speak of a construct of the human mind, and in *that* sense always a 'human' world? So how should we define 'the world'? I will devote the first section to this question, and I will argue for a fairly intuitive notion of the world, the core of which is 'out-there-ness', i.e. the commonsensical idea that there is a world 'out there' that has a certain 'hardness' to it and that offers 'resistance' to our actions and theories – a quality that we ignore at our peril, as the current climate change attests. This seems to me to be a notion of the world that can and should be upheld without falling into the trap of a naive realism that assumes too simple a connection between our perception and conceptions of (things in) the world and the world 'out there' *or* the Cartesian trap of forgetting that we are part of the very same world we perceive. The notion of the world I propose to use is also inclusive in the sense that it allows for 'ideal' objects to be part of it – but of course without collapsing into idealism or pure constructivism. Although I take it to be an intuitive notion of the world, it is important to explicate it and flesh it out, because only then can we appreciate the complexity of this notion that we normally rely on implicitly, and become aware of the various types of worldliness it includes.

What Is 'the World'?

The world – the notion of 'the world' – is necessarily central to education, and to thinking about education. Whether one conceives of education as transmission of the (or a) world, as adjusting to, introducing to, initiation into, constructing, preparing for, or opening up the world to children, the world, however conceived, is the 'other' that children are taught about and enabled to relate to in specific ways.

The notion of the world has also always been central to philosophy, and always problematic; but arguably the explicit problematization of 'the world' and our relation to it began with Enlightenment philosopher Immanuel Kant, and his idealist view provides a useful starting-point here.[1] Naturally, I cannot provide an overview of the history of philosophical thinking about the world in this paragraph, nor would this be helpful, so I will limit myself to a presentation of some contrasting positions that have left their mark on philosophy of education, beginning with Kant.

Kant famously drew attention to the active role of our minds in the construction of the world. More specifically, he claimed that it is due to innate mental categories and concepts that the world appears to us as an orderly whole; without them, we would be confronted with a chaotic barrage of experience (if this could still be called 'experience'). This idealist view ('idealist' in the philosophical sense that reality is seen as either mental or immaterial in itself or

1 See Sean Gaston, *The Concept of World from Kant to Derrida* (New York: Rowman and Littlefield, 2013).

to an important extent constructed by the mind) has exerted a powerful influence over subsequent philosophical thinking, but it runs counter to a common-sense view of the world according to which the world is material and simple 'out there'.

Many people, confronted with the question 'what is the world', would probably be inclined to try a purely 'objective' definition first, something like 'the world is everything that exists'. Of course this requires us to define 'existence', so problems arise immediately. If we wish to avoid tautology ('existence means being there') we need to come up with a *mark* of existence, for instance: everything exists that can be detected through the senses or technological extensions of the senses. Does this work for everything? What about the (in)famous sound a tree makes (or does not make) when there is no one to hear it fall? All the vibrations in the air that would produce the sound if they met an ear exist and can be detected by technological means if there's no-one around, but it seems that the actual *sound* (a qualitative aspect of experience, a 'quale' in the language of philosophy of mind and philosophy of consciousness) only exists if there is someone to receive those vibrations. So a beginning of idealism inevitably creeps in. Things become even more complicated when we introduce abstract 'things' like beauty, love, justice, democracy, masculinity and femininity, or – to draw from another register – biological species, time, gravity. A purely 'objective' (tangible-furniture-of-the-world) definition of 'world' cannot deal with such 'things' in an adequate way; if we (want to be able to) see them as part of the world we need a different concept of the world.

In the *Tractatus Logico-Philosophicus* Wittgenstein explicitly rejected the idea that the world is the sum of all existing things, stating first: 'The world is all that is the case.' And then: 'The world is the totality of facts, not of things.'[2] The difference is that '[t]o say that the world is a totality of things would be to leave out that things fit together'.[3] The cat lies in the chair, and the chair stands by the fire, and the fire warms the cat. These are 'facts in logical space', they are states of affairs that are logically possible and that may or may not actually be the case – but their being possible is inherent in them. Chairs can be sat or lain in (by certain creatures at least), and cats can be warmed. Linguistic statements about states of affairs (purport to) represent or picture the world;

[2] In the original German: 'I. Die Welt is alles, was der Fall ist.' And: 'I.I. Die Welt ist die Gesamtheit der Tatsachen, nicht der Dinge.' Ludwig Wittgenstein, *Tractatus Logico-Philosophicus (Werkausgabe Band 1)* (Frankfurt am Main: Suhrkamp, 1993), 11. I have here given the English translation used in H. O. Mounce, *Wittgenstein's Tractatus: An Introduction* (Oxford: Basil Blackwell, 1981), which is Ludwig Wittgenstein, *Tractatus Logico-Philosophicus*, trans. D. F. Pears and B. F. McGuiness (London: Routledge & Kegan Paul, 1974).

[3] Mounce, *Wittgenstein's Tractatus*, 18.

they can be true or false, depending on whether the world is as stated (is the cat really in the chair?). Ultimately, the point of contact between language and world is 'the relationship between a simple name and a simple object', where no further description is needed.[4] A chair is not a simple object, since it consists of identifiable parts. In fact, Wittgenstein was unable to give an example of a simple object or of a name (or 'elementary proposition'), but just reasoned that the regression (from a complex object to its parts, to parts of those parts, and so on) must stop somewhere, because otherwise we would be unable to say anything about the world – and his main purpose was to explain how language could say something about the world, how linguistic statements could be 'true'. As it turns out, this required (in his view) a very restricted notion of both language and world. The world is what can be spoken of, and everything that cannot be spoken of ('das Mystische', the mystical) lies outside the world. Only propositions that can be true or false, that state possible facts about the world, make sense. Statements about what lies beyond the limit of language (like Wittgenstein's own *Tractatus*, as he himself observed) are 'nonsensical' ('unsinnig') – meaning that even though they may look like they can *say* something about the world (be true or false) they actually cannot. But they can *show* something. For according to Wittgenstein, '[t]here are, indeed, things that are inexpressible. They *show* themselves. They are what is mystical'.[5] In short, for Wittgenstein the world is not the totality of everything 'there is' – in fact, everything that matters to us, everything 'higher', all value, beauty, and meaning, 'must lie outside the world'.[6] In Wittgenstein's view, any attempt to say something about the *meaning* of life, or about the mystical fact *that* the world exists (rather than how it exists, i.e. what it is like, the domain of natural science), runs up against the limits of what we can say. They are wonder-inspired attempts to express the inexpressible, 'a tendency in the human mind,' Wittgenstein said, 'which I personally cannot help respecting deeply and I would not for my life ridicule it'.[7]

Although there is ample space for wonder in Wittgenstein's thought, and there are considerable similarities between what I said about wonder in the previous

4 Ibid., 21.

5 This is K. T. Fann's rendering of T. 6.522, the original of which reads: 'Es gibt allerdings Unaussprechliches. Dies *zeigt* sich, es ist das Mystische.' K. T. Fann, *Wittgenstein's Conception of Philosophy* (Oxford: Basil Blackwell, 1969), 24; Wittgenstein, *Tractatus (Werkausgabe Band 1)*, 85.

6 Wittgenstein, *Tractatus (Werkausgabe Band 1)*, 82, 6.41: 'Der Sinn der Welt muß außerhalb ihrer liegen. In der Welt ist alles, wie es ist, und geschieht alles, wie es geschieht; es gibt *in* ihr keinen Wert – und wenn es ihn gäbe, so hätte er keinen Wert.' Ibid., 83, 6.42: 'Darum kann es auch keine Sätze der Ethik geben. Sätze können nichts höheres ausdrücken.'

7 Ludwig Wittgenstein, 'A Lecture on Ethics', *Philosophical Review* 74, no. 1 (1965): 12.

chapter and Wittgenstein's views, the question whether wonder 'says' something about the world would be meaningless for him. The term 'reveals' (being more like 'shows', Wittgenstein's preferred term) would be more congenial to him, but if wonder could show anything it would be something that lay *outside* of the world.[8] So the price we have to pay for clarity about what the world is, and about what we can and cannot 'say', in (the early) Wittgenstein's thought, is that we have to think of 'the world' as just one domain of reality, as the domain of fact as opposed to value. In other words: the world we actually live in – a place that feels to us as suffused with value of all kinds, that we think we are talking about not just in physics but also in ethical and political debates – is not 'the world' in Wittgenstein's sense. But why would we surrender 'the world' to the natural sciences (and even to those sciences understood in a particular, also contestable way)? Why not simply accept that 'the world' is a complex notion that gathers up in itself all kinds of 'facts' and experiences, that the world is both familiar and strange, knowable and mysterious, transparent and opaque? This is, after all, what the world is for us.

In Wittgenstein's later work, in particular the *Philosophische Untersuchungen* (*Philosophical Investigations*), arguably without having changed his fundamental outlook on life and reality, he abandons the correspondence theory of meaning of the *Tractatus* in favour of one that emphasizes the pragmatic and social nature of language: the meaning of words and utterances lies in their use and depends on the practice or 'language-game' that forms the context of the utterance.[9] The meaning of the words 'own goal' is very different, depending on whether they are part of a commentary on a football match or a person's explanation of what she is trying to achieve in life. Accordingly, for the later Wittgenstein there is no single limit to language and no single or absolute sense of 'sense' and 'nonsense', since things only make sense in particular language-games.[10] The problem with 'metaphysics' (philosophizing about the ultimate

[8] That Wittgenstein valued wonder is evident not only from what he says in the *Tractatus*, but also from remarks he makes elsewhere, for instance: 'That is the fatal thing about the scientific way of thinking (which today possesses the whole world), that it wants to respond to every disquietude with an explanation', and 'The insidious thing about the causal point of view is that it leads us to say: "Of course, it had to happen like that." Whereas we ought to think: it may have happened like that – and also in many other ways.' Ludwig Wittgenstein, *Wittgenstein's Nachlass: The Bergen Electronic Edition. Text and Facsimile Version* (Oxford: Oxford University Press, 2000), 219 81 (i.e. typescript 219, page 81), and Ludwig Wittgenstein, *Culture and Value*, rev. 2nd ed., ed. G. H. von Wright, trans. Peter Winch (Oxford: Blackwell, 1998), both cited in Kevin M. Cahill, *The Fate of Wonder: Wittgenstein's Critique of Metaphysics and Modernity* (New York: Columbia University Press, 2011), 51.

[9] Ludwig Wittgenstein, *Philosophische Untersuchungen*, in Wittgenstein, *Tractatus (Werkausgabe Band 1)*, 225–485; Ludwig Wittgenstein, *Philosophical Investigations*, trans. G. E. M. Anscombe (Oxford: Basil Blackwell, 1982).

[10] Fann, *Wittgenstein's Conception of Philosophy*, 83.

nature of reality, about the meaning of life, about moral value) is that it is confused about language games; it uses an 'empirical' form of expression where only poetry and such forms of expression are apt.[11]

Wittgenstein's work contributed greatly to the 'linguistic turn' in philosophy, and was thus an important influence on the work of Richard Peters (one of the founding fathers of analytical philosophy of education).[12] Peters praises Kant for providing a necessary corrective to the empiricist 'tabula rasa' view of experience and education, but observes that both the British Empiricists (Locke, Berkely, Hume) and Kant (as well as later Kantians such as Piaget, who mapped the development of the categories Kant presumed to be innate) failed to appreciate that 'the development of mind is the product of initiation into public traditions enshrined in a public language'.[13] Without denying 'the importance of individual centres of experience', which Peters felt received undue emphasis in empiricism but too little attention in the post-Kantian philosophy of people like Hegel and Marx, Peters stresses the intentionality of consciousness, the fact 'that consciousness (…) is related in its different modes to objects', and the fact that '[t]he objects of consciousness are first and foremost objects in a public world that are marked out and differentiated by a public language into which the individual is initiated'.[14] The objects of consciousness are not private, though each individual has a private perspective; nor are they simply out there. They arise as one learns a language: 'The learning of language and the discovery of a public world of objects in space and time proceed together.'[15] To initiate children into such a public world – into a 'form of life', a Wittgensteinian term Peters also uses – is what education 'essentially' consists in.[16]

This intersubjective world that education is about (that is, 'the content that is handed on and (…) the criteria by reference to which it is criticized and developed'), Peters says, is 'what D.H. Lawrence called "the holy ground" that stands between teacher and taught' (idem).[17] This is a suggestive phrase, for it raises the question what is 'holy' about the public world that children are initiated into and why. Is it the fact that this public world – whichever public

[11] Ibid., 93.

[12] He has also been criticized for abandoning his early commitment to a Wittgensteinian 'functionalist' approach to meaning in favour of an essentialist form of conceptual analysis, however; see Peter Gilroy, 'The Aims of Education and the Philosophy of Education', in *The Aims of Education*, ed. Roger Marples (London and New York: Routledge, 1999).

[13] Peters, *Ethics & Education*, 49.

[14] Ibid., 50.

[15] Ibid.

[16] Ibid., 52.

[17] Ibid.

world – is the world children get to live in? But is it indeed the case that there is no world outside of the public world opened up – but also created – by the language (or languages) children are taught? Peters admits that there may be a few 'natural' or 'universal' objects (such as the mother's breast) that infants in the early stages of development discover by taste and touch. The 'human world', however, in contrast to the child's initial 'amorphous world', 'is largely a selective world of social artifice', created by 'rules and customs' (idem). Hence '[t]he working class man (…) who has access only to a limited vocabulary and to a limited set of symbolic structures, literally lives in a different world from the professional man who has a much wider and more varied vocabulary and whose education in the various differentiated forms of thought has continued for nearly a decade longer'.[18] The working class man literally – not metaphorically – lives in a different world from the professional man, Peters says (and note that this is long before the standard everyday use of 'literally' became a hyperbolic use in cases like 'I literally died', where this obviously did not happen). Peters thus defends a form of linguistic idealism: Kant modified by Wittgenstein.

There is a sober realism, even a profound truth, I think, in Peters' observation. To say that the world merely *looks* different to 'the' working class (wo)man than to the more highly educated (wo)man does not cover it, it is too superficial; the difference – the divide – goes deeper than that. Yet at the same time it seems to me that we lose something important if we leave it at this – different people living in different worlds (even if they are somehow, perhaps due to overlaps between them, still fairly well coordinated). What we lose – or would have to give up – is precisely that insistent intuitive idea that the world is also in a sense just 'out there', that it is independently real – independent, that is, of what we make of it. We lose this, in particular, if we locate the difference between the world of the 'working class man' and the 'professional man' *entirely* in language, in the vocabularies they have at their disposal. The differences are much more 'real', more tangible, than that – they can be seen on the table and in the food cupboard or fridge, in their holiday photo albums, in the softness or hardness of the skin on their hands.

In Peters' work language can divide people, in a way enclosing them in different worlds, as well as create a public or common world. Continental philosophers like Martin Heidegger and his student Hannah Arendt, too, stress the fact that, despite the reality of subjective perspectives, people do also inhabit a common world. Heidegger wrote that '[t]he surrounding world is different in a

[18] Ibid., 52–3.

certain way for each of us, and notwithstanding that we move about in a common world'.[19] He stressed our fundamental engagement with or embeddedness in the world; the world is not something we must establish a relation with, or can either relate or not relate to, but we are always already in-the-world, and not in a simple spatial sense, because that would suggest a contingent relation between us and the world – and we cannot *not* be in the world.[20] Language plays a constitutive role in Heidegger's analysis of Being, it is 'the house of Being', and thus has a world-creating role.[21] In Arendt's philosophy – influential in the work of an increasing number of philosophers of education (Gert Biesta, Jan Masschelein, Maarten Simons, Joris Vlieghe, among others) – the term 'world' primarily denotes a sphere created by communal effort. The world arises out of 'work' by which people create things and institutions with a certain stability and durability; it is the result of the human transformation of the earth into the spaces we inhabit, into our common world, which is a world of plurality, a world in which everyone can (in principle) introduce something new. This is where we act, where we show 'who we are' as we engage with others and take responsibility for the maintenance and renewal of the world.[22] For Arendt (famously) the task of education is 'to prepare [children] (...) for the task of renewing a common world'.[23] As Biesta notes, 'world' receives a very specific meaning in Arendt's thought. 'It is not just any social or physical environment, but points to a certain quality of social interaction that is expressed in an orientation towards the enabling and maintenance of plurality'.[24]

19 Martin Heidegger, *The Basic Problems of Phenomenology*, trans. Albert Hofstadter (Oxford: Blackwell, 1988), 164, cited in Peter Ashworth and Man Cheung Chung, 'Conclusion: Phenomenology and Psychological Science', in *Phenomenology and Psychological Science: Historical and Philosophical Perspectives*, eds. Peter Ashworth and Man Cheung Chung (New York: Springer, 2006), 201.

20 See Martin Heidegger, *Sein und Zeit* (Tübingen: Max Niemeyer Verlag, 1984), 52ff.

21 Martin Heidegger, 'Letter on Humanism', trans. Frank A. Capuzzi and J. Glenn Gray, in *Martin Heidegger: Basic Writings; Revised and Expanded Edition*, ed. David Farrell Krell (London: Routledge, 1993), 217, cited in Michael Wheeler, 'Martin Heidegger', *The Stanford Encyclopedia of Philosophy* (Winter 2018 edition), ed. Edward N. Zalta. https://plato.stanford.edu/archives/win2018/entries/heidegger.

22 See Hannah Arendt, *The Human Condition* (Chicago: University of Chicago Press, 1958), and Natasha Levinson, 'The Paradox of Natality: Teaching in the Midst of Belatedness', in *Hannah Arendt and Education: Renewing Our Common World*, ed. Mordechai Gordon. (Boulder, CO and Oxford: Westview Press, 2001).

23 Hannah Arendt, 'The Crisis in Education', in Hannah Arendt, *Between Past and Future* (New York: Penguin Books, 2006), 193.

24 Gert Biesta, 'De School als Toegang tot de Wereld: Een Pedagogische Kijk op Goed Onderwijs', in *Wat is Goed Onderwijs: Bijdragen uit de Pedagogiek*, eds. Ruud Klarus and Wim Wardekker (Den Haag: Boom Lemma, 2011), 29.

What is striking in the work of Peters, Heidegger, and Arendt alike is what might be called their 'humanism' or 'anthropocentrism', depending on one's point of view – their 'world' is predominantly a *human* world. By 'anthropocentrism' I do not mean to suggest that these authors necessarily placed human interests above those of other beings, or even that it would not be possible to develop and justify a non-anthropocentric ethic from a point of view inspired by their thinking. What I do mean is that these thinkers show a (common) preoccupation with the human world, with human activity in the world, and with what makes this possible. Humanity is placed in a realm of its own, and this is due to its possession of language, self-consciousness, its ability to think; however much we are in-the-world, we are in a sense still not entirely *of* this world (or we are in a world of our own). Three philosophers of the late nineteenth and first half of the twentieth century that, each in their own way, rejected such a view and rather stressed our continuity with the rest of the world, our embodiment, and the primacy of perception or experience, are Maurice Merleau-Ponty, John Dewey, and Alfred North Whitehead. Each of them showed that it is not just through language that we inhabit a common world, but also through our being essentially, even physically, interwoven with the world. For Merleau-Ponty perceptions are not private, nor are they communicable because they involve 'ideas'; rather, it is our being *embodied* that gives us an openness to the world and that is the reason why we can speak (with each other) of a world.[25] For Dewey the significance of the development of the discipline of biology, and in particular of the theory of evolution, lay 'precisely in its emphasis upon continuity of simpler and more complex organic forms until we reach man'. According to Dewey, its 'effect upon the theory of knowing is to displace the notion that it is the activity of a mere onlooker or spectator of the world', because it shows 'that the living creature is part of the world, sharing its vicissitudes and fortunes, and making itself secure in its precarious dependence

[25] Maurice Merleau-Ponty, *The Primacy of Perception and Other Essays on Phenomenological Psychology, the Philosophy of Art, History and Politics*, ed. and intr. James M. Edie (n.p.: Northwestern University Press, 1964), 17. See also Maurice Merleau-Ponty, *The Visible and the Invisible*, ed. Claude Lefort, trans. Alphonso Lingis (Evanston: Northwestern University Press, 1968), in which the notion of 'the Flesh' becomes the 'primordial' notion that connects us (our bodies) and the world. Heidegger's concept of Being-in-the-world is clearly present in Merleau-Ponty's thought, but the important difference is that Merleau-Ponty moved away from the traditional emphasis on consciousness and thought and stressed corporeity instead. Hubert Dreyfus calls Merleau-Ponty's philosophy a 'nonmentalistic phenomenology of perception that parallels Heidegger's philosophy of action in seeking a radical break with subject/object thinking'; Hubert L. Dreyfus, *Being-in-the-World: A Commentary on Heidegger's Being and Time, Division I* (Cambridge, MA and London: The MIT Press, 1991), 346n15. The relation between Heidegger's and Merleau-Ponty's work is complex, though; see Douglas Low, 'Merleau-Ponty's Criticism of Heidegger', *Philosophy Today* 53 (Fall 2009).

only as it intellectually identifies itself with the things about it.'[26] Whitehead, in his process philosophy (which was influenced by Dewey's thought, among others), used the *distinction* between subject and object, but rejected the *division* between them that characterizes much of Western philosophy; he expresses his view by contrasting it with Kant's (idealism): 'For Kant, the world emerges from the subject, for the philosophy of organism, the subject emerges from the world … '[27] Whitehead also stressed the continuity between human beings and the rest of nature: 'Undoubtedly the body is very vaguely distinguishable from external nature. It is in fact merely one among other natural objects.'[28] And: 'The human body is that region of the world which is the primary field of human expression.'[29] Against Hume, Whitehead defended our perception of causality – we *feel* that we are influenced by the world outside us. Whitehead's example is of a man in a dark room where the electric light is suddenly turned on, making the man blink. According to Hume the man perceived the flash and then the blink, as well as the *habit* of blinking after flashes – it is just an association, no actual causality can be inferred, let alone experienced. Whitehead dismisses this as nonsense, a mere dogmatic insistence that all experience is of one kind only, namely ordinary sense perception. Instead he accepts the man's claim that the flash *made* him blink – for this is simply what we feel in such a situation: we feel that we are influenced by – that is to say we feel that we are *part of*, rather than separate from – the world.[30] This means that the 'out-there-ness' of the world does not exclude, in fact necessarily includes, 'in-and-through-me-ness' as well – the world neither begins nor ends at the 'limit' formed by our skin.

Note that this also emphasizes a certain priority of the world over our linguistically constituted world. Our access to the world is to an important extent mediated by language (or our world is in part constituted by language), but there is also a 'prelinguistic' world that makes itself 'known', that 'presences', from time to time – a world that is always in the background, for example in how our bodies 'feel' because of gravity (something we tend not to notice but which astronauts are acutely aware of). It is not because we possess a *concept* of the sun that we blink when we look right into it; and a warm – but not burning – sun

26 John Dewey, *Democracy and Education* (New York: The Free Press, 1997), 337–8.

27 Alfred North Whitehead, *Process and Reality: An Essay in Cosmology* (New York: The Free Press, 1985), 88.

28 Whitehead, *Modes of Thought*, 114.

29 Ibid., 22. Cf. also ibid., 115: 'The body is that portion of nature with which each moment of human experience intimately coöperates [*sic*].'

30 Whitehead, *Process and Reality*, 174–6.

on our skin is as agreeable to *us*, possessors of linguistic concepts, as to the cat drowsing on the windowsill.

The upshot of this brief foray into the philosophy of 'the world' is that, in most of its uses – in the everyday uses I am interested in – 'the world' is a complex notion; it is neither a simple notion nor (does the word refer to) a simply locatable thing. And when our experiences of wonder prompt us to ask whether wonder reveals something about the world, or when our reflection on wonder leads us to ask about the way we relate to the world in wonder, we need to retain this complexity, these various layers, for they are also contained in the experiences that engender the question. We must retain both the subjective (the world as felt and interpreted by us) and the objective (the world from which we emerge, that makes itself felt, that is 'stubborn fact'[31]); both the human and the non-human, both the importance of language and the notion of a world behind and beyond language. This tension between the world as constructed and at the same time independent of our constructions is nicely illustrated in Olga Tokarczuk's recent Nobel lecture. On the one hand, she writes: 'The world is a fabric we weave daily on the great looms of information … When this story changes, so does the world. In this sense the world is made of words'. Yet at the same time she acknowledges the world's independence of our narrative constructions when she observes that our problem today is that 'we do not yet have ready narratives (…) for the ultra-rapid transformations of our world', 'we lack new ways of telling the story of the world', and that the world is vulnerable to what we do to it – which calls for tenderness, 'a way of looking that shows the world as being alive, living, interconnected, cooperating with, and codependent on itself'.[32]

So it is both true that the world is a field of experience – especially if we do not limit the meaning of experience to human experience – and that it has an objective 'hardness' to it. But that quality is not limited to rock-solid objects; social norms, for instance, exert real pressure, too. The world is the material-experiential space we are born into and grow up in, in which we learn to distinguish between different modes of existence – various physical modes (solidity, fluidity, gaseousness), various (non-exclusive) abstract modes (conceptual, dreamlike, intersubjective), and various experiential modes (sensorial, emotional, cognitive, and other bodily modes) – and their interrelations: some things exist as illusions or falsehoods, other things exist independently of us, though *as we know them*

[31] Ibid., 43.

[32] Olga Tokarczuk, 'The Tender Narrator', in *Nobel Lecture by the Nobel Laureate in Literature 2018* (n.p.: Svenska Akademien/The Nobel Foundation, 2019), 3, 24.

they do not. The difference between things 'out there' and things 'as we know them' is a clearing where wonder often resides. Part of what makes wonder interesting is that it is a phenomenon of the limit or the threshold between these poles, and it is this position that provides the key to answering the question(s) that concerns us in this chapter. But before we move there I propose a change of register to look at wonder as a 'natural' phenomenon that arises from our being embodied, evolved and evolving creatures in an evolving world, because it is important to see what we may and may not glean from this.

Wonder and Emotion: An Evolutionary Perspective

My main source for this paragraph is Robert Fuller's *Wonder: From Emotion to Spirituality*. In that book, Fuller argues on the basis of findings from the natural and social sciences (in particular, evolutionary science and biology, and various branches of psychology, including social psychology and neuropsychology), that wonder is a principal source of spirituality, eliciting 'belief in the existence of a more-than-physical reality'.[33] Furthermore, he argues for the normative claim that 'a life shaped by wonder is qualitatively "better" than a life that is relatively devoid of this emotion', as well as for a further normative claim that wonder 'not only is but also *should* be a principal source of personal spirituality', because it allows for a richer and more fulfilling life than a purely secular outlook, while avoiding the risk of dogmatism religion in a narrow sense suffers from.[34]

Fuller does not hesitate to call wonder an emotion, even 'a common human emotion'; but he observes also that 'not one major Western theorist in the past hundred years has explicitly listed wonder as one of the principal primary or secondary emotions'.[35] One reason for this neglect, in science, at least, Fuller suggests, is that biologists and psychologists rarely study emotions with no immediate survival value.[36] Indeed, the working definition of emotions used in an important psychological handbook is that emotions are 'multi-component responses to challenges or opportunities that are important to the individual's

[33] Fuller, *Wonder*, 1.
[34] Ibid., 2 (my italics).
[35] Ibid., 9.
[36] Another reason is that scientists have tended to focus on emotions that '(1) manifest themselves over a short duration of time, (2) give rise to visible facial expressions or bodily gestures, and (3) orient people to concrete features of their physical environment. None of this,' Fuller notes, 'bodes well for the study of wonder as an emotional experience'; ibid., 31.

goals, particularly social ones'.[37] Martha Nussbaum, as we have seen, also noted wonder's peculiar place among the emotions as a non-eudaimonistic emotion; this means, among other things, that there is no immediately obvious advantage to wonder, it is not obviously functional or adaptive.

Why is it interesting, in the context of this chapter, to ask whether wonder is adaptive? Because one important reason why emotions can be adaptive is that they 'tell us' something about the world. As I noted in the opening paragraph, emotions might be adaptive or functional for other reasons as well. If parents have an emotional response to their newborn that makes them want to protect and care for their baby, this response is functional from an evolutionary perspective: parents that have this response are more likely to raise their child to an age at which it will in turn procreate, and are therefore more likely to pass on their genes. Thus, assuming a (partly) genetic basis for the emotional response, this emotion is selected for in evolution. But the emotion is adaptive *regardless* of whether it reveals something about their baby. Emotions like fear and disgust, however, seem to have been selected for at least in part because they are 'informative'. Fear alerts us to danger, the risk to our lives posed by a wildfire or a wild animal, for instance. Disgust helps us avoid other dangers, like the risk posed by noxious substances. Could the same be true for wonder? Is wonder an emotion like fear or disgust? Is it an emotion at all?

For Fuller wonder is an emotion, but his understanding of this is nuanced. He acknowledges that there may not be 'a single essence that is a necessary and sufficient condition for all instances of wonder', but maintains that 'there are prototypical characteristics of certain human experiences that make it meaningful to speak of wonder as a distinct emotional response'.[38] He also notes that 'wonder is first and foremost an experience', that experiences are shaped by 'the neural structure of our brains as well as our personal histories of interaction with our social and cultural environments' and that therefore 'it is probably more helpful to think of wonder as an emotional experience (i.e., an activity whereby an organism responds to its environment) rather than as simply an emotion (i.e. a noun or separate entity somehow isolated from the multiple contexts in which it emerges)'. He warns against the tendency to reify wonder, and proposes a definition of wonder as 'the feeling state that accompanies the total organism's

[37] Keith Oatley, Dacher Keltner, and Jennifer M. Jenkins, *Understanding Emotions*, 2nd ed. (Malden: Blackwell Publishing, 2006), 29.

[38] Fuller, *Wonder*, 33.

response to something novel and unexpected (especially those things that strike us as especially powerful, real, true, and/or beautiful)'.[39]

As long as we think of emotions in this nuanced way, Fuller is happy to speak of wonder as an emotion. There are a number of elements in his view that I am very much in agreement with: wonder is not a 'thing', and we need to take care to always be aware of the complex experience behind the word; wonder is a response; the term 'wonder' covers a great variety of experiences. I also agree that the variety is not such that it becomes meaningless to speak of wonder as a distinct type of experience (in the way I have done in the previous chapter). But a lot of these things could equally well be said about fear or joy or some other emotion; and to my mind wonder differs from what are typically called emotions in an important respect not sufficiently addressed by Fuller, namely that, apart from a sense of puzzlement or mystery, *wonder has no unique and stable affective signature*, but varying affective valences. I do not want to overemphasize this point, since there are a number of recognizable affective features that typically make us reach for the word 'wonder': a sense of puzzlement, a certain felt distance from the object, the sense of a pause or break in the flow of events, et cetera – but the further affective quality of wonder can range from fear to joy, from a sense of absurdity to something approaching awe or admiration. So if we speak of wonder as an emotion, we should take care not to assume that it has a single affective signature the way typical emotions do. (The variety between instances of fear, for instance, is of a different order than that between instances of wonder.)

A second point worth noting is that the common distinction between emotions (as short-lived affective states) and moods (longer-lasting states, 'sometimes as a low-intensity background', that lack an intentional object)[40] is more difficult to maintain in the case of wonder. Wonder typically does have an intentional object, but, as I noted in the previous chapter, when wonder becomes dispositional it can be somewhat like a mood, in the sense that it is an affective tone in the background without a specific object.

With these qualifications in mind, let us see what can be said about wonder from an evolutionary perspective on emotions. Firstly, Fuller notes that if we look at wonder as an emotion it must be a *secondary*, not a primary emotion. Primary emotions are supposed to be 'hardwired', innate, and universal evolved human responses with a low susceptibility to conscious control; secondary emotions

[39] Ibid.
[40] Oatley, Keltner, and Jenkins, *Understanding Emotions*, 30.

are seen as 'combinations or permutations of the primary emotions', 'more influenced by social forces and individual experience', and 'more susceptible to conscious thought and control'.[41] Secondly, unlike fear and disgust, wonder is not an *avoidance* emotion, but belongs to a class or family of emotions said to include also curiosity, enthusiasm, interest, and attraction.[42] These mobilize very different behaviours than avoidance emotions; they 'motivate sustained involvement with one's surroundings'.[43]

These points are central to Fuller's account of wonder, which is summarized in the following quote:

> Wonder (...) does not display the 'prototypical characteristics' associated with the evolutionary-adaptive model underlying most contemporary discussions of the emotions. Experiences of wonder do not, for example, ordinarily lead to the kinds of facial and physiological expressions found in the primary emotions studied by most researchers. Nor do they contribute to the survival tasks closely linked with hunting and gathering. Indeed, the experience of wonder has relatively little adaptive significance for single individuals in the short run. Yet (...) experiences of wonder may prompt individuals over time to develop moods and attitudes that serve the adaptive needs of the wider community. They can also give rise to religiously charged philosophical orientations that might possibly serve the long-term survival of the human species. The study of wonder thus prompt reflection on the fairly narrow understandings of 'useful' and 'adaptive' that the sciences traditionally bring to their study of emotional experience. Seen in wider anthropological context, experiences of wonder evoke moods and attitudes that lead to what may well be humanity's highest levels of fulfillment and well-being.[44]

The adaptiveness or functionality of emotions is usually seen along the lines of the adaptiveness of *primary* emotions, i.e. in terms of immediate survival value. Fuller questions this narrow understanding of adaptation: '[T]he role of wonder in our lives alerts us to a broader understanding of adaptation', for 'adaptation requires receptivity as well as activity, creative ways of sensing one's connectedness with the world as well as ways of establishing a safe distance from potential danger'.[45] Wonder differs from emotions with an immediate survival

[41] Fuller, *Wonder*, 28–9.
[42] Ibid., 35.
[43] Ibid., 36.
[44] Ibid., 54–5.
[45] Ibid., 12.

value in two ways, Fuller says: firstly, it is not an avoidance emotion, but one that makes us approach things and connect with things; and secondly, wonder 'awakens our mental capacity for abstract, higher-order thought' and 'seems to direct our cognitive activities to construct models of a greater whole in terms of which the parts of our lives might be seen to have meaning and purpose.'[46] In individuals' psychological development to adulthood wonder, like curiosity, 'is a prime motivating factor in the acquisition of higher-order conceptions of reality', it 'is an emotional experience that invites us to entertain belief in the existence and causal activity of an order of reality that lies beyond or behind sensory appearances'.[47] But why would this be adaptive? Fuller suggests that wonder's adaptive value lies in the fact that it makes us engage with the world, promoting an open and receptive stance, rather than a utilitarian one.[48] 'This last feature of wonder – the temporary deactivation of our utilitarian striving and the creation of a sense of our participation in a more general order of life – is crucial to understanding how wonder guides our adaptation to the wider interpersonal, moral, and cultural environments we inhabit.'[49] Wonder, Fuller suggests, may inspire and contribute to personal attitudes towards others and the world that in the long run benefit all, promoting peace and human flourishing.

Although Fuller's analysis of wonder is very sophisticated and his critique of conventional evolutionary perspectives on emotions quite plausible, I am not entirely convinced by his argument for wonder's adaptiveness. One strand of the argument is that it is adaptive to construct higher-order conceptions of reality, that wonder stimulates the construction of higher-order conceptions of reality, and that wonder is therefore adaptive. But there are many different kinds of higher-order conceptions of reality, and it is not self-evident that all of them will be equally adaptive. Newtonian and Einsteinian physics are (both still quite useful) higher-order conceptions of reality, but so are the myriad of religions the world contains. Throughout his book Fuller uses terms that connect wonder with the object of religion and metaphysics; wonder is said to stimulate 'conceptualization [of] a more-than-physical order of reality', a 'metaphysical order of existence', it 'entices us to consider the reality of the unseen, the existence of a more general order of existence from which this world derives its meaning and purpose', and

[46] Ibid., 60.
[47] Ibid., 13; Fuller refers to the work of Piaget here.
[48] Ibid., 37.
[49] Ibid., 41.

it is therefore 'one of the principal sources of humanity's spiritual impulse'.[50] The question is whether the construction of *this* type of higher-order conception is adaptive, and it seems equally well possible to think of arguments that support this claim as arguments that undermine it.

This is where another strand of the argument comes in. Fuller enters into debate with thinkers like Steven Pinker and Richard Dawkins for whom religion and philosophy (in the sense of metaphysics) are non-adaptive by-products of evolution, misguided attempts to apply 'mental tools to problems other than the problems they were designed to solve'.[51] He argues that '[w]here Pinker, Atran, and Dawkins prove unhelpful is their peculiar insistence that the only proper domain of adaptation is the immediate physical environment. (…) Our brains coevolved with our cultural experience and symbolic communication. Higher-order cognition made cultural life possible even as cultural life in turn selected for brains capable of engaging in abstract, higher-order thought.'[52] We adapt to a dynamic, social environment that is 'abstract rather than solely physical, and striving toward future possibilities rather than composed only of present realities'.[53] Wonder, on Fuller's account, is functional in this context because it stimulates us to look beyond our own plans and interests and to form conceptions of a larger whole, a reality behind the physical, that we are part of, and to search for meaning and the realization of moral and aesthetic ideals – things in which we find the highest fulfilment. In particular, it balances an 'active' mode of adaptation through mastery of our environment with an equally necessary 'receptive' mode of adaptation through adjustment, a mode that enables us to 'break out of our constructed world from time to time and gain a larger vision of the full range of our needs and interests'.[54]

The difficulty with this argument is that it is hard to see whether the adaptiveness Fuller claims for wonder is still an *evolutionary* adaptiveness; i.e. the question is whether wonder could be a trait selected for in evolution in virtue of the features Fuller mentions. I cannot think of any way to decisively settle this question. To see a value (for individuals or communities) in having a sense of wonder does not yet establish its evolutionary adaptiveness; and it is one thing to make a case for the adaptiveness of being able to construct higher-order conceptions of reality, and of being interested in the world and motivated to

50 Ibid., 13–15.
51 Ibid., 56.
52 Ibid., 58–9.
53 Ibid., 59.
54 Ibid., 62.

engage with it; but it is another thing altogether to extend that case to include the adaptiveness of the peculiar response to the world we call wonder. It *is* true that wonder is part of the part-biological, part-cultural evolved make-up of human beings and human societies today; but this is not necessarily *because* wonder is functional or adaptive. It remains possible to see wonder – and the metaphysical constructions or spirituality Fuller says it inspires – as non-adaptive by-products of traits that *are* adaptive.

Recall, however, that the purpose of this section was not so much to establish whether wonder is adaptive or not, but rather whether it might be adaptive *because it tells us something about the world*. Thus, the first question is only important if the answer to the latter might be positive. Although Fuller regularly uses 'realist' language in connection with wonder ('response', 'recognition of the intrinsic significance of the stimuli at hand', 'open up certain kinds of realities') he does not pursue this question so much.[55] He defends a Jamesian, pragmatic view of the value of wonder as a source of spirituality and religion, and therefore the question whether the beliefs it inspires are true in the sense that they correspond with objective features of the world is in the end irrelevant – what matters for Fuller is that wonder (if it is balanced with curiosity) promotes a rich, philosophically reasonable, and morally valuable life.[56] He does consider the 'object' of wonder in this context, but says that 'this object in some fundamental way eludes literal designation'.[57] Wonder, he says, citing Rachel Carson, 'incited in her a passion for "some universal truth that lies just beyond our grasp (…) [a meaning that] haunts and ever eludes us, and in its very pursuit we approach the ultimate mystery of Life itself."'[58] So wonder is connected with a quest for meaning, but what we encounter on this quest – even at its end, if we do not give in to false certainties – is mystery.[59] If wonder 'tells us' anything, it seems, it is that the world is mysterious. Someone might counter that the mystery is merely a function of (the limits of) our capacity to understand the world. But this either-or is unhelpful; the world is such that it – its *being*, and the being of everything we encounter – cannot be understood in the way we normally, in our everyday lives, understand things. Our categories of explanation, causality, and origination break down. As I wrote elsewhere, 'when we try to think about [the]

[55] E.g. ibid., 41, 155.
[56] Ibid., 152–8.
[57] Ibid., 157.
[58] Ibid., citing Carson, *The Edge of the Sea*, 250; see also Fuller, *Wonder*, 109.
[59] I have explored the connections between wonder, mystery and (the search for) meaning in Schinkel, 'Wonder, Mystery, and Meaning'.

origins [of the world] and the possibility of non-being we become hopelessly entangled in logical contradictions', and in that sense the being of the world is inherently mysterious.[60] Wonder is the awareness that accompanies the event of such a break-down.

The problem with an evolutionary approach to wonder is that it is at risk of falling into the either-or trap according to which wonder is either adaptive and useful or a useless by-product of an evolutionarily adaptive trait or tendency. For Fuller it is adaptive as a source of spirituality and an inspiration for religious or metaphysical higher-order conceptions of reality; for people like Pinker and Dawkins its tendency to inspire such things is a sure sign that it is a useless by-product of an in itself adaptive cognitive–affective system that helps us understand and get around in the world. I would like to propose a middle road. To say that wonder (that is, the type of wonder that is a source of spirituality) is a by-product of such systems is to marginalize it too much, and to sever its intrinsic connection with those systems. But Fuller's argument for its adaptiveness remains underdetermined; it wants to prove too much, and in order to do so it has to overload wonder with positive (substantive and valuable) content. But what if we were to emphasize the fact that wonder is 'essentially', or first and foremost, a phenomenon of the *limit*? That it is, as Wittgenstein suggested, where we run up against the limits of our understanding, which are at the same time the limits of 'the world' as we know it? Wonder brings these limits into view, reminds us of our limitations, and at the same time reveals that there is (a) 'world' beyond our image of the world. It is (at least in part) because the world is too much for our ability to comprehend it that we experience wonder; and at the same time this is possible because our cognitive–affective system is sophisticated enough to allow its limits to come into view. This is the view I will develop in the remainder of this chapter.

Wonder as a Phenomenon of the Limit

The world as a whole, and existence as such, Hepburn said, is the 'finally secure object of wonder'.[61] But what, if anything, does wonder reveal to us about the world, about existence, about being? And more broadly, what forms of connection to the world does wonder make possible? Wonder does not connect us to the

60 Schinkel, 'Wonder, Mystery, and Meaning', 24–5.

61 Hepburn, 'Wonder', 9.

world through a 'signalling' function the way certain (avoidance) emotions do, but rather through a specific type of *attention* – so if we want to explore this more fully, we need to turn to a phenomenological approach that can elucidate what happens when we attend to the world in this way.

To start, it is important to be aware that the 'finally secure object of wonder' of which Hepburn spoke is not an object like other objects. This is the important point expressed by Heidegger in terms of the distinction between the ontic and the ontological; wonder is not concerned with *beings* and whatever characterizes them or happens to them, but with *being*, and this is of a different order altogether. For the same reason it is important not to misunderstand the 'limits' I spoke of at the end of the previous section. The limits of our understanding intended there are not contingent limits that might expand (or contract) in the way we might move the fence around a meadow, but limits that confront us however much we know, whichever way we look, as soon as – for whatever reason – the world appears to us *in a certain way*, i.e. as soon as our everyday comportment towards the world falls away and we are left to gaze upon it 'naked'. The nakedness is ours as much as the world's, because without our knowledge and our explanations we feel exposed, vulnerable. But the being of the world beyond our ordinary understanding of *how* it is, is a bare 'presence' that is never present in the way objects *in* the world are normally present to us. The world beyond our perception of it is – by definition – imperceptible.

The danger with a distinction like that between the ontic and the ontological is that we reify these terms, turning them into signs that refer to separate metaphysical realms. My view is rather that there are 'only' the world (or reality) – that we are part of – and the ways in which we relate to it (or, if this suggests too much distance, are bound up with it). When we do chores, pursue goals, act on concerns in daily life the world appears to us in a particular way that does not foreground the mystery of its being. But when we suddenly wonder at the inexplicability of our doing the dishes (not because we always leave them for our partner to do, but for instance because we experience a zooming out and marvel at the phenomenon of doing dishes as something that is *real* in one tiny corner of the galaxy) the world appears to us fundamentally differently. The activity is stripped of its meaning – its normally unnoticed, taken-for-granted meaningfulness – and this opens a realm of possibility (it sounds rather grand in connection with doing the dishes, but still): we can relate to what we are doing anew, with more awareness and more purpose – we are engaged in an activity of 'maintenance', by which we maintain the conditions of possibility for living our (working and family) lives – or we can, if only momentarily, reject it as an absurd waste of time. At any rate our attunement to the mystery of being does not mean that we enter a different realm of existence, but that our awareness of the world has changed – has become deeper and fuller, and cut loose from habitual, conventional, and goal-directed ways of acting, feeling, and perceiving – and that we have thus entered into a different type of connection with the world. The difference between the ontic and the ontological is a matter of the direction and quality of attention. The question to be answered is how we (can) relate to the world through the mode of attention that is wonder.

Wonder as Encounter

Phenomenologically, wonder has the character of an *encounter*. As Jeff Malpas writes: 'it is the encounter – and the character of that encounter as a revealing, an opening up, of things and the world – that seems to lie at the heart of the experience of wonder.'[62] He goes on to explain that wonder is not a response to 'any particular appearance or set of appearances' (although wonder is always triggered by a specific appearance), but rather 'the response that is evoked in us by the very recognition of appearance as such' – we are 'brought to a halt by the appearance, and forced to attend to it, not because it shows something else (…), nor because of anything that explains how it is (…), but merely by the fact that it is'.[63]

Terms like 'encounter' and 'response' may sound 'objectivist', in the sense that they seem to presuppose some *thing* that we encounter or respond to – rather than leaving open the possibility that wonder is entirely internally generated, and illusory in so far as it seems to connect with something, be informed by something, or tell us something about the 'external' world. The encounter, however, while certainly not illusory, is not with an 'object' (in the sense of an existing entity) but with *appearance*, which in more ontological terms means to say that it is with being – with the sheer fact of 'there-being-things', things appearing to us – as such.

Drawing on Levinas, Malpas compares the experience of wonder with that of light, of opening one's eyes:

> Just as the experience of opening one's eyes is an experience of the immediate coming to visual presence of things – not the experience of the establishing of some relation, but of things being, simply, 'there' – so the experience of wonder

[62] Malpas, 'Beginning in Wonder'.
[63] Ibid.; emphasis in original.

> is the experience of ourselves as already in the sway of wonder, of ourselves as already 'there' along with the wondrous.

And he adds that 'the encounter that wonder brings into view is just our being already with things, already given over to them and them to us'.[64]

While Malpas is right in saying that wonder makes us aware of the fact that we are *normally* always co-present with things – they form a stage, as it were, without a backstage; a stage we cannot leave – he fails to point out that wonder *creates* a certain distance to its 'object' – or that part of the experience of wonder is the experience of a certain distance – that (subsequently) enables us to *establish* a *relationship* with that with which we are already bound up. This is not to establish a relationship where there was no connection before, but to deepen it, or add a new layer of meaning (whether affirmative or negative), to a pre-existing connection. Wonder thus opens up the possibility of *reconfiguring* our everyday connections with the world, of reweaving the pattern of our interwovenness with it – *and* it helps us to live in a fuller awareness of the world, and of the paradox inherent in the sense of normality that pervades our day-to-day dealings in the world: this is at the same time illusory and justified, both contingent and necessary.

Wonder as Revelation

Compared to other 'subjective' responses to the world (joy, fear, melancholy) wonder is special because it opens the inner world to the outer world. Wonder opens the world by opening us; though phenomenologically it is rather the case that the *world* opens *us* – it breaks in, as if to let us feel that it is more and always other than we thought or thought we knew. Whereas (other) emotions are determined by particular organismic or personal goals or desires, focus our attention on specific aspects of the world relevant from the perspective of those goals and desires, and thus determine our response, wonder sets in motion a widening, rather than a narrowing movement. It entails a receptive type of attention – not directive, not projecting, but opening up and preparing to receive.

Sometimes – and I'm sure many readers will recognize this – when I am on my way to work, joining in the ranks of the disciplined army of employees that obeyed their alarm clocks to catch their transport so as to present in time wherever they are stationed, I am struck by the contrast between this way of life and that of all of humankind for 99 per cent of its history (counting only

[64] Ibid.

the roughly 200,000 years that *Homo sapiens* has had so far, not our human ancestors before that). And I can imagine a high school student, who is being prepared for this life by having to structure her life in a similar way, having the same experience. Virtually nothing of what occurs every weekday morning and evening existed for our hunter-gatherer ancestors or for the early farmers. From a biological or evolutionary perspective – looking at human beings over a long period of time, and as one species of animal among countless others – our modern way of life appears as extraordinary and extraordinarily unlikely, and such a perception easily leads to wonder, to a state in which any and all explanations of why things are (now) the way they are fall short, and are in fact utterly beside the point.

When the everyday meaningfulness of what we are doing and what is happening around us falls away this can be a dizzying experience. We suddenly sense a depth to existence that is normally hidden from view, and in the same stroke we are revealed to ourselves as 'superficial' creatures: most of the time we skim across the surface of things, barely aware of their presence. It is as if we spend our days in a boat drifting on the surface of an ocean, constantly looking to the horizon, but afraid to plumb the depths of the ocean beneath us, as if the mere awareness of them might sink us.

And even when our engagement with things is not superficial, it is still most of the time reductive. A scientist may spend a lifetime developing one particular perspective on some phenomenon; and we all view the people in our lives in a particular way, we have opinions about them – which is to say we see and know them incompletely. When we read the newspaper and get worked up about the stupidity or wickedness of some politicians our perception presupposes and is based on a 'world' of ideas and feelings, on our vague and probably in many ways incoherent construal of the world.

Wonder does not offer us a 'true' perception of the world, it does not, as is sometimes suggested, show us things 'as they are', but it can nevertheless be said to be 'revelatory' in two ways. Firstly, wonder reveals to us most clearly the fact that 'the world' as we normally perceive it is always an interpreted, even appropriated world, and that our interpretations must not be mistaken for the world as such. Secondly, by pointing out the inadequacy of our interpretations it confronts us with an elusive world 'behind' or 'beyond' our perception. We do not *perceive* this world, it is not revealed to us what it looks like; only its presence – *that* it is there, *that* there is something beyond our perception – is revealed to us. As Malpas writes: 'In wonder, our "being there" is suddenly "lit up," and yet in being illuminated, it is also shown as essentially dark – while we can "see into" the intricacies of the world and our situation in it, that there is a world, and that we are already given over to it, is absolutely impenetrable.'[65] Wonder, another author wrote, '*thaumazein*, (…) both opens our eyes wide and plunges us into the dark'.[66]

So in wonder we arrive at the limit of what we can perceive and make sense of. Jean-Luc Nancy writes: 'In the final analysis wonder is nothing other than that which happens or arrives at the limit. Wonder itself is a kind of sign without signification, and the sign – the index or the signal – that signification is verging upon its limit, and that sense is laid bare.'[67] 'Sense is laid bare' – sense, the French *sens*, can mean both meaning and (sense) perception. 'Bare' can mean dry, barren, infertile, but also naked, open, in plain view. Thus the limit of what we can think, grasp, perceive, and express, is also a place of possibility. Through wonder it is possible to relate to the world differently, to 'establish anew our relations with the world'.[68] As Nicola Gess and Mireille Schnyder write, when one recognizes that there is a limit ('Grenze') to one's understanding of the world – or to the world as one understands it – the possibility of going beyond the limit ('Grenzüberschreitung'), of transgression or transcendence, also arises.[69] In wonder we become aware of a limit, but it is also an experience of being touched by, and standing on the threshold of, the limitless, which has no definition and is therefore undefinable; it can be experienced both as sheer actuality and as sheer possibility.[70]

This may seem obvious for inquisitive wonder, in cases where in wonder we are confronted merely with the limits of our present understanding, but not the limits of understanding per se; but much less obvious for deep wonder. What kind of space of possibility is opened up by deep wonder? It can hardly entail the possibility of a better understanding, or can it? I think it can, in a way. Firstly, wonder at being as such also sensitizes us to the fallibility of views that *can* be improved by new knowledge and more adequate understanding. It invites a

[65] Malpas, 'Beginning in Wonder'.
[66] John Llewelyn, 'On the Saying that Philosophy Begins in *Thaumazein*', in *Post-Structuralist Classics*, ed. Andrew Benjamin (London: Routledge, 1988), 173, cited in Hove, 'The Face of Wonder', 459n1.
[67] Jean-Luc Nancy, *L'Oubli de la Philosophie* (Paris: Galilée, 1986), 104/67, cited in Rubenstein, *Strange Wonder*, 125.
[68] Hove, 'The Face of Wonder', 458.
[69] Nicola Gess and Mireille Schnyder, 'Staunen als Grenzphänomen. Eine Einführung', in *Staunen als Grenzphänomen*, eds. Nicola Gess, Mireille Schnyder, Hugues Marchal, and Johannes Bartuschat (Paderborn: Wilhelm Fink, 2017), 7.
[70] Wonder is thus an experience of the *coincidentia oppositorum*, the unity (the coinciding or meeting) of opposites – a concept most strongly associated with the philosophy of Nicholas of Cusa, who described God in these terms; God was therefore beyond human understanding. See Nicholas Cusanus, *Of Learned Ignorance*, trans. Germain Heron (Eugene: Wipf & Stock Publishers, 2007).

change of perspective that opens new vistas. Secondly, deep wonder and the experience of mystery it entails impresses upon us an awareness of the *inevitable* fallibility and the limited nature of any conception of the world we construe; this pertains to the limits of understanding per se. More positively, it orients us towards the world behind that conception, a world we can 'know', however, only in non-cognitive ways. Yet our intuition of that world still underlies new attempts to understand or to organize the world. These attempts are inevitably also imperfect, but they may achieve a more refined ignorance – an ignorance that incorporates an awareness of its own limitations and a sense of the 'other' that escapes it.[71] Whitehead said that philosophy begins in wonder, but when the philosopher is done the wonder remains; but what has been added is 'some grasp of the immensity of things, some purification of emotion by understanding'.[72] But apart from the possibility of a new understanding, there is also the possibility of a different *world* – and that is at least as important an aspect of the space of possibility opened up by wonder. In wonder we become vividly aware of the current world as a contingent possibility, and therefore of the fact that the world could have been and could be different.

Wonder and the World

Wonder entails an openness to 'phenomena', to that which shows itself to us; it is a receptive mode of consciousness in which our interpretative frameworks are bracketed, even broken down. For this reason it also tends to promote a second kind of openness, directed inward: an anti-dogmatic stance. Since dogmatic adherence to beliefs hinders education, this is one reason why wonder has educational importance. For the same reason, and with equal educational importance, wonder fosters intellectual humility and modesty. As a phenomenon of the limit it makes us strongly aware of the limits of our understanding – in fact, of the *limitations* of our (faculty of) understanding; though here we might as well say that wonder is where we become aware of the irreducible mystery of existence – the muchness of the world spills over our categories and overwhelms us. We are out of our depth or, as Hove put it, 'at our wits' end'; the world, on this level at least, resists and exceeds understanding.[73] There is a danger in

[71] I have made this point before, in particular in relation to love for and wonder at another person, an 'other' who/that always escapes us, in Schinkel, 'The Educational Importance of Deep Wonder', 549–50.

[72] Whitehead, *Modes of Thought*, 168–9.

[73] Hove, 'The Face of Wonder', 450.

emphasizing understanding, and the connection of wonder with the limits of understanding, too much: it suggests that wonder is only the *end* of something, whereas (as pointed out by Gess and Schnyder) it may also be the *beginning* of something. Wonder is the mode of consciousness we are in when we find ourselves on the threshold between our everyday mode of consciousness and relating to the world and an as yet undetermined new mode of consciousness, attention, and relation – a threshold, of course, that we may or may not cross. Also, it risks neglecting the aesthetic dimension of many experiences of wonder; the limit of one form of perception may not be the limit of 'perception' per se.

In virtue of the various aspects of the nature of wonder described above, wonder, especially if it becomes dispositional, may (gradually) transform the way we relate to the world and act in it in further ways. At the very least, wonder shows us the world as an interesting place; as long as we wonder, we cannot escape a sense of importance. In its most affirmative form, it may be akin to love.[74] Hepburn noted that wonder is a point of view from which compassion readily flows.[75] Though it can on occasion be intense, even rapturous, it is generally a calm state, naturally associated with patience and opposed to a readiness to judge. But none of this is *guaranteed*. Dwelling in wonder may also foster frustration with the (human) world, and an impatience with people who approach the world in a purely practical-utilitarian fashion – people who see only problems and solutions, questions that admit of answers (that, if they do not have them yet, they will surely find). Gabriel Marcel distinguished between problems and mysteries; whereas a mystery is something 'in which I find myself caught up, and whose essence is therefore not to be met before me in its entirety', a problem 'is something met with which bars my passage' and 'is before me in its entirety'.[76] The world that we become aware of in wonder, the world *in the way we become aware of it* in wonder, is never before us in its entirety – that is, it can never be 'in our view', laid out before us.[77] It is not seen or grasped, but *sensed*, like a vibration that continues in us, at the moment we leave the world 'in its entirety' behind us and stand on the threshold of a groundlessness that yet

[74] Schinkel, 'The Educational Importance of Deep Wonder'.

[75] Hepburn, 'Wonder', 15.

[76] Gabriel Marcel, *Being and Having*, trans. Katherine Farrer (Boston: Beacon Press, 1951), 100, cited in Malpas, 'Beginning in Wonder', note 26. Malpas also notes that the same distinction was taken up by Merleau-Ponty.

[77] Note that this is completely compatible with the fact that wonder involves a 'holistic' rather than analytic perception of things; in fact, it is exactly *because* wonder involves a holistic awareness rather than one in which we perceive the separate components of which things are made up that we cannot *grasp* the world in its entirety: we cannot gain an *overview* of all it contains.

grounds everything; though we may not be able to see reason in it, yet the world *is* – and at least sometimes has rhyme to it.

Therefore, wonder may also dispose us to be more mindful of the *many* ways in which we are (potentially) 'in touch' with the world, apart from the traditionally dominant seeing and thinking. We 'know' the world in many ways before we come to know it, simply because we are part of it, the 'border' not even being clear (when does the air we breathe stop being part of the external world to become part of us?). We 'feel' it even before we sense it with one of our five senses – in the pull of gravity, a lurching stomach, or a feeling of light-headedness. One of the challenges for the next chapter, in which I discuss the connection between wonder and the general aim of education, is to address the question how this, too, might be educationally important.

Let me in closing return to a close relative of the question whether wonder tells us something about the world. What of someone who does not recognize all of the above, who is either never aware of any absolute limit to his or her understanding, or is aware of such a limit but not in this way, not in or with wonder? What if someone is incapable of experiencing wonder at the mystery of being, or at any particular being's being just as it is? Would there be something 'wrong' with this person, or could we say that (s)he failed to 'see' something? In other words: is such wonder (at least sometimes) a fitting or even a required response to the world, and are there times when other responses would be inadequate? Or if there is no particular time or moment when it would be appropriate, is it nevertheless 'inappropriate' to never experience such wonder? I would not hesitate to say that there is something amiss when someone does not recognize at all that the world exceeds our capacity to understand it; but conceivably someone could recognize this without experiencing wonder, but in a more matter-of-factly way. It seems to me, however, that this would have to be a purely 'intellectual' understanding that is as incomplete as a similar understanding of love or mortality is when neither have been *experienced* in a meaningful way, or as an intellectual understanding of morality that is uninformed by moral feelings and emotions. If it has not evoked wonder, the mystery of being has not truly sunk in.

Conclusion

While the sense that in wonder we 'see things as they are' is not exactly true, it nevertheless contains an important element of truth. The appearance of wonder is at the same time the disappearance of our ordinary ways of interpreting the world, which means that we now perceive them both unhelped and unhindered by those interpretative frameworks. Insofar as these frameworks involved distortions, which they inevitably do, in wonder we are rid of those, and are enabled to become aware of aspects of the world that we were not – and could not become – aware of before. Wonder is itself a particular mode of experiencing the world and thus cannot claim to reveal it 'as it is', and yet it is revelatory not only because it makes us aware of the fact that the world we live our everyday lives in is always in some sense an interpreted, constructed world, but also and even more importantly because it reveals to us that there is a world *beyond* those constructions, albeit one we can by definition never perceive with the clarity that characterizes our ordinary conscious perception of the world (a clarity and distinctness that is not a mark of truth, but of the operation of our mental structures). In wonder we *sense* a world beyond our constructions, beyond everyday appearances; we are confronted with the world's – and our – simply being-there, with appearance as such. This is a living, vibrant reality that touches us, but does not allow us to grasp it. And yet, as I will argue in the next chapter, this type of wonder is – counterintuitively, perhaps – intimately connected with the aim of education.

3

Wonder and the Aim of Education

What is the aim of education? For some this question won't make sense because education – obviously – has many aims, not just the one. Others may find the question not merely nonsensical but positively objectionable, because it seems to presuppose an essentialist view of education, and thus one that does violence to the plurality of everything we (or some people) call education. I am going to ask the question anyway. More specifically, I will ask what the *general* aim of education is – which provides at least part of an answer to the first objection, because we can then readily admit that on a more concrete or specific level education has many aims – and, as explained in the introduction, I will be asking this for a specific sense of the term 'education' – which should at least diminish the concern about essentialism. The value of formulating a general aim of education as such is threefold: firstly, it will allow us to see connections, important commonalities, between various types of educational activity; secondly, it can help to explain or ground intuitions and ideas about when and why a specific type of education or educational effort fails; and thirdly, because it provides us with an independent standard it offers some protection and autonomy vis-a-vis politicized views of the aims of education (by which I here mean ideologically informed views that serve particular political interests).[1]

1 As Barrow notes: 'The vacuum that is left by an abandonment of inquiry into the aims of education is all too readily filled by the imposition of extraneous ends by various interested parties. Thus it is that the nature of education is increasingly dictated by the demands of industry, government, religious pressure groups and the like. The various demands of such interest groups might conceivably be reasonable and possibly should be a concern of the schooling system. But even when the demands are reasonable they are not a substitute for specifically educational demands. Without an educational ideal, we have no argument to support those specifically educational demands.' I wholeheartedly agree. See Robin Barrow, '"Or What's a Heaven For?" The Importance of Aims in Education', in *The Aims of Education*, ed. Roger Marples (London and New York: Routledge, 1999), 20.

But in the context of this chapter it has a more specific value, because my aim in this chapter is to show the deep, intrinsic connections between wonder and what education (again, in a particular sense of the term) *is*, or what 'it is about'; and formulating a view on the general aim of education will help me do so.[2] In doing so I will develop the idea of the mutual importance of wonder and education put forward in the introduction, and lay the basis for the two chapters that follow, on wonder and moral education and wonder and political education, respectively, as well as for the concluding chapter, in which implications for policy and practice are discussed.

The outline of this chapter is as follows. I will begin by discussing a number of influential views on the aim of education: first Richard Peters' 'intrinsic' or liberal-educational view, then some variants of the view that human flourishing should be the aim of education, and finally Gert Biesta's Arendtian proposal that education should open up the world to children. I then explain my own view of the aim of education, which also foregrounds the notion of 'opening up the world', but depends on a different conception of 'world' than Biesta's view, and incorporates elements from all of the discussed views. The third section is devoted to the intrinsic connections between wonder and (the aim of) education. I conclude with a brief summary.

Some Views on the Aim of Education

The 'Intrinsic' View: Richard Peters

In the 1960s a new type of philosophy of education developed, of which Richard Peters was one of the founding fathers (Samuel Scheffler and Paul Hirst being others). This 'analytical' philosophy of education moved away from direct reflection on what the aims, subject matter and form of education should be, and instead concentrated primarily on an analysis of the central concepts associated with educational practices – beginning, of course, with the concept of education itself. Peters contrasted the type of philosophy of education he advocated with an older type that 'consisted in the formulation of high-level directives which would guide educational practice and shape the organization of schools and

2 From now on I will use 'the aim of education' to refer to the general aim of education.

universities'.[3] He reformulated the task of philosophy of education as follows: 'Philosophers make explicit the conceptual schemes which [educational] beliefs and standards presuppose; they examine their consistency and search for criteria for their justification.'[4] And this is exactly how he himself approached the concept of education and, bound up with this (for him, at least), the question of the aim(s) of education.

Peters never claimed to offer an analysis of *the* concept of education, but in *Ethics and Education* he distinguished between 'central and peripheral usages of the term' and it was his view that his analysis pertained to central uses of the term. In later writings he acknowledged more clearly that what he first deemed to be peripheral uses were actually much more widespread, but critics still felt that he did not sufficiently do justice to the conceptual plurality hidden behind the word 'education', and that what Peters had actually done was analyse and elucidate one particular concept, namely that of *liberal education*.[5] This seems a fair assessment – *if* it is at the same time acknowledged how influential this concept (still) is in the Western world.[6] Both in his earlier and, with more emphasis, in his later work he contrasted *education*, as implied in the phrase 'the educated man' with *training*, showing that his concern was with education as something that engages and changes the whole person, and transforms a person's outlook on the world. This is indeed central to the concept of liberal education. And in fact, as early as *Ethics and Education*, Peters himself observed that the concept of education he developed there 'is almost indistinguishable from that of "liberal education"'.[7] The function of the term 'liberal', Peters suggested, might in fact merely be to 'emphasize one or other' of the criteria which in his view activities or processes had to satisfy in order to count as educational 'in a context where these were being made difficult to realize'.[8] So what are these criteria?

'Education', Peters noted, does not pick out any specific activity as the word 'gardening' does; it is something that can occur or that one can do by oneself or in a group, and through various types of activity. What the word does, instead, is 'lay down criteria to which activities or processes must conform'.[9] These

[3] Peters, *Ethics & Education*, 15.
[4] Ibid., 16.
[5] Mike A.B. Degenhardt, 'Richard Peters: Liberal Traditionalist', in *The SAGE Handbook of Philosophy of Education*, eds. Richard Bailey, Robin Barrow, David Carr, and Christine McCarthy (London: Sage, 2010), http://dx.doi.org/10.4135/9781446200872.n9
[6] See Barrow, 'Or What's a Heaven For?'.
[7] Peters, *Ethics & Education*, 43.
[8] Ibid.
[9] Ibid., 24–5.

criteria are threefold: education (1) 'implies the transmission of what is worthwhile to those who become committed to it'; (2) 'must involve knowledge and understanding and some kind of cognitive perspective, which are not inert'; (3) 'at least rules out some procedures of transmission, on the grounds that they lack wittingness and voluntariness on the part of the learner'.[10] So activities and processes can only count as educational (in the sense of the word that Peters is interested in) if something of value is inherent in them, a value that is (at some point at least) also appreciated by the learner; if what is acquired in them goes beyond mere factual knowledge or specific skills, but includes a deeper understanding of the material, that influences the way in which an educated person perceives the world and is fruitful in interpretation of and action in new situations; and if they respect the person of the learner, rely on their assent and appeal at least minimally to their reason and understanding.[11]

The notion of *aims* of education is connected with the first criterion, with the normative dimension of education. Peters notes that because the concept of education implies 'the intentional bringing about of a desirable state of mind' people may easily mistake it for 'a neutral process that is instrumental to something that is worthwhile which is extrinsic to it'.[12] But on Peters' view this is confused for two reasons. Firstly, because if the 'aim' – the 'desirable state of mind' – were not attained in a particular person's case (despite years of participation in supposedly educational activities), we would not call the person 'educated', which shows that the aim is *intrinsic* to education, rather than extrinsic to it. Secondly, because when we say, for instance, that the aim of education is to make sure children will get jobs, we are using the term 'aim' inappropriately, or at least in an unusual sense. Whereas terms like 'purpose' and 'motive' pertain to *why* a person does what she does, the term 'aim' refers to the *internal* target or point of the activity. A comparison with the aim of a game may be instructive here. The aim of a game has to be described in terms of what players of the game, those who are on the inside of the practice, so to speak, are trying to accomplish. Furthermore, the aim lies *within* the game, and is not something attained after the game has ended; hence it is described in the rulebook, as the statement of the point of the game, or what the game is about. The aim of chess

10 Ibid., 45.

11 It seems to me that the qualification 'to those who become committed to it' in the first criterion actually introduces something of the second and third criteria into the first. Peters only introduces it after discussion of the second and third criteria; before that he only speaks of the transmission of what is worthwhile.

12 Ibid., 27.

is to 'capture' the opponent's king (that is, to attack it, while at the same time preventing its escape, thus immobilizing it in a position of being under attack); it is not to win a tournament or prize money, though that may be a player's purpose or motive to play chess. In the same way, getting a job is not the aim of education, nor can any other goal that is extrinsic to the educational activities be called their aim. 'To ask for an aim is to ask for a more precise specification of what an action or activity is.'[13] Or, in other words, '[a]sking a person about his aims is a method of getting him to concentrate or clear his mind about what he is trying to do'.[14]

Aims of education can be more or less specific, they can be abstract or more concrete, but they are never explanations of *why* educators are doing what they are doing, but more precise specifications of their activity. The aim of a history teacher may be to make children acquainted with the complex origins of the First World War, or to develop their understanding of human conflict in general. The teacher's motives for formulating these aims may be of many different kinds: to make sure they do not fail a general examination, in which these topics are addressed; a hunch that the students will be more motivated to study these things with enthusiasm than some other topic; a personal fascination with the theme; and perhaps also a sense that this is knowledge and understanding worth having in and for itself. But in so far as the teaching is to count as educational, only the latter point matters: the activities are understood as intrinsically valuable.

This raises the important problem of justification. As explained in the previous chapter Peters argued that education is a matter of initiation into worthwhile modes of thought and activity, and that this initiation into 'a public world picked out by the language and concepts of a people', 'a public inheritance', was necessary for the development of mind.[15] Children do not develop consciousness, 'the hall-mark of mind' just naturally. 'The objects of consciousness are first and foremost objects in a public world that are marked out and differentiated by a public language into which the individual is initiated.'[16] So education clearly presupposes a world that transcends and precedes the individual – an intersubjective world. The lack of a clear awareness of this was a defect shared, Peters noted, between the 'moulding' and 'growth' models of education; both saw the educator 'as a detached operator who is working for some kind of result in another person which is external to him'.[17] They ignore

13 Ibid., 28.
14 Ibid.
15 Ibid., 52, 53.
16 Ibid., 50.
17 Ibid., 51–52.

'the holy ground' (D.H. Lawrence) 'that stands between teacher and taught': the content of education, that precedes and transcends both teacher and learner, and the criteria on the basis of which this content is assessed and developed over time.[18] All this may be so, but it is a fact that in millennia of recorded history people have developed many traditions that are sometimes, from an ethical or an educational point of view, diametrically opposed to each other; aristocratic and egalitarian traditions, imperialistic and isolationist traditions, traditions of war and traditions of peace. Furthermore, there is an enormous range of social practices, some very ancient, into which people have initiated their children; practices ranging from yodelling to bull-fighting and from gardening to safari hunting. Into which traditions, social practices, or forms of life are children to be initiated? In other words: what makes education – as a practice centrally concerned with the development of knowledge and understanding – particularly valuable? And what should be on the curriculum, and how can we justify this?

Peters offered a transcendental justification, a justification based on the presuppositions of the demand for justification itself. In essence it came down to this: when we ask for a justification, when we ask 'why do this rather than that?', a concern for truth is presupposed, and thus the intrinsic value of knowledge and understanding is presupposed. In other words, it is not possible to seriously ask for a justification and at the same time deny or question the importance of knowledge and understanding.[19] This justification has been much criticized.[20] Degenhardt notes that it has been remarked that 'to love poetry because it instantiates rationality is not to love poetry'; but this choice of words – 'because it instantiates rationality' – does not do Peters justice; he was very explicit about his view that understanding was not just a cool, rational affair.[21] A more serious problem is that to establish that a concern for truth is *presupposed* in asking for a justification, and that therefore the value of truth and of the practice of justification is presupposed, is not yet to establish the *actual* value of truth or of

[18] Ibid., 52.

[19] Peters offers such a justification in *Ethics & Education* and again in a 1973 article republished as Richard S. Peters, 'The Justification of Education', in *Education and the Education of Teachers*, ed. Richard S. Peters (London: Routledge & Kegan Paul, 1977). For a fuller rendition and very precise analysis of Peters' transcendental argument see Stefaan Cuypers, 'R. S. Peters' "The Justification of Education" Revisited', *Ethics and Education* 7, no. 1 (2012).

[20] Peters himself also wrote: 'I tried but failed to give a convincing transcendental justification of "worthwhile activities", such as science or agriculture as distinct from Bingo or playing fruit machines, which I thought relevant to the curriculum.' Richard S. Peters, 'Philosophy of Education', in *Educational Theory and Its Foundation Disciplines*, ed. Paul H. Hirst (London: Routledge & Kegan Paul, 1983), 37, cited in Cuypers, 'R. S. Peters' "The Justification of Education" Revisited', 4.

[21] Degenhardt, 'R.S. Peters'.

justification.[22] Peters' ultimate answer to the question why we value justification was that we simply are reason-responsive creatures; the demand for justification and a concern for truth are 'immanent in human life', 'woven into the fabric of human life', which would be 'unintelligible' without it.[23] On one interpretation this simply assumes the intrinsic value of truth and reason-giving, and therefore of knowledge and understanding. But, as Cuypers shows, another interpretation is also possible, one in which Peters' justification – or at least the intention behind the project – is seen as 'broadly perfectionist' rather than transcendental.[24]

Whereas narrow perfectionism (in the sense in which Thomas Hurka uses the term) entails the view that what we should aim at in life – what is good for human beings – is the perfection of human nature (i.e. of certain capacities deemed essential and valuable), broad perfectionism is not committed to a view of what human beings 'essentially' are, and does not tie a view of the good life to human nature.[25] It may, however, appeal to certain general facts about the human condition that help explain why certain things are important to human beings. And this is exactly what Peters does – somewhat implicitly in earlier work, and more explicitly in later texts. He argues that education 'is concerned with developing knowledge and understanding which is relevant to people's lives, in the sense that it should enable them to grasp how they are placed in the world'.[26] Education should not just enable people to make a living, but it should be concerned with *quality* of life, and that means it should take account of the human condition – in fact, education should develop (deepen, expand, refine) our awareness of the human condition, of phenomena of the natural, interpersonal, and social-political world, phenomena like birth and death, ageing, the tides, the seasons, the dark, friendship, loneliness, violence and so on.[27] Because these things are part of the human condition and thus to a great extent determine the quality of our lives, an understanding of them is valuable; and to think of this as an *instrumental* type of value is to fail to see

22 Cuypers, 'R. S. Peters' "The Justification of Education" Revisited', 8.

23 Peters, 'The Justification of Education', 102–5, cited in Cuypers, 'R. S. Peters' "The Justification of Education" Revisited', 7.

24 Cuypers, 'R. S. Peters' "The Justification of Education" Revisited', 12.

25 Thomas Hurka, *Perfectionism* (Oxford: Oxford University Press, 1993).

26 Richard S. Peters, 'Farewell to Aims?' *The London Educational Review* 2 (1973): 3.

27 See Richard S. Peters, 'Ambiguities in Liberal Education and the Problem of Its Content', in *Education and the Education of Teachers*, ed. Richard S. Peters (London: Routledge & Kegan Paul, 1977), Richard S. Peters, 'Dilemmas in Liberal Education', in *Education and the Education of Teachers*, ed. Richard S. Peters (London: Routledge & Kegan Paul, 1977), and Richard S. Peters, 'Democratic Values and Educational Aims', in *Essays on Educators*, ed. Richard S. Peters (London: George Allen &; Unwin, 1981).

the extent to which the need for such understanding – being able to *make sense* of the world and of others – is integral to human life. '*[R]eason-responsiveness*,' Cuypers explains, 'is the typical way in which humans react to the pressures of their predicament, as it is instinctive reaction for animals. Confronted with their condition and motivated by their concerns for survival and the quality of life, humans, as rational beings, are creatures who place themselves under the demands of reason'.[28] This explains, and justifies (in a broadly perfectionist way), the intrinsic value of education. It also seems to close at least some of the distance between 'the intrinsic view' of the aim of education and a different, currently influential type of approach, to which I now turn.

Human Flourishing as the Aim of Education

A number of authors, Doret de Ruyter, Harry Brighouse, John White, and Kristján Kristjánsson being among the most prominent, have defended variants of a different type of view on the aim of education, a type of view that starts from a different interpretation of the question as to the aim of education and therefore arrives at a rather different answer: education should aim at human flourishing. Peters contrasted his own view with instrumentalist views of education according to which it 'must be *for* something else, must get people somewhere – as if, ultimately, there is somewhere to get'. He summarized that perspective in the phrase: 'The kingdom of heaven lies always ahead', and noted that this kingdom usually took the shape of 'better-paid jobs, more prestige, more opportunities for pleasure, pastimes and possessions – perhaps, even, the greatest good of the greatest number or the class-less society'.[29] In contrast, Peters went on to ask, not what education is *for*, but what it *is*, and interpreted the question as to the aim of education accordingly. Times have changed, but much has also remained the same: the complaint that what education is (or should be) about tends to be forgotten can be heard as loudly now as in Peters' day; only the direction in which proposals for improvement are taken differs. Let us take a quick look at the four most prominent defenders of human flourishing as the aim of education.[30] In White's view the current (which is to say the traditional) school curriculum lacks a true rationale, an aim that actually guides policy

[28] Cuypers, 'R.S. Peters' "The Justification of Education" Revisited', 13.

[29] Peters, 'Farewell to Aims?' 2.

[30] These are also discussed extensively in Lynne Wolbert, 'Flourishing, Fragility and Family Life: Critical Reflections on Human Flourishing as an Aim of Education' (PhD diss., Vrije Universiteit Amsterdam, 2018), who offers a number of valuable meta-perspectives on the debate on flourishing as the aim of education.

and practice; instead, recently introduced overarching aims (in the UK) have simply been tacked on to the existing curriculum, which according to White is an outdated inheritance of eighteenth-century puritanical thinking. So he says: 'The most important question to ask about school education is "What is it for?"'[31] Kristjánsson speaks of the 'growing disillusionment in educational circles with mere grade attainment and high achievement in PISA scores as the be-all and end-all of schooling', in light of which 'the time is ripe to revisit some perennial questions about the role of education in helping students flourish overall as human beings'.[32] Brighouse also situates his contribution to the debate in the context of an educational system that seems primarily geared towards meeting the demands of our economy.[33] (That leaves Doret de Ruyter, who seems to be the exception here; her interest in flourishing as the aim of education has always been connected at least as much with upbringing as with schooling, and with the role of ideals in the good life.[34])

It is not my intention to discuss all these views of human flourishing as the aim of education here; my interest lies in the structural differences and similarities with Peters' view. At first sight these authors do exactly what Peters despaired of: they seem to seek a 'kingdom of heaven' that 'lies ahead' of education. But this is not actually the case. None of these authors is concerned only with children's *future* flourishing, nor do they see flourishing as something that merely *results* from education, rather than being intrinsically connected with it. Kristjánsson, for instance, explicitly states that he takes 'good education to be part of the good life, rather than just a preparation for it'.[35] This draws support from the idea that virtue is its own reward (i.e. is intrinsically valuable and constitutive rather than instrumental to flourishing), since an important part of what goes on in schools is the practicing (in both senses of the word) of virtue.[36] Moreover, Kristjánsson understands flourishing as a 'developmentally progressive activity' that 'actualises satisfactorily an individual human being's natural capacities', and thus establishes a natural link with education.[37] De Ruyter, too, thinks of

31 John White, 'What Schools Are for and Why', *Impact* 14 (2007): 5, cited in Wolbert, 'Flourishing, Fragility and Family Life', 4.

32 Kristján Kristjánsson, *Flourishing as the Aim of Education: A Neo-Aristotelian View* (London and New York: Routledge, 2020), 1.

33 Harry Brighouse, *On Education* (Abingdon and New York: Routledge, 2006.

34 See, for instance, Doret J. de Ruyter, 'Pottering in the Garden? On Human Flourishing and Education', *British Journal of Educational Studies* 52, no. 4 (2004), and Doret J. de Ruyter, 'Ideals, Education, and Happy Flourishing', *Educational Theory* 57, no. 1 (2007).

35 Kristjánsson, *Flourishing as the Aim of Education*, 1.

36 Ibid., 17.

37 Ibid. N.B. This merely picks out two elements of his much more encompassing definition of flourishing.

children's flourishing not only as something that lies in their future, but also as something to be realized while they are students; and at least some of the goods she sees as constitutive of flourishing (e.g. being able to reflect on one's own good) are also instantiated in education.[38] White concurs: 'Children come to know what a meaningful life is by engaging in one.'[39]

It is also worth noting that these authors have far from abandoned the view that knowledge, understanding, and gaining a cognitive perspective are essential to education. Brighouse opposes an overly instrumental view of education with the idea that it should be life-enhancing, i.e. promote children's flourishing, and claims that 'schools need to emphasize the intrinsic value of intellectual pursuits to serve this end'.[40] Reiss and White argue that, connecting and underpinning the aims of 'equipping every student to lead a personally flourishing life' and 'equipping every student to help others lead personally flourishing lives' is a third aim: 'helping every student develop a broad background of understanding' – a background understanding of the world, the society they live in, and their own place in both.[41] In Kristjánsson's view education should aim at *phronetic* virtue rather than merely habituated virtue; that means that an important role is reserved for the reflective capacity for judgement.[42] De Ruyter, too, emphasizes that children should be able to interpret and reflect on their own good, and that parents should 'assist children to become practically wise adults'; this practical wisdom goes beyond 'being knowledgeable and intelligent' to include a commitment to what one perceives as valuable and a willingness to act in accordance with one's understanding of this.[43] But this is exactly how Peters explained Whitehead's idea that knowledge should not be inert: it should 'characterize [a person's] way of looking at things rather than be hived off' *and* 'involve the kind of commitment that comes from being on the inside of a form of thought and awareness'. For Peters, what distinguishes education from training, or the knowledge involved in the former from that involved in the latter, is that education involves the cultivation of insight and skills not for a single narrow purpose, but 'as a necessary foundation for a balanced way of life'.[44]

38 De Ruyter, 'Pottering in the Garden?'.

39 John White, 'Education and a Meaningful Life', *Oxford Review of Education* 35, no. 4 (2009): 429. Meaningfulness, for White, is a necessary, but not a sufficient, condition for flourishing.

40 Brighouse, *On Education*, 4; see also 54.

41 Michael Reiss and John White, *An Aims-Based Curriculum: The Significance of Human Flourishing for Schools* (London: Institute of Education Press, 2013), 9, 11.

42 Kristjánsson, *Flourishing as the Aim of Education*, 17.

43 De Ruyter, 'Ideals, Education, and Happy Flourishing', 34.

44 Peters, *Ethics & Education*, 31, 34.

This brings me to the last commonality between the four authors discussed in this section and Peters: the idea that education should be relevant to living one's life and living it well. This was central to Peters' understanding to education, as we have seen, and the same holds for the authors discussed here. It lies behind White's rejection of the idea that subject knowledge is valuable *per se*: '*Why* introduce children to the best literature, history, science, or mathematics, unless this is in some way *personally beneficial* to themselves or others?'[45] And it is, of course, simply inherent in the idea that education should aim at enabling children to flourish now and in the future.

So the authors discussed here do not differ as strongly from Peters as it might seem at first sight. They share his rejection of an exclusively extrinsic view of the aim(s) of education, and agree at least in part on what education should be about and should try to accomplish. Nevertheless, they do ask a different question: not 'what is the (intrinsic) aim of education?' or 'what is education?', but 'what is education *for*?' They are interested in the ultimate end to be served by education, and they do not see an analysis of the concept of education as a particularly useful approach to that issue. Both Kristjánsson and White speak of flourishing as the *overarching aim* of education, to distinguish it from more concrete aims; this overarching aim provides the rationale for the proposed content and form of education.[46] While this is perfectly legitimate – one can hardly question the appropriateness of asking what schools are for or what parental education should aim for – I think we should not be too hasty to abandon Peters' project. Barrow notes that '[m]any would perhaps accept that schools should have a responsibility for developing the physical health and the mental health (…) of individuals as well as socialising them. But such concerns seem distinct from the business of educating them.'[47] This is not just a point about how we should use the term 'education', but more fundamentally a point about (the idea of) a specific type of *practice* that may be worth preserving. If the criterion of a 'successful' education becomes whether it enables a person to flourish (however this is to be determined), we lose something that was central to the concept of education Peters defended, and that is central, I believe, to many people's understanding of education today. Unless we define 'flourishing' in such a way as to include all of those intrinsically valuable features of education Peters identified, making flourishing the aim of education means letting go, at least

45 John White, *Exploring Well-Being in Schools* (Abingdon and New York: Routledge, 2011), 121.

46 Ibid., 125; Kristjánsson, *Flourishing as the Aim of Education*, 1.

47 Barrow, 'Or What's a Heaven For?', 17.

to some extent, of a concern with what distinguishes *educational* experiences, moments, activities, and processes, in Peters' specific sense of the word, from noneducational ones. Why would this matter? One could argue that it would only matter if it made a difference to people's flourishing. But that would amount to saying that *any* value is only really a value if it is constitutive of or at least conducive to flourishing. The concept of flourishing would usurp the concept of value. There are reasons to reject that idea; one is that one can think of other candidates for the overarching aim of education than human flourishing (i.e. the flourishing of individual human beings).[48] Another is that it forces us far beyond common understandings of what 'flourishing' means – it is not difficult to conceive of someone flourishing in a perfectly understandable and non-trivial (even quite demanding) sense of the term, while at the same time conceding that some types of value are not realized in this person's life. And vice versa, I can also imagine someone valuing being 'educated' while at the same time being hesitant to conclude that this furthered his or her flourishing – to put it very crudely, it is not at all obvious that it is all things considered 'better to be a human being dissatisfied than a pig satisfied, better to be Socrates dissatisfied than a fool satisfied'. As Aldo Leopold wrote: 'One of the penalties of an ecological education is that one lives alone in a world of wounds'.[49] In short, a reasonable (but obviously non-Aristotelian) understanding of flourishing is possible that does not make it the only or the ultimate value.

But even if we accept the view that flourishing *is* what matters, ultimately, so that any value inherent in 'education' must be understood as being either constitutive of or conducive to flourishing, we have good reason to try not to lose sight of the question as to what makes certain experiences and activities 'educational'. For this question foregrounds a valuable *phenomenon* – and (as with wonder) it is the phenomenon rather than the concept that matters. This is a phenomenon that (probably) all educators know and hope to see: that someone who was at first 'on the outside' of a particular mode of thought or awareness – or a particular understanding within such a mode – comes to be

48 Haji and Cuypers suggest social welfare and world betterment as options; see Ishtiyaque Haji and Stefaan Cuypers, 'Ultimate Educational Aims, Overridingness, and Personal Well-being', *Studies in Philosophy and Education* 30, no. 6 (2011). Defenders of human flourishing as an aim of education would probably see such aims as ultimately derivable from or reducible to human flourishing. So a better alternative might be an aim that went beyond the flourishing of human beings.

49 Aldo Leopold, *A Sand County Almanac* (New York: Ballantine, 1966), 197, cited in David W. Orr, *Earth in Mind: On Education, the Environment, and the Human Prospect* (Washington/Covelo/London: Island Press, 2004), 22.

'on the inside' of it.[50] I was tempted to write 'by some miracle comes to be on the inside of it', because this, or at least the completion of this process, has the character of an event that can be neither predicted nor forced. In formulating his three criteria Peters tried to capture essential elements of this phenomenon. In doing so he linked up – and this is also an important part of the point of Barrow's remark cited above – with educators' self-understanding. Educators, in particular school teachers who teach particular subjects, if asked what they were doing and why, would not readily come up with talk of human flourishing; they would be much more inclined to describe their activity in terms of acquainting children with certain aspects and features of the world, and helping them understand these. And they will know the difference between 'successful' instances of education – where 'education' truly happened – and cases where children's 'knowledge' remained inert.

A World-oriented View: Gert Biesta

Concern about the present state of education and government policy on education fuelled Gert Biesta's work at least as much as that of the previously discussed authors, but his reflection on what education is and is for is also prompted by the observation that traditional 'pedagogical' thinking is no longer adequate to the world children are born into today.[51] Central to the European Enlightenment 'pedagogical' tradition is the notion of rational autonomy, the idea that the development from childhood to adulthood should be one of increasing independence and competent and reasonable self-determination, and that education is what enables this transition – an idea that is present as much in the German Bildung tradition as in the Anglo-Saxon tradition of liberal education. Without rejecting the value of the notions

[50] Yannis Hadzigeorgiou offers some great examples of this in 'Fostering a Sense of Wonder in the Science Classroom', *Research in Science Education* 42 (2012): 1000, with many students commenting (in journals they kept) after particular classes: 'Now I understand … ' or 'But it was after (…) that I really understood' (with clear implied emphases on 'now' and 'really').

[51] 'Pedagogical' should here be understood in the Continental sense (German 'pädagogisch', Dutch 'pedagogisch'); there is no perfect English translation for this term, which highlights a 'shaping' dimension of child-rearing and education that is not captured by those terms as they are commonly used. Parents do not just tend to their children's needs; they also guide and influence their development as persons, attempting to steer this in a direction they consider desirable. The Dutch verb for this is 'opvoeden', the German 'erziehen'. Education (in schools) can have – and in fact normally has – such a dimension as well; if this receives explicit attention, we can speak of 'vorming' in Dutch or 'Bildung' in German; see Gert Biesta, 'De School als Toegang tot de Wereld: Een Pedagogische Kijk op Goed Onderwijs', in *Wat Is Goed Onderwijs? Bijdragen uit de Pedagogiek*, eds. Ruud Klarus and Wim Wardekker (Den Haag: Boom Lemma, 2011), 21.

of independence and reasonableness, Biesta notes that this view of education and what it is for is not without its problems. 'Reason' has been shown not to be the universally good thing it was once held to be, for rational thinking (of a kind, e.g. in science) was implicated in the atrocities of twentieth-century history; the border between rationality and irrationality is contestable and a site of the exercise of power and the exclusion of 'undesirables'; to make the development of rational autonomy the end of education relegates childhood to a 'not yet' status which the child needs to be emancipated from (which would constitute progress); and in the current global context we need to recognize that the Enlightenment ideal of rational autonomy does not signal the emancipation from tradition but itself constitutes (the heart of) a particular tradition of thought.[52]

In light of these problems Biesta identifies three challenges for 'pedagogy' (again, in the Continental sense of 'Pädagogik', in German, or 'pedagogiek', in Dutch). The first is to no longer exclusively think about 'education' (in the sense of 'Erziehung', 'opvoeding') in terms of realizing reasonable independence or rational autonomy, but to approach it in a 'radically open way', 'not in terms of what must or shall be, but in terms of the new beginning that wants to come into the world'.[53] The second challenge is to see if it is possible to no longer exclusively think of education in temporal, developmental, and progressive terms and the concomitant 'not-yet' of childhood. And the third relates to the distinction between socialization and subjectification, which was traditionally made in terms of the child's development into an independent, reasonable, self-determining being: can we maintain the distinction between socialization and subjectification without taking recourse to that concept?[54]

In order to meet these challenges Biesta develops a conception of the aim of education centred around the notions of 'coming into the world' and 'uniqueness'. 'Coming into the world' is a notion inspired by Hannah Arendt's work, as well as that of Jean-Luc Nancy.[55] Biesta notes that whereas many philosophers emphasize human beings' mortality, Arendt emphasizes *natality*, 'the fact that human beings are *born* into the world', that with every birth something *new*

[52] Biesta, 'De School als Toegang tot de Wereld'; Gert Biesta, *The Beautiful Risk of Education* (London and New York: Routledge, 2016).
[53] Biesta, 'De School als Toegang tot de Wereld', 26 (my translation).
[54] Ibid., 26–7; Biesta, *The Beautiful Risk*, 142.
[55] Nancy's term is 'coming into presence'; see Biesta, *The Beautiful Risk*, 143.

enters the world – or at least a *potentiality* for renewal.[56] For natality, Natasha Levinson explains, is Arendt's term for 'the human capacity for renewal'.[57] The important question for adults, and for educators in particular, is how to deal with the new – how to make sure that the promise of renewal can be fulfilled. In Arendt's terms, this comes down to the question how the older generation can ensure that the new generation can come into the world. This is not simply up to the newcomers, since whether their initiatives will take hold and bear fruit depends on how others take these initiatives up. One could attempt to control those responses, but that would mean, as Biesta explains, that only one person would be free, would be able to *act*, whereas the others could merely follow suit. Against this Arendt introduces the notion of *plurality* as 'the condition of human action'.[58] It is only when we safeguard the possibility for people to develop and express (in word and action) their own perspectives on the world 'that *everyone's* beginnings can come into presence'.[59] The implications for 'pedagogy', for the thinking and the practice of educators (parents and teachers) are that they need to perform a difficult balancing act; they need to 'mediate between the old and the new'.[60] On the one hand they need to protect the new against being crushed by or made to fit the mould of the old; on the other hand they need to protect and preserve the old, the world that forms the precondition for the appearance of anything new. It is only by caring for both and taking responsibility for both that the world can be renewed. As Biesta says, 'a pedagogical orientation to the coming into the world of the new *also* demands attention and care for a certain "quality" of the world', which might be called a 'worldly' quality – i.e. the quality of a world of plurality, one that offers the conditions for everyone to introduce or initiate something new.[61] Education, then, for Biesta, should offer access to the

[56] Biesta, 'De School als Toegang tot de Wereld', 27; Arendt, 'The Crisis in Education', 171. It seems to me that Arendt's emphasis on this was probably inspired by John Dewey's work, Martin Buber's, or both. For Dewey wrote that living things distinguish themselves from inanimate ones by the fact that they 'maintain themselves by renewal' and that '[w]hat nutrition and reproduction are to physiological life, education is to social life'; and Buber began his 1925 lecture 'Über das Erzieherische' with a reflection on the fact that every minute, all over the world, 'specific and yet specifiable' people are born, writing also: 'In every hour the human race begins.' Dewey, *Democracy and Education*, 1, 9; Martin Buber, *Reden über Erziehung* (Heidelberg: Verlag Lambert Schneider, 1962), 98. Arendt had certainly read Dewey, and was probably also familiar with Buber's educational writings. See also Anders Schinkel, 'Education as Mediation between Child and World: The Role of Wonder', *Studies in Philosophy and Education* (online first, October 2019).

[57] Levinson, 'The Paradox of Natality', 13.

[58] Arendt, *The Human Condition*, 8, cited in Biesta, 'De School als Toegang tot de Wereld', 28, and *The Beautiful Risk*, 143.

[59] Biesta, *The Beautiful Risk*, 143.

[60] Arendt, 'The Crisis in Education', 190; see also Schinkel, 'Education as Mediation between Child and World'.

[61] Biesta, 'De School als Toegang tot de Wereld', 29.

world in the sense of enabling children to 'come into the world', and this requires (also) care for the world; it entails a responsibility both for the new inherent in the children and for the worldly quality of the world. In this sense Biesta (refreshingly, we might say) offers a *world-oriented* rather than a child-centred view of the aim of education.

But it is at this point that Biesta observes, as noted in the previous chapter, that 'world' receives a very specific meaning in Arendt's work: 'It is not just any social or physical environment, but points to a certain quality of social interaction that is expressed in an orientation towards the enabling and maintenance of plurality.'[62] In light of Biesta's Arendtian view of subjectification, where being a subject means to act, and thereby to show who you are, 'in public', the orientation to the 'world' in this sense is understandable and perhaps appropriate; but as I argued in the previous chapter it is important to remember that accepting such a conception of the world entails a significant loss: it makes it much more difficult to recognize both our (bodily) rootedness in the world, and the fact that the world (in a more common understanding of that term) precedes not just the present generation of human beings, but human beings in general; and that it transcends us, and – despite the fact that we are part of it – to some extent always eludes us.

The second key notion in Biesta's proposal for an alternative view of the aim of education is 'uniqueness'. He develops this as an alternative to the notion of rational autonomy or reasonable independence, the notion traditionally used to distinguish socialization from subjectification. Since Enlightenment thinking, rather than transcending all tradition, constitutes a tradition of its own – with the implication that education for autonomy is itself (now) a form of socialization rather than subjectification – we need a new way of thinking about subjectification. This is where the idea of 'uniqueness' comes in, a notion Biesta takes from Levinas' work, but that also has clear connections with Arendt's (existentialist) notions of freedom and action. We tend to think of an individual's uniqueness in terms of how (s)he is distinct from others, i.e. in terms of a difference in characteristics. Biesta rejects such a conception of uniqueness, because he sees it as bound up with problematic notions of identity (politics) and an instrumental relation to others.[63] The Levinasian notion of uniqueness he favours turns neither on what distinguishes us from others nor on how we distinguish ourselves, but on situations in which it matters that *I*

[62] Ibid.
[63] Ibid., 31.

am there, and therefore on *uniqueness-as-irreplaceability*.[64] In Levinas' ethical ontology it is in situations where the other calls upon, singles us out, demands a response from us – of care, of attention, of justice – that 'I', my uniqueness, can become real. At this point we have to decide whether we will act, whether we will respond – take responsibility for our responsibility – or not.[65] Uniqueness is thus a 'fragile possibility', not something that can be 'produced' by education. It is also something that, once again, demands attention to the 'worldly quality' of education, since 'it is only in a situation of plurality, where the encounter with the other [person, AS] and the other [in general, AS] is a real possibility, that uniqueness is itself a possibility'.[66] The addition of 'the other' in general, or the non-human other (in Dutch: 'het andere'), as distinct from the other *person*, is significant, since for Levinas the other is another *person*, and the encounter with others under conditions of plurality in Arendt's work is also a strictly human affair. Biesta's addition therefore accentuates (although it could work to obscure) the same limitation in Levinas' work that I noted earlier with regard to Arendt's notion of the world.

To sum up: Biesta offers us an interesting alternative conception of the aim of education (including, but not limited to, schooling), which is to give children access to the world, to enable them (or at least preserve the possibility for them) to 'come into the world' as unique human beings. It is, in a specific and limited but nevertheless important sense, a world-oriented proposal, one that shifts at least some of our attention to what is needed to preserve the possibility for children and for the new to come into the world.

The Aim of Education: To Open Up the World

My aim in this chapter is to show deep, intrinsic connections between wonder and education. The understanding of education – or better, the *phenomenon* – I am interested in, which was already briefly described in the introduction to this book, is very close to Richard Peters' understanding of education. I readily admit that this is a historically and culturally contingent understanding, but that does not mean it does not pick out, or attempt to articulate, a phenomenon worth defending, caring about, and striving to bring about – as educators in

64 Biesta, *The Beautiful Risk*, 144; Biesta, *Good Education in an Age of Measurement*.
65 Biesta attributes the phrase 'taking responsibility for our responsibility' to Zygmunt Bauman.
66 Biesta, 'De School als Toegang tot de Wereld', 33.

fact do. My view of the aim of education, then, is also quite similar to Peters'. However, considering the idea of human flourishing as the aim of education helped to gain clarity, on the one hand, about what we are *not* asking – at least not directly – when we ask what the intrinsic aim of education is, and therefore it helped place this question into perspective. On the other hand, it made clearer what such views could more easily lose sight of, namely the question as to what makes a particular practice or experience *educational* in a specific but important sense. And we have also seen that these types of view, despite their differences, show considerable overlap when it comes to the idea that and the way in which education ought to be relevant to life. Biesta's 'pedagogical' approach to the aim of education is important because it offers a correction to the (over)emphasis on autonomy that characterizes the liberal educational tradition, and furthermore because it encourages us to attend to the conditions of possibility for children's coming into the world. Moreover, the view that education is about enabling children to come into the world very clearly establishes an intrinsic connection between the question what education *is* with the question what it is *for*, and I take this to be a desirable feature of an educational theory. The proposal that follows builds strongly on Peters' work, but attempts to incorporate some of the valuable features of the other approaches.

Education as Opening Up the World

Schools are commonly seen as the places *par excellence* where education ought to occur. What is it people assume – or hope – happens there? What is it teachers hope to accomplish? Peters' proposal still seems largely adequate to answer these questions: we hope that children gain knowledge and understanding of things that matter – *true* knowledge and understanding, meaning that they involve cognitive perspective, knowledge that is not 'inert', and an understanding that is the child's *own*, which means that she has 'seen' something for herself (a point I will come back to). A great advantage of formulating the aim of education in this way is that it links up with educators' self-understanding and their understanding of what they are doing. A disadvantage is that it draws attention only to what happens in the child, and in itself says nothing about what it means to gain such understanding. There is a directionality, a movement, in education that is not captured in this formulation; this is its orientation towards the *world*, understood not in the Arendtian sense, but in the sense explained in the previous chapter. This orientation has two aspects: first, there is the teacher's attempt to draw the child's attention to something 'out there', something to be understood, some subject matter – the 'holy ground' that both Peters and Whitehead take from D.H. Lawrence. There is something to be known and understood there. When the child soaks some of this up, her world will be larger, in a qualified way; but only when 'the penny drops', when she 'sees' for herself, for instance, that what she was told is indeed true, will she actually experience an 'opening up' of a new part of the world. This is what education aims at: to open up the world, to further the extent to which children (or adults, for that matter) have 'access' to the world.

Importantly, this is not just a human world – it is not the public world of which Arendt spoke, nor is it merely a humanly constructed world. Human constructs offer particular forms of access to the world, but we are not imprisoned by those constructs, and the contact we make through them or sometimes despite of them is real.[67] The world that education should help children to perceive more of and make sense of is multifarious; it is sound and light; hardness, softness, roughness, smoothness; colour and tone and taste; pain and pleasure; pains of many kinds, pleasures of many kinds; voices human and non-human; bodies and their borders: hairless, furry, feathered, and scaly skins; animals and plants and fungi and things that elude classification; classifications and taxonomies and critiques of taxonomies and classifications; natural events, historical events and human actions, and questions about the difference; things that just happen and disasters; life and death; being alive and being particularly alive; waking and sleeping and states in between; the sun and the moon, and suns and moons; time and the lack of it, and moments that reside outside of time; love and heartache; love at a distance and love touching; sex and desire and longing; birth and abortion; opinions and arguments and hatred; violence and the violent repression of violence; order and chaos; order in the human world and order in the universe, and chaos in both; rhythm and pattern; stability and change; change and identity; the riddle of the self, the question of the importance or unimportance of the self. The world is endless.

But is it possible to lead children to a world, rather than initiate them into a particular world*view*? Martin Buber raises this question as a possible objection to his own idea that education ('Bildung') should be concerned with 'the world'. Do educators not always, inevitably, present some *aspect* of the world to their pupils or students? Is it possible and would it be desirable to educate in a 'neutral'

67 My understanding of 'opening up the world' is thus different from Biesta's, but very similar to that defended in Jan Masschelein and Maarten Simons, *In Defence of the School* (Leuven: E-ducation, Culture & Society Publishers, 2013) – which is surprising, in a way, since their work is strongly inspired by Arendt's as well; but they have not adopted Arendt's specific notion of (the) 'world'.

way, unbiased by a particular worldview? Buber answers that this is neither possible nor desirable; but the point that matters is whether one's worldview fosters real engagement with the world, or instead takes the place of the world. The point of a worldview is to nourish a love of the world, such that one does not tire of seeing what is there to see, of noticing what can be noticed; the point is to be 'true' to the world, whatever your worldview – the word 'true' here points to the connection between loyalty or faithfulness (to the world) on the one hand and truthfulness and being real on the other.[68]

The task of education is to open up the world to children, meaning that children gain in understanding, in their ability to make sense of it and connect with it emotionally, and in freedom to operate in it. It also means to nourish a disposition to return again and again to the world behind our worldview, behind our constructs, behind the concepts that give us access to the world but may also obscure it. For what it's worth – and there are certainly good arguments to be made for forms of education that transcend disciplinary boundaries – the school curriculum tracks the various forms of access to the world developed in Western societies over the course of their history: languages, scientific disciplines, artistic disciplines, and physical disciplines. For instance, the subject of biology, firstly, provides access to the world *through* (the lens of) the study of biology (its concepts, techniques, and instruments), and secondly, provides access to the world *of* biology, to the discipline, the literature, the scientific community. The latter becomes increasingly important as the pupil progresses in the subject, and especially at university. The same applies to the other subjects on the curriculum. What teachers ultimately try to do, I believe – but I am aware that everyday practice often looks very different – is to open up worlds: the world of plants and animals, the world of rocks and rivers, the many worlds of history that are both past and somehow still present at the same time. An old schoolbook I have at home makes this very plain; it is called *The Earth Shown to the Children*; and it is telling that in its introduction it speaks both of the 'wonders' treated in the book and of 'wondering' (about mountains, rivers and seas, whether they have always been as they are now).[69]

There are many forms of access to the world, and many ways of gaining access to the world: initiation into a language (learning to speak, read and write) is an important one. Language is an imperfect tool, yet it is one of our main windows onto the world. Beyond being a tool it also to an important extent

[68] Buber, *Reden über Erziehung*, 53–4.
[69] Ellison Hawks, *The Earth Shown to the Children* (London and Edinburgh: T.C. & E.C. Jack, 1914).

shapes our 'world' – to such an extent even that we sometimes forget that there is a world beyond what our language reveals to us. Language allows us to express ourselves and communicate with others. It thereby opens up further possibilities: expanding one's world through newspapers, television, the internet and other media, through novels and poetry – the world of books is opened, and each book contains a world of its own that is also a window onto the 'real' world. Other examples are a carpenter's apprentice learning to recognize different kinds of wood and their particular characteristics, a mechanics student getting to grips with the way a car engine works, a child mastering a musical instrument. Access to the world, then, can be more intellectual or more physical; and even if it is intellectual it is still embodied and still also affective. In music, but also in sports, science, and probably any other area, *gifted* children appear now and then; these are children that, due to their native talent, enjoy *privileged access* to the world. They effortlessly reach places that others only get to with extreme difficulty and through very hard work; and they can go places that are unattainable to others because they have a natural feeling and aptitude for the activities in question.

The kinds of access to the world that education aims at, although it is certainly not a purely cognitive or intellectual matter, do all essentially involve understanding of some kind. Not all advances in 'access to the world' are educational accomplishments. A child that learns to walk gains access to the world – and sometimes perilously so. But learning to walk is not education. It becomes (physical) education only when our bodily interaction with the world and the access to the world our bodies provide are thematized and become the object of deliberate influence.[70] Moreover, simply by growing taller and stronger children do gain access to the world (although they also lose certain kinds of access), but this obviously has nothing to do with education. The understanding involved in education can be matter of acquiring a *feel* for something, which involves tacit knowledge, but it can also involve a much more explicit grasp of a certain subject matter. Understanding and access to the world in the fullest sense intended here differ from 'mere' knowledge: one may know something without *really* knowing it – hence the experience I assume we all have from time to time, of suddenly grasping something we already 'knew'. Similarly, seeing and seeing are two: a lot of the time we see things without *really* seeing them; instead, we note their presence, we recognize them, sort them under a certain label, and nothing more. Education does not aim at the ability to do this; rather, it struggles

[70] On this topic see Margaret Whitehead, 'Meaningful Existence, Embodiment, and Physical Education', *Journal of Philosophy of Education* 24, no. 1 (1990).

to counter our apparently natural tendency to 'see' in this superficial way – a tendency that appears with age and experience; young children are not troubled by it. The aim of education is to make us 'truly' see things, which means that we know them in a way that always has an element of wonder mixed in – i.e. an element of not-knowing, of mystery.

Understanding involves seeing how things hang together, how one thing connects to another.[71] This means understanding is by definition incomplete or imperfect. '[A] complete understanding is a perfect grasp of the universe in its totality. We are finite beings; and such a grasp is denied to us.'[72] Therefore 'understanding is never a completed state of mind' but 'always bears the character of a process of penetration, incomplete and partial'.[73] A gain in understanding may take the form of 'progressive' illumination of the area (around that which) we are trying to get to grips with – so that our access to the world increases and we are able to venture further in it, and to move in between things. But it may also be a matter of something that was dull beginning to glow, to become illuminated from within, which in turn heightens our interest. Understanding is thus intrinsically connected with being *interested* in the world, not only because as Whitehead said 'there can be no mental development without interest', but also because understanding, as well as subjective interest, requires *inter-esse*, a venturing among and being in the midst of things.[74] This also involves a real 'contact' with the world, whether physical or not – though in the end all our contact is embodied, of course. We truly 'see' things, rather than superficially noticing them; we *respond* to them, and therefore become able to act 'responsibly'. Access to the world involves *attention* that has a particular quality, attention that is both exclusive and receptive.

With a variation on something Bergson said about philosophy, we might say that education requires the reversal of the normal direction of the workings of thought.[75] As noticed in the introduction to this book, we have an innate tendency to deal 'efficiently' with information; anything we already know is quickly labelled as uninformative. The result is that we see less and less, as we recognize more and more. Novelty wears off swiftly. Things that start out as

[71] Hence the notion of understanding is closely related to that of meaning; or understanding is one dimension of meaning; see Baumeister, *Meanings of life*, 15–17, White, 'Education and a Meaningful Life', and Anders Schinkel, 'Education and Ultimate Meaning', *Oxford Review of Education* 41, no. 6 (2015): 719.

[72] Whitehead, *Modes of Thought*, 43.

[73] Ibid., 43.

[74] Whitehead, 'Rhythmic Claims', 48.

[75] Henri Bergson, *Introduction to Metaphysics* (New York: Philosophical Library, 1961), 64.

exciting quickly become boringly familiar. This highlights the importance of education that is imaginative, and specifically of art in education: sometimes we need artists who place objects (the extreme example is 'ready mades') in museums for us to be able to really see them again; artists, therefore, are also educators. The phrase 'anything we already know' requires explanation, for 'knowing' here really means nothing more than 'being familiar with'; it need not entail any real knowledge or understanding of this thing we are familiar with. I know very little about how my computer works (or about how anything works, to be honest), but it does not surprise me that it works (most of the time), I simple take it for granted. Education counters this tendency; it is inversely related to the extent to which we merely take things for granted. Or at least it is opposed to taking things for granted without being able to justify – by our knowledge and understanding – that we do so.

By 'justify' I do not mean that 'true' knowledge and understanding are distinguished by the fact that they are backed up by proof, because proof, in the strict sense of the term, as Whitehead says, is 'a second-rate procedure'. 'When the word *proof* has been uttered, the next notion to enter the mind is halfheartedness.'[76] What we are after instead is self-evidence. Strange as this may sound it is not difficult to see what Whitehead meant. Recent news in the medical sciences is that some mouth-dwelling bacterium may be linked to the development of Alzheimer.[77] A Harvard blog says that 'the hypothesis is not conclusively proven and many questions still remain'. But what does that mean, 'conclusively proven'? How many 'facts' in the history of science were not once deemed conclusively proven but were overtaken by the facts nonetheless? Questions are always possible about the basic assumptions of the study, the methodology used, the instruments involved (were they functioning properly?), the interpretation of the findings, and so on. Whenever something is too small, too large, or too complex to perceive immediately and in its entirety – whenever, therefore, the sense that something is the case must be established by inferential steps and the accumulation of evidence, any sense of certainty we achieve will be tentative. In the ideal case, the proof is a ladder that can be thrown away at the end; this is when it 'has produced self-evidence and thereby rendered itself unnecessary'.[78] Compare a child that immediately sees that $4 \times (5 - 3)$ is exactly

[76] Whitehead, *Modes of Thought*, 48.

[77] Veerasak Srisuknimit, 'Oral Bacteria May Be Responsible for Alzheimer's Disease', *Science in the News* blog, 7 February 2019, http://sitn.hms.harvard.edu/flash/2019/oral-bacteria-may-responsible-alzheimers-disease/

[78] Whitehead, *Modes of Thought*, 48.

the same as $(4 \times 5) - (4 \times 3)$ with a child that needs to work out both sums to see that, indeed, the answer in both cases is 8. The latter child now has proof that it is true, but unless this has resulted in self-evidence, her understanding will not have the same quality as that of the first child. My point is that the kind of understanding educators hope to promote in children involves a form of intuition, an immediate (though not necessarily in the temporal sense) 'grasp' of things. This applies to the understanding involved in being able to follow a train of thought – a logical sequence of reasoning – as well as that involved in the ability to follow *someone else's* train of thought that led him to act in a certain way – the kind of understanding at stake when someone explains to us why he did or did not or failed to do something, needing us to understand.

To the extent that the world is opened up to children, to the extent that they gain access to the world in the sense that they have *live* knowledge and understanding of it, their outlook on the world will be transformed. As Masschelein and Simons point out, education is not just learning as an additive process, but *formation*, in which the world that is opened up to us also forms us; the 'I and one's life-world are brought into constant play'.[79] Apart from the criteria for the *concept* of education this seems to me the main element in Peters' liberal *conception* of education worth retaining: the idea that central to education is the change in people's outlook on life and the world it brings about. I am not particularly interested in the notion of 'the educated man' (or woman) and all this implies; it is neither necessary nor desirable that everyone becomes a 'cultured' person, and no educator should be disappointed simply because a student did not develop into such a person. But it would be odd, firstly, for an educator to be completely satisfied before a student truly understands the material taught, and thus is – even if imperceptibly, when it comes to a particular, limited gain in understanding – to some extent changed, no longer exactly the same person (s)he was before. (This goes a long way towards explaining why being a teacher can be such a frustrating job – a frustration that is often mirrored by that of the student, of course.) And secondly, if education is (a quality of a) process that brings about a change in outlook, this means it changes people in a stronger sense as well. Part of the aim of education is a 'personal' change; Whitehead expressed this by saying that more important than knowledge is 'the way in which knowledge is held', which he called 'wisdom', which 'concerns the handling of knowledge, its selection for the determination of relevant issues, its

[79] Masschelein and Simons, *In Defence of the School*, 45.

employment to add value to our immediate experience'.[80] I take this to include a sense of perspective, of the importance of things and of oneself, and of the extent of one's understanding. For example, wisdom implies knowing when to speak and when to remain silent. The notion of education, then, brings with it that of intellectual virtues like intellectual humility, open-mindedness, fair-mindedness, and a love of truth.

At this point it is worth pausing to consider the notion of *autonomy* that plays such an important role in liberal conceptions of education. If the aim of education involves that students come to understand something *for themselves* – i.e. that they have not merely memorized some facts plus someone else's understanding of how they are connected, but have established these facts and their interconnections for themselves – then education will also entail fostering a corresponding disposition.[81] '[T]he search for reasons for action [and, presumably, belief; AS] is the hall-mark of the autonomous person. He is not prepared to accept authoritative pronouncements and is unhappy about simply doing what others do without inquiring any further.'[82] Valuable as such a disposition may be (not least in an educational context), it seems to me that to label the desired dispositional state 'autonomy' has some unfortunate consequences. Firstly, the term 'autonomy' brings with it a strong association of voluntarism, of deciding at will, which could be confusing in a context where people are trying to determine, to the best of their abilities, 'how things are' (however problematic that notion obviously is) – the term is not meant to imply that one decides for oneself what is the case, irrespective of the evidence, of course, but it is easy to lose sight of the appropriate context of application of the term. Secondly, and more importantly, the emphasis on autonomy casts the student in an active role, one in which she is in control and refuses to be controlled; but while that can be valuable – within limits – in the context of the relationship with educators, it is at the same time not at all the right state to be in in relation to the subject matter. In relation to the *world*, it is something much more like *heteronomy* that education demands. We want to foster a disposition to 'submit' to the reasons for belief and action that the world affords, to be moved by those reasons (which, of course, often involve feeling as well). If we want to understand the world better, we need at least part of the time to adopt a receptive and responsive stance, in order to

[80] Whitehead, 'Rhythmic Claims', 46.

[81] Education would entail fostering such a disposition as a *prerequisite* for education, not as an aim in itself; see Michael Hand, 'Against Autonomy as an Educational Aim', *Oxford Review of Education* 32, no. 4 (2006).

[82] Peters, *Ethics & Education*, 196.

make sure that we project as little of our own preconceptions onto the world as possible. In this sense heteronomy is a proper aim of education, a natural companion of opening up the world.

The idea that the aim of education is to open up the world presupposes that it is *valuable* to have the world opened up for oneself, to have more 'access' to it. This is not indiscriminately so. This is the problem Peters also struggled with: for example, acquiring an in-depth understanding of the most productive way to 'charm' worms (i.e. to get them to surface from the ground) may increase one's access to the world, but few people would consider it the business of education to promote this. (There are actually competitions in this. Most participants appear to see the joke, but some get really serious.) The value of particular knowledge and understanding, then, is not a given, but depends on its contribution to a person's understanding of the human condition as well as her own specific situation in life. This criterion does not even exclude that much (which is good), but it does relegate some things to the sphere of infotainment rather than education.

But there is another aspect to the idea that it is, in principle, valuable to open up the world; this is the assumption that there is value to be *found* there: beauty and complexity to be appreciated, goodness to be admired, truth to be discovered. Their opposites are also there, but the suffering this brings with it only strengthens the case for a world-oriented education that helps us – in so far as the world and our 'design' allows – make sense of the human condition, and at the same time draws us out of ourselves and our daily pre-occupations, with the inflated and distorted perspectives these often involve, and draw our attention to the world that is – mysteriously and perhaps bizarrely – out there. Education entails the aim at two closely related things: abilities and opportunities for the appreciation and evaluation of what the world has to offer; and abilities and opportunities for value creation. The two go hand in hand: the ability to create value depends on the ability to appreciate value, and the latter is enhanced by the former. The 'sense of disclosure' that Whitehead spoke of is closely linked to creativity. In a sense, one can only fully appreciate something when one knows what it takes to create it, or for it to come into being. Value, of course, can be of many kinds: intellectual, moral, aesthetic, religious, artistic, emotional, historical and so on, which means that education cannot limit itself to any one of these.

To conclude this section I would like to point out something that many people will have become increasingly aware of over the last decades, namely the *fragility* of all these kinds of value, and their dependence on the complex natural system that our world is. This highlights also another kind of value: the value of life and of the diversity of life. Human life with all the particular kinds of value that may be realized in it is just one form of life, utterly dependent on the flourishing of other types of life and on the existence of conditions favourable for those and our kinds of life. This supplies us with an important reason to adopt a world-oriented view of the aim of education, 'world-oriented' in a much wider sense than Biesta's proposal; a reason why preserving the conditions of possibility for coming into the world needs, in the present global context, to be understood much more broadly. The natural world that we inhabit should indeed be treated as 'holy ground'.

The Intrinsic, Extrinsic and Overarching Aims of Education

In the last paragraphs of the previous section I established a link between the intrinsic aim of education – to open up the world to children, or to promote their access to the world – and what we might see as its overarching aim: to contribute to the quality, not only of the lives of those who are educated, but of *all* of life by 'maintaining' the world. Large as this aim sounds, I do intend it in a modest way, in the sense that we should not so much seek to *improve* nature (we have done enough of that, and see where it has brought us) but to foster an attitude of appreciation, of care, and a willingness to *maintain* the world on which all of life depends to the extent to which this is within our control, which of course is very limited – an attitude informed by knowledge and understanding, and inspired by love for the world, not in the sense in which Arendt used the term (i.e. in connection with her specific use of the term 'world'), but in the more encompassing sense of 'world' I use here.[83] Ideally, one's view of the intrinsic aim of education connects meaningfully with one's view of its overarching and its extrinsic aims. It would be a shame if one's answer to the question what education *is* had no real connection with one's answer to the question what it is *for* or what reasons there are for engaging in the practice. So in this section I briefly show how these types of aims are linked, in my view, as well as how and why they are inevitably in (some) tension with each other.

When we recognize some practice or some experience as educational and ask what it is that makes it so, my answer is that it opens up the world – in some

[83] See Schinkel, 'Education as Mediation between Child and World'; for world-affirming pedagogies inspired by Arendt's notion of love for the world see, apart from Biesta's work, Naomi Hodgson, Joris Vlieghe, and Piotr Zamojski, 'Education and the Love for the World: Articulating a Post-critical Educational Philosophy', *Foro de Educación* 16, no. 24 (2018) and Joris Vlieghe and Piotr Zamojski, *Towards an Ontology of Teaching: Thing-centered Pedagogy, Affirmation, and Love for the World* (Cham: Springer, 2019).

aspect, and to some degree – to the person(s) who are educated. When we ask *why* we would try to do this, it seems to me that the answer is threefold, comprising (again) the *intrinsic aim* of education, as something that is intrinsically valuable, *extrinsic aims*, such as the reproduction of society, maintaining its important institutions, enabling people to make a decent living, and so on, and an *overarching aim*, which I explained above in terms of 'maintaining' the world and fostering the quality of life. Extrinsic aims can be seen as secondary to or derivable from the overarching aim, but in practice they function as independent justifications of education. The overarching aim of education requires its intrinsic aim to be what (in my view) it is; and education's intrinsic aim is ultimately justified, to a large extent, by its overarching aim. The extrinsic aims express a recognition that a certain level of 'access to the world' (in the sense explained above) is necessary for another type of access to the world: the diplomas gathered over the course of one's educational career open (career) doors that would otherwise remain closed; and education enables a person to function in society in a way that contributes to its maintenance (or reform, as the case may be). (But it is worth noting that 'education' here does not necessarily mean education in the normative sense employed in this chapter and throughout this book; at least when it comes to diplomas it is clear that these can be gained without education in the full sense of the word.)

Education's overarching aim as well as its extrinsic aims to some extent impose limitations on education's intrinsic aim: what access to the world we wish to provide or promote is partly determined by value judgements derived from the overarching aim to which education is ultimately expected to contribute; and it is partly determined by another type of value judgement that is derived from education's extrinsic aims. Ideal-typically, we may label the former type of value judgement as judgements of *importance* and the latter as judgements of *relevance*: education is to provide children with such access to the world as we deem it important to have, in light of the overarching aim of contributing to the maintenance of the world and fostering the quality of life; and education is to provide children with such access to the world as we believe it is relevant to have in light of certain extrinsic aims that determine what kinds of knowledge, understanding, skills, capacities, et cetera, are necessary for individuals to function well in society and to maintain societal functioning.

However, since neither the overarching aim nor any extrinsic aims constitute *intrinsic* aims of education – which is another way of saying that education preserves a certain *autonomy* with regard to these aims – there will in practice always be a tension, firstly, between the attempt to realize the aim of education and the striving to ensure that education contributes to overarching and extrinsic aims. In the case of extrinsic aims the tension clearly exists in practice *and* in theory, because having the education system deliver people that can keep our economy going (an extrinsic aim) may even be logically at odds with the intrinsic aim at authentic and therefore potentially critical (or subversive) understanding. There are ways to formulate education's legitimate extrinsic aims that would lessen the tension, but it is doubtful it could be get rid of entirely. I have formulated the overarching aim of education in a way that minimizes the tension with its intrinsic aim (among other things by distinguishing education from other phenomena, such as infotainment), but it is still impossible to exclude the possibility of tension between them – or at least I am unwilling to *define* education in terms of only those experiences that contribute to education's overarching aim. Some experiences may be educational, even deemed valuable, that may lead some people to despair. Also, human beings have an inclination to explore the world, even where it may be suspected that this may not contribute to, or even be detrimental to, the maintenance of the world and the flourishing of life in it. (Think of Adam and Eve.) One could say that when that is the case this shows a defect in some aspect of their education, such as their *moral* education; but even if we were to concede that (since education, like understanding, is inevitably imperfect), this would not render the rest noneducational. Truly educated people have done a lot of damage in the world.

The Intrinsic Connections between Wonder and (the Aim of) Education

It is well known that the word 'education' can be traced back (as desired) to two very similar Latin roots with rather different meanings: *educare*, meaning to train or to rear, and *educere*, meaning to lead out. The second will sound more sympathetic to many people today, but it can be interpreted in at least two different ways: (1) to bring forth from the student what is already (embryonically) present in the student, to bring out a person's talents; (2) to lead the student out into the world. It is this world-oriented conception of the meaning of 'education' that I have stressed in this chapter; and this links it closely to wonder as a mode of consciousness characterized by centrality of the 'object' and a forgetting of the self. Refracted by wonder 'leading out into the world' becomes 'leading *out of the self* and into the world'. In this section I will highlight – and distil from the foregoing – a number of ways in which wonder is intrinsically connected with education. By 'intrinsically connected' I mean a connection in the nature of the phenomena, such that it is very difficult to think of the one occurring in complete absence of the other. I also mean that the relation between the two is not incidental or contingent, but to be expected given the ways these 'experiences' influence a person. In the first subsection below I focus on the aspect of openness to the world that characterizes both wonder and education. The three subsections that follow link up with Peters' criteria of education. In the final subsection I discuss wonder in connection with understanding, feelings, and the imagination.

Interest in and Openness to the World

The most important contribution of (deep/contemplative) wonder to education is that it sparks, sustains, or, if necessary, revives our interest in the world – an interest in things for their own sake, not because we want something from them.[84] With wonder comes a sense of importance; it *is* a way in which the world is important in us, a form that the feeling of importance takes. And interest is the subjective side of importance; it emphasizes the subject's inclination towards the object, rather than the object's impact on the subject. Education shares – and, in practice, often builds on – wonder's orientation towards the world. It is unthinkable without an interest in the world for its own sake, and although wonder is not the only form that such an interest can take (certain forms of love and care are others) it is hard to imagine education without the particular type of attention wonder entails. This has to do with a peculiar combination of elements that we see in wonder: the epistemic element (of puzzlement or a sense of mystery) that characterizes even deep or contemplative wonder, the 'impractical' nature of wonder, its opposition to determinacy and closure. In wonder we are confronted with a mystery that engages us, even though we know that it cannot be resolved – the silent questions implied in it ('How can it be that … ?', 'How is it possible that … ?') merely look like their counterparts in the realm of answerable questions. Even though we do not seek *answers* or *solutions* our imagination still seeks ways to 'grasp' that which lies beyond our ability to understand – it reaches beyond the limit. As long as our 'outlook' on the world is informed by wonder, we are 'forced' to keep it before us as something we *long* to understand, while we are at the same time acutely aware that it *eludes*

[84] Schinkel, 'The Educational Importance of Deep Wonder', 550.

our understanding. The form that our interest (in things for their own sake) takes is not bound up with action in the way that care is, but it remains tied in a paradoxical way to our striving for understanding. Whereas inquisitive wonder works towards new and more adequate understanding, deep wonder provides a crucial qualification or modification of our understanding; it emphasizes its temporary, tentative, imperfect nature by placing it in the perspective of what lies fundamentally *beyond* our understanding. Wonder's reminder that *perfect* understanding is forever out of reach tempts us to keep refining our understanding – or, depending on the perspective taken – our ignorance. An 'educated' person will always be aware of the non-definitive nature of her knowledge and understanding of the world.

Value

Implicit in, but central to, the normative concept of education is the idea that it involves engagement with something of value. The experience of wonder involves a sense of importance, and hence of value – the sense that something matters, which at the very least entails the sense that something is worth attending to for its own sake. And in many cases the experience of wonder goes beyond this, suggesting that what is encountered in wonder *is* valuable. In education we are looking for what matters, and wonder is one of the things that gives us a sense of what matters. It fosters our sensitivity to value, and beyond that it often actively heightens our appreciation of value that we encounter – for instance in the forms of the beauty and complexity we find in the natural world, or in the ways we can be affected by art, ways that mimic the effects of confronting the mystery of (things in) the world. Needless to say, wonder is also a place from which we may be inspired to *create* value, whether in the form of art or in how we act in the world. Wonder is therefore a close companion both of our ability to appreciate value and of our ability to bring value into the world.

Education entails the development, not just of a sense of value and of the abilities to appreciate and create value, but also of a 'tragic' sense of value. Dramatic as that may sound, it is part and parcel of any sense of value worth the name, simply because the *fragility* of value is inherent in the nature of the phenomenon. That is to say, the realization of value is always merely a *possibility*, and even 'actual' value (so an instance of the actualization of the possibility of value) retains that character of possibility, in the sense that it can fade, disappear, be destroyed or be obscured. Value is never *certain*, never to be taken for granted. (And when we *do* take something absolutely for granted, this also means that we do not appreciate its value.) Wonder strongly fosters our sensitivity to the fragility of value, because in wonder we experience things as radically contingent – we appreciate that they could have not-been, and could also not-be. When we experience nature, life, existence in wonder we are acutely aware of its extraordinariness, its not-to-be-taken-for-granted-ness and often (when wonder takes its most affirmative form) its preciousness.

(Cognitive) Perspective and Outlook on the World

Martin Opdal, inspired by Richard Peters, argued that 'perspective development' (rather than just the accumulation of knowledge) is the ultimate aim of education, and he argued that for this reason wonder has a central role to play in education.[85] As discussed in Chapter 1, Opdal saw it as the distinguishing feature of wonder as opposed to curiosity that whereas the latter involves questioning *within* accepted interpretative frameworks, wonder raises questions about the frameworks themselves. In other words, experiences of wonder make one question the adequacy of one's perspective on some particular thing, or even of one's outlook on the world as a whole. A child whose understanding of the behaviour of solids placed in water is framed in terms of weight, solidity and hardness alone may experience wonder on perceiving that a boat shaped from modelling clay can float.[86] The child has not just learned something new, she cannot simply add a new fact to her existing stock of knowledge, but she is 'forced' to question her framework of understanding and to adjust this in order to be able to accommodate the new fact.

Since my understanding of education has also been inspired by Peters, I am largely in agreement with Opdal. However, to my mind Opdal places too much emphasis on the cognitive aspect of 'perspective' and with that on the role of wonder in developing a 'more extensive, consistent, and integrative' perspective; and as a corollary of this Opdal seems to identify wonder with inquisitive wonder and therefore to forget that wonder does not always (immediately) involve or lead to questioning, i.e. that there is also such a thing as deep or contemplative wonder. So we need to modify Opdal's view somewhat: education aims to open up the world, and wonder furthers this aim – or in fact has the effect of opening up the world – in a number of ways: by stimulating perspective development

85 Opdal, 'Curiosity, Wonder, and Education'.

86 Yannis Hadzigeorgiou, 'Wonder, Its Nature and Its Role in the Learning Process', in *Wonder, Education, and Human Flourishing*, ed. Anders Schinkel (Amsterdam: VU University Press, 2020).

in Opdal's sense, by driving a change of outlook on the world (which is not necessarily the same thing), and – which is the starting point for both – by bringing (some aspect of) the world into full awareness. Hadzigeorgiou's empirical research again offers some good examples. Students who were already familiar with the law of gravity, and who already knew that it was the weakest of all forces, 'understood it better' when their wonder was evoked by a simple experiment, in which a small magnet was shown to be able to attract a paperclip up to itself that the whole earth was pulling on from below. And students' journals were filled with similar expressions, inspired by other wonder-evoking experiments: 'Now I begin to understand … ', 'Now I understand … ', 'It was after (…) that I really understood … '.[87] These are not examples of situations in which existing frames of interpretation were challenged, but examples of 'shocks of awareness', as Hadzigeorgiou says, citing Maxine Greene: 'A great part of our everyday life is not lived consciously, and since nothing makes an impression, the world seems bland, muffled, and vague. Now and then, however, there are exceptional moments, moments of response to "shocks of awareness"'.[88] This links up with the first point discussed in this section, that wonder sparks or revives our interest in the world; wonder can make the unremarkable – or at any rate unremarked – interesting, extraordinary, indeed remarkable. That is to say, wonder *is* the experience of something *as* remarkable in some way, but even once the wonder has passed it can leave behind – like treasure left on the beach by the retreating waves – a sense that what we are perceiving or contemplating *is* remarkable.

While it is obvious that inquisitive wonder is closely related to 'opening up the world' because it entails a drive in the person experiencing the wonder to do exactly that for and by herself, the examples above show that there is an important role for deep wonder here, too, and that this, too, is intrinsically connected with the aim of education. 'Opening up the world' should not be seen merely as expanding the territory in which someone is able to move around, but also – and perhaps even more – as a *transformation* of the world someone experiences. A world that was at first dimly perceived, that was in effect like a door one knew to exist but never bothered to open, is transformed by wonder into a vibrant reality. One's outlook on the world has changed, but this phrase, 'outlook on', fails to capture all of what happens here; it is too distant, too cold.

87 Hadzigeorgiou, 'Fostering a Sense of Wonder', 999–1000.
88 Maxine Greene, *Landscapes of Learning* (New York: Teachers College Press, 1978), 185, cited in Hadzigeorgiou, 'Fostering a Sense of Wonder', 999.

The 'shock of awareness' experienced in wonder is a visceral experience, and it establishes an emotional connection with the world.

One more aspect needs to be added to this: wonder often involves a widening of one's perspective that changes – at least temporarily – one's sense of the importance of things.[89] It is hard to imagine that when someone experiences deep wonder as she gazes up into the Milky Way, sensing without grasping the immensity of scale of time and space, this will not affect, if only momentarily, her perception of the importance of the 'pressing' chores that are waiting for her in the office the next morning. Does wonder give us a 'correct' perspective, a view of how important things 'really' are? That is a difficult question, which I dare not answer affirmatively.[90] But it is educationally valuable to be able to leave one's everyday perspective, if only because this opens up space to consider alternative ways of looking at things.

Voluntariness and Wittingness

Peters' third criterion of education was that it 'at least rules out some procedures of transmission, on the grounds that they lack wittingness and voluntariness on the part of the learner'. Education is therefore incompatible with (for instance) indoctrination, at least when that is seen as a process of belief-formation (e.g. by a 'teacher' in 'students') that bypasses students' ability to assess the plausibility of those beliefs, and that shields beliefs from or immunizes them against future assessments of their plausibility. There is nothing wrong or anti-educational per se about accepting on authority that the distance from the earth to the sun is 149,600,000 kilometres; but when someone is made to believe this in a way that places it beyond the possibility of correction in the face of contradictory evidence, this is uneducational. The positive corollary of this is that education involves fostering a disposition to 'submit' to the reasons for belief and action that the world affords; this 'heteronomy' (which in philosophy of education, as noted, is more commonly expressed in terms of autonomy) simply comes with the world-oriented nature of education. The aim is not just for students to accept, say, that technological developments are important forces in history, but for students to come to see this for themselves – which is to say that their

[89] See Chapter 4.

[90] I explore it a bit more, but still only tentatively, in Schinkel, 'Wonder, Mystery, and Meaning'. And see the previous chapter for a discussion of the more general question whether wonder tells us something about the world, and the next chapter for the question whether wonder reveals value.

attention is (ultimately) diverted away from the school book or the teacher (or *through* those) to the world. Only contact with the world can enable *educational* experiences.

Paul Kingsnorth wrote: 'Experiences changes you. Nothing else changes you.'[91] This is true, unfortunately, for both educational and noneducational experiences. Fear of a teacher may well change you – even for the rest of your life. And this change may involve that you will never be able to shake certain beliefs entirely. The truth of what Kingsnorth says lies in the fact that 'experience', as he uses the term there, involves emotion. Not anything counts as experience, only things that, because of their affective charge, affect you. (Thus, the idea that 'only experience changes you' is a tautology, but a fruitful one.) Wonder, if not 'an emotion', still has a (variable) emotional aspect. This consists of a complex mixture of puzzlement, surprise (sometimes), a sense of importance, a feeling that something is extraordinary, interest and a form of attraction, sometimes also admiration, awe, or a sense of beauty, or something leaning towards those things; and sometimes fear and an uncomfortable feeling of uncertainty. Wonder also implies an intensification of the present and a heightened awareness of things – as if they have come alive – and this, too, is part of its complex and variable affective signature. Wonder, therefore, is certainly a candidate for the kind of thing that 'changes you' – but does that make it a (potentially) educational experience?

I would argue that wonder can indeed be an educational experience (and that it is unlikely to be the opposite), and that wonder can help transform noneducational experiences and (intended to be) 'educational' nonexperiences into educational experiences. On the one hand the increased awareness – even 'shock of awareness' – wonder brings with it are intrinsically connected with the experience of 'true' understanding and 'seeing for oneself'. And on the other hand wonder is *not* the type of emotional experience that immunizes or shields beliefs against future assessments of their plausibility, but rather the opposite. Wonder not only vivifies the experienced world, but – except perhaps in young children – also heightens one's awareness of the experience of 'learning' or '(trans)formation' itself. Since it also motivates and inspires engagement with the world, wonder fosters both 'wittingness' and 'voluntariness'.

91 Paul Kingsnorth, *Confessions of a Recovering Environmentalist* (London: Faber & Faber, 2017), 16.

Understanding, Feelings and the Imagination

Kieran Egan has arguably done more than anybody else to show the importance of imagination to education. He does not conceive of imagination as a special faculty, but rather sees it as the heightened functioning of all one's mental capacities, as 'a particular flexibility which can invigorate all mental functions'.[92] He endorses Alan White's definition of imagination: 'To imagine something is to *think of* it as possibly being so.'[93] This captures both imagining things that are not the case (such as how the world *might* be, and how we would like it to be) as well as trying to imagine how things actually are (as scientists often do). He rejects a Humean conception of imagination as a mysterious faculty necessary to be able to think or make sense of anything at all, and instead favours a conception that is closer to our everyday understanding of the term, namely of imaginative activity as a special form of mental activity. Egan summarizes his conception of the imagination as follows: '[I]magination is the capacity to think of things as possibly being so; it is an intentional act of mind; it is the source of invention, novelty, and generativity; it is not implicated in all perception and in the construction of all meaning; it is not distinct from rationality but is rather a capacity that greatly enriches rational thinking.'[94] (My brief comments on the place of the imagination in the phenomenology of wonder are largely in agreement with this conception of the imagination, but unlike Egan I would not say that imaginative activity is necessarily a consciously willed activity. Egan says that daydreaming 'slides over into imaginative activity only when we assume the director's seat'; I would say that experiences of wonder are good examples of cases where the imagination is active, and where we may be aware of this on some level, without being in the director's seat.[95])

Given this description of imagination it is not surprising that Egan sees it as central to education. Linking up with Plato's, Rousseau's, and Dewey's educational philosophies, which though very distinct share 'a concern to stimulate in students the ability to think of things as possibly being so, with all that implies in terms of flexibility, richness and freedom of mental activity'.[96] Egan notes that for these thinkers it is not so much ignorance that is the

92 Kieran Egan, *Imagination in Teaching and Learning – Ages 8 to 15* (London: Routledge, 2001), 36.
93 Ibid. The quotation is from Alan R. White, *The Language of Imagination* (Oxford: Blackwell, 1990), 184.
94 Egan, *Imagination*, 43.
95 Ibid., 38.
96 Ibid., 47.

sign of the failure of education, but rather the imprisonment of the mind by conventional ideas. Likewise, to 'know' a lot – to be unbeatable in trivia quiz-shows – is not yet to be educated, if this knowledge is inert, if it is not 'one's own', and if, therefore, one cannot transcend conventional ideas. Egan therefore sees it as justified to describe education as 'a process that awakens individuals to a kind of thought that enables them to imagine conditions other than those that exist or that have existed', a definition which immediately highlights the centrality of the imagination to education.[97] The imagination is key to a 'real', personal engagement with educational subject matter; in part through our sense of what is possible (and therefore of contingency) it heightens our awareness of what we perceive or are contemplating, it enables the 'utilization' of knowledge in the Whiteheadian sense, and it enriches the meanings we create as we learn.[98]

Egan's understanding of education is fully in line with that defended in this chapter, so I need not dwell on this and can proceed to highlight the connections between wonder and the imagination. Egan discusses these himself as well, but his use of the term wonder differs from mine. Egan distinguishes between wonder as 'the emotion evoked by perceiving something as extraordinary or strange, or as an extreme achievement' from awe, 'the emotion evoked by the perception that beyond or behind or beneath the real, tangible world around us we are adrift in an ocean of mystery'; whereas wonder, for Egan, is 'concerned with the real world', awe 'is the sense of mystery that underlies existence' and 'is evoked by a vivid awareness of all that lies beyond our comprehension, beyond thinking about, and beyond explaining'.[99] Clearly, what Egan says about awe largely matches my description of deep or contemplative wonder (while what Egan calls wonder cannot simply be identified with what I call inquisitive wonder, since Egan's wonder is also an aesthetic response, that not necessarily involves or issues in a drive to investigate). Egan therefore observes about awe what I observed about deep wonder, namely that it's 'use' or educational importance is not immediately obvious. Yet he suggests that it is 'fundamental to understanding', because a person familiar with it 'is less likely to be a victim of surprise at the way life happens to clobber out events' and 'provides an even wider context than does knowledge of the limits and extremes of reality for enabling us to ascribe meaning to the details of our lives and the world around

[97] Ibid.
[98] Ibid., 51.
[99] Ibid., 78.

us'.[100] If I interpret him correctly, the point Egan makes here – a point I agree with, apart from the terminological difference – is that a sensitivity to the mystery of being changes your outlook in life in such a way that you will be less easily taken aback by occurrences in the contingent and unpredictable stream of events that any life is. Deep wonder fosters a certain equanimity: mental composure, and a measure of control over one's emotions. And by placing our lives in the context of the larger narrative of the evolving universe such wonder can also heighten our sense of the significance of things, and open up new ways to give meaning to or find meaning in our lives – though this, as I noted in Chapter 1, is not guaranteed.

The imagination breathes life into things that otherwise would 'tell no story'.[101] Imaginative activity can therefore lead (through 'romance') to wonder; and in turn when wonder strikes it often sparks the imagination. In many cases being in a state of wonder coincides with experiencing a play of the imagination. When wonder becomes more than something that suddenly strikes, now and then – when it becomes dispositional, or at any rate a formative influence, this means that everything comes to be seen, as it were, under the sign of the possible. It is, mysteriously, but might not have been – while in another sense it was perhaps inevitable. This fosters a richer understanding, since it extends the connections we dimly perceive between things into the deep past, into the deep future, and into the realm of unrealized possibilities. It fosters a richer understanding, while at the same time we encounter the limits of our understanding, limits that the imagination tries to reach beyond. Our understanding here becomes enriched not so much through cognitive progress but by feeling, by a change in the 'non-cognitive' dimension of our connection with the world. In wonder – in the mode of consciousness or attention that is wonder – we become (more than usually) aware of our presence, our bodily participation, in a whole that defies comprehension. As dreamy a reputation as wonder may have, it is in my view a 'grounding' experiential state. As such it can play an important role in the prevention of damaging, superficial ways of engaging with and 'understanding' the world, ways that are made possible by an overly rational, what we might call a 'voyeuristic' conception of knowledge and understanding in which as human beings we observe nature from a stance outside of it, a realm of our own.[102]

[100] Ibid., 79.

[101] Cf. Pedersen's discussion of Warnock's view of the imagination as 'animator'; Pedersen, *Balanced Wonder*, 104; Mary Warnock, *Imagination* (London and Boston: Faber and Faber, 1976).

[102] For the (educationally and generally) harmful separation of intellect and feeling see Orr, *Earth in Mind*, especially part I.

Conclusion

In his essay 'Democratic Values and Educational Aims' Richard Peters writes:

> In many the contingency, creation and continuance of the world, which are beyond the power of man to comprehend, give rise to awe and wonder. The human condition is viewed in a wider perspective, under 'a certain aspect of eternity', and ways of life are generated that transcend and transform what is demanded by morality and truth. Others are content to operate within the limits of human understanding and are unmoved by reflection on the order of the world that makes such understanding possible. But both types of reaction are available only for those who have had their awareness extended in this dimension by education.[103]

What I take this to mean is that both a religious or spiritual response to the world, affectively charged by awe and wonder, and a more 'this-worldly' (for want of a better word) response to the world are – as authentic, reflective responses – only possible as a result of education. With regard to wonder this is quite a modest claim. I hope to have shown in this chapter that education is hardly conceivable without wonder, that education makes it more likely that wonder will happen, and that wonder certainly makes it more likely that education will happen. Wonder opens up the heart and mind, and opens these up to the world; it is therefore an essentially educational experience or mode of awareness. And the change of outlook that education seeks – that is the hallmark of education – is unlikely to occur unless students are sensitized by wonder to the world's extraordinariness. The following two chapters explore the implications of this view for moral and political education, respectively.

[103] Peters, 'Democratic Values and Educational Aims', 41.

4

Wonder and Moral Education

'A child's world is fresh and new and beautiful,' Rachel Carson writes in the 1965 classic *The Sense of Wonder*, 'full of wonder and excitement. It is our misfortune that for most of us that clear-eyed vision, that true instinct for what is beautiful and awe-inspiring, is dimmed and even lost before we reach adulthood'.[1] I expect many readers will recognize what Carson expresses here; that is, many people will share the intuition that a sense of wonder is a good thing, that it comes quite naturally to children, and that in many cases it becomes muted as we grow to adulthood. The ability to experience wonder – at (objects or events in) the natural world, at existence as such, at anything new and surprising one cannot make sense of – does indeed seem valuable in itself, as well as instrumentally, in fuelling a drive to understand and explain things. But the question I wish to address in this chapter is the more specific one whether we should stimulate the sense of wonder, and provoke experiences of wonder, in education, with a view to its *moral* effects or importance. Are there moral effects of wonder – or does wonder have a moral significance – that give us a (further) reason to promote children's sense of wonder and to attempt to elicit the experience of wonder in children? And if so, will *any* experience of wonder do, from a moral perspective, or do only *some* experiences of wonder – in specific contexts, or with a specific object – have the desired effect? One way to approach this question is to ask whether there are moral spillover effects from what are by themselves morally neutral experiences of wonder, or morally limited ones, in the sense that their moral charge is limited to a specific domain (such as one's attitude towards nature). For example, does wonder elicited by the view of a sunlit mountain peak have (a wider) moral import? Does it (or can it) contribute to a child's

This chapter is a revised and expanded version of Schinkel, 'Wonder and Moral Education'.

[1] Rachel Carson, *The Sense of Wonder* (New York: HarperCollins, 1998), 54.

moral development? Another way to approach the issue is to ask whether, if we want children to develop morally desirable attitudes (of care, compassion and respect, for instance) towards certain things or beings, fostering a sense of wonder towards those things or beings is a good step to take.

I will argue in this chapter that wonder can be morally important and that therefore fostering wonder can indeed be part of moral education, even that fostering a particular kind of wonder should ideally be part of moral education. But I will also argue that the issue is to be approached with caution; it is by no means obvious that wonder is necessarily a moral attitude or that it cannot but support and enhance moral virtues and morally virtuous emotions. In the second section following this introduction I will outline the claims various authors have made for wonder's moral potential, i.e. the potential for wonder to support morally desirable emotions, attitudes, and actions. This will be followed by a short section in which I show by means of an example that the relation between wonder and morality is more complicated than is often acknowledged. Next I offer an evaluation of wonder's moral importance, followed by a close look at the relation between wonder and 'otherness', and in the final section (before the conclusion) I outline my view on wonder's potential role in moral education. But I will begin by elucidating my understanding of moral education.[2]

Moral Education

As explained in the previous chapter I understand education as a practice that opens up the world, that 'gives access to' the world by enabling children (or adults, for that matter) to perceive more and to understand more, to act in the world more adequately and effectively, but also more 'responsibly' – i.e. in true 'response' to the world. 'Opening up the world' is a matter of establishing a *relationship* with the world. At the same time, therefore, education implies a going 'beyond the surface', beyond mere familiarity with things, beyond mere acceptance that things are as they are, or that they are a certain way because

[2] As readers familiar with that literature will no doubt notice, my understanding of morality and moral education has been influenced by the work of Martin Buber, Raimond Gaita, Iris Murdoch, Simone Weil, and Nel Noddings (among others). See Martin Buber, *I and Thou*, (London and New York: Continuum, 2004), Raimond Gaita, *Good and Evil: An Absolute Conception*, 2nd ed. (Abingdon: Routledge, 2006), Iris Murdoch, *The Sovereignty of Good* (London: Routledge & Kegan Paul, 1980), and Simone Weil, *Simone Weil: An Anthology*, ed. and intr. Siân Miles (London: Virago Press Limited, 1986); Nel Noddings, *Educating Moral People* (New York: Teachers College Press, 2002).

someone else says so. Education is a process that is inversely related to the extent to which we take things for granted, and therefore wonder, in which we experience the familiar as strange or mysterious in some way, is intimately connected with it.

Specific types of education, whether in mathematics or history, aesthetics or morality, should not so much be seen as each taking care of a particular part of the world partitioned off from the others – partial views that together give us a 360-degree vision –, but rather as offering different perspectives on the world as a whole. Moral education discloses the world in a particular way; it sensitizes us to value and cultivates dispositions to respond to value in appropriate ways. Like other types of education this involves initiation into a language that shapes how we perceive the world and into particular ways of doing and being. Moral education is not just socialization; it is not just a matter of 'catching' the moral system of one's group and adapting to that.[3] Firstly, moral education, as I understand it, is education in an 'ideal' morality – it implies the idea that there is something *beyond* the sets of moral values, rules, principles, and so on accepted by particular groups of people in any time or place. It implies, in other words, that when we know the answer to the question whether some action is seen as morally right, acceptable, or praiseworthy by some group or community, we may still wonder whether it *is* actually morally right, acceptable, or praiseworthy.[4] Secondly, moral *education* implies that the person who is educated becomes aware of and comes to appreciate what morality is about and thereby becomes able to see the sense and nonsense of accepted moral systems, and to question accepted justifications on the basis of his or her own moral experience and reasoning. Moral education aims at openness to a value dimension of the world that is *aided* by the existing moral vocabulary and grammar, but not limited to it. More concretely, it entails the cultivation of emotional sensibilities, beliefs and dispositions to act that aim to further and protect life and its enjoyment, beauty,

[3] Michael Hand describes one argument for the idea that we can do without moral education (an idea he rejects) as 'the suggestion that morality is caught rather than taught', i.e. acquired informally rather than through 'deliberate facilitation by adults'; Michael Hand, *A Theory of Moral Education* (Abingdon: Routledge, 2018), 7–8. I largely agree, but I would note that deliberate moral education by adults is not always necessary for children to become 'morally educated' persons; some people achieve this by themselves, educated by experience, taught by the world and by themselves (sometimes in spite of an indoctrinatory type of education).

[4] My use of 'moral' here is thus close to what Bernard Gert called the normative as opposed to the descriptive sense of the term; see Bernard Gert and Joshua Gert, 'The Definition of Morality', *The Stanford Encyclopedia of Philosophy* (Spring 2016 edition), E. N. Zalta (ed.), http://plato.stanford.edu/archives/spr2016/entries/morality-definition. I say 'close to' because I do not fully subscribe to the role of 'rationality' in Gert's normative definition of morality. I do wish to retain the idea here of an 'ideal' morality as opposed to the sociological notion of a morality, which in theory can have any content whatsoever.

love, and other forms of value and importance in the world; and as a corollary it involves promoting an appreciation of *moral* value(s), such as the values of honesty, justice and care.

To explain further how I conceive of moral education it is helpful to compare and contrast it with the view defended, in an extremely lucid way, by Michael Hand in his recent work on the subject – a view with which I concur to some extent, but also disagree on fundamental points.[5] For Hand, morality is 'in whole or in part, a matter of subscribing to moral standards and believing them to be justified', so moral education is 'in whole or in part, education in or about this matter'.[6] More specifically, in line with the two parts of morality he mentions, moral education consists of two parts, which he calls *moral formation* and *moral inquiry*. The former entails the cultivation of 'the conative, affective and behavioural dispositions that constitute subscription to moral standards', while the latter is about facilitating 'the formation of beliefs about the justificatory status of moral standards'.[7] Now, the central purpose of Hand's book is to tackle the problem of whether and how moral education, understood in this way, can be justified, given that reasonable disagreement exists about the content and justification of morality, and that 'teaching propositions as true, or standards as justified, when there is reasonable disagreement about them, is indoctrinatory' (and indoctrination is undesirable, and at odds with the idea of education, since it means that someone comes to hold beliefs 'non-rationally, on some other basis than the force of relevant evidence and argument').[8] Hand's solution to this problem, in short, is to invoke a (contractarian) argument to establish that the scope of *reasonable* disagreement about morality is limited, and that therefore moral education that aims at 'cultivating full moral commitment', i.e. at 'bringing it about that children subscribe to moral standards *and* believe them to be justified' is a legitimate practice; and to show that a rational justification of basic moral standards is available, so that aiming to persuade children of their validity is not indoctrinatory.[9] The core of the former argument is that human social groups need to deal with permanent threats to the social order (having

5 Hand, *A Theory of Moral Education*. The revisions I made for this chapter to the article on which it is based have been made largely in response to Michael Hand's provocative but sympathetic critique of that article, for which I am very grateful: Michael Hand, 'Wonder and Moral Education: A Reply to Anders Schinkel', paper presented at the conference Wonder, Education, and Human Flourishing, Amsterdam, the Netherlands, 5–6 April 2019. An excellent summary of Hand's view, of which I have also made use, is provided by Johannes Drerup, 'A Theory of Moral Education', *Educational Theory* 68, no. 4–5 (2018).

6 Ibid., 29.

7 Ibid., 29–30.

8 Ibid., 5–6.

9 Ibid., 43 and ch. 6.

to do with limited sympathies and limited resources, among other things), and that this requires 'universally-enlisting and penalty-endorsing subscription to certain standards of conduct', i.e. 'moral' subscription.[10] In short, basic moral standards, such as prohibitions against killing, stealing and lying, are necessary and justified because without them it would not be possible for people to live together (in social groups) peacefully.[11]

As said, I concur with Hand that moral education (properly understood) goes beyond socialization. As a deliberate practice, moral education should aim at more than, or something other than, making sure children internalize and abide by the moral norms of the social group they belong to.[12] Education aims not just at the ability to do something, but at understanding what one is doing (or thinking, or feeling), the kind of understanding that enables a person to make exceptions to rules if the situation demands it. I also agree with Hand that moral education is justifiable, but like Drerup I am not convinced that the philosophical justification of morality Hand offers is also *educationally* the best way to justify subscription to moral standards. Drerup rightly notes that we 'do not usually teach children to be moral primarily by referring to the functional importance of the universally-enlisting and penalty-endorsing subscription to moral standards in social groups'.[13] In response Hand might admit that we do not teach children to *be* moral that way, but that when it comes to educating them about the *justification* for being moral we should refer to morality's function in dealing with the problem of sociality. But this would underestimate (the importance of) the difference between Hand's theory and the practice of moral education. In everyday life parents and educators also *justify* subscription to moral standards (and penalizing transgressions) in a different way than Hand proposes. In 'discipline encounters' parents often make use of 'induction', i.e. when a child transgresses a moral norm, for instance by hitting another child (for no good reason), they encourage the child to take the victim's perspective, point out that the victim is hurt, and that this was caused by the child's hitting the other.[14] In other words: the moral norm (of not hurting innocent others)

[10] Ibid., 67.

[11] To this might be added that living in social groups is the default situation for human beings and that doing so is, except perhaps for a small number of adults, necessary in order to survive and live well.

[12] I realize that the notions of belonging to a social group and of 'the norms' of a social group are fraught with difficulties, since in our world it is only in exceptional cases that a person can clearly be said to belong to one social group only, and that a social group can be said to have one clearly delineated set of moral norms, values, and practices; but I will leave this aside here.

[13] Drerup, 'A Theory of Moral Education', 582.

[14] Martin L. Hoffman, *Empathy and Moral Development* (Cambridge: Cambridge University Press, 2000), chapter 6.

is justified *directly* by appeal to what it means to be hurt (which involves pain, distress, social anxiety, and so on). It is the 'bad' nature of that state that provides the reason not to cause others to be in that state. No detour through the contractarian countryside is taken, and none seems necessary.

An obvious response is open to Hand, of course: that we offer different justifications in practice does not mean that they are better than the one he proposes; in fact, if we want to have a justification that does not appeal to controversial meta-ethical positions (because we do not want to engage in indoctrination) we should steer clear from the idea that there is something *intrinsically* bad from a moral perspective about causing hurt without good reason. In my view, however, this is too large a sacrifice to make – we would sacrifice too much on the altar of an ideal rationality. What we would sacrifice – what *I* feel I would have to sacrifice, at least, but I have no doubt that many people would feel the same way – is what moral experience tells us, namely that we should not hurt others or treat others unjustly, because of what it *means* to do so. This is revealed to us superficially in ordinary instances of empathy, but more deeply in the (rarer) experiences we have in those moments when we meet another person's or another creature's gaze and hurting them becomes unthinkable or the knowledge of having hurt them deeply painful. In these moral events, these encounters, we 'perceive' and respond to something we may express abstractly (and never fully satisfactorily) with words like 'inherent value' or 'intrinsic value' or, in one of Raimond Gaita's terms, 'infinite preciousness'.[15] In Albert Schweitzer's case such an experience led to him formulating his famous notion of 'reverence for life'.[16]

Most people, I trust, will at minimum be able to experience the 'badness' involved in injustice or in causing hurt without justification, and will not require a different justification of the basic moral rules and principles pertaining to this. (Moral nihilists might, but they are just as much – or little – a problem for Hand's view as for mine.[17]) And many people will at least occasionally experience or have experienced a moral encounter of the kind described above, and for them, too, a contractarian justification of morality may perhaps have its use in

[15] Gaita, *Good and Evil*, xv (among other places). Gaita makes explicit that he uses different terms, depending on the context; sometimes he speaks of 'unconditional respect' rather than 'infinite preciousness' or 'inalienable preciousness'.

[16] Albert Schweitzer, *Die Ehrfurcht vor dem Leben: Grundtexte aus fünf Jahrzehnten* (München: Verlag C. H. Beck, 2003), 20.

[17] See Hand, *A Theory of Moral Education*, 69–72 for his response to the problem of moral nihilism.

a political context, but ultimately misses the point. From the point of view of moral experience, it is 'one thought too many'.

Morality, as I see it, is about what we do with our freedom to *respond* to others and to the world – to respond or not to respond at all, and to respond in ways that enhance value (life, love, beauty) or diminish it. Response-ability and responsivity are thus central to the moral life. This has important implications for how we see the relation between moral education and indoctrination (and, of course, the relation between wonder and moral education). For Hand the harm of indoctrination is that 'indoctrinated beliefs are thought-stoppers'; 'holding beliefs on a topic non-rationally,' Hand writes, 'is a serious impediment to thinking clearly about that topic, to engaging critically and open-mindedly with evidence and argument bearing on it, and to moderating or relinquishing beliefs that turn out to be unwarranted'.[18] While I do not think Hand is wrong in saying this, I would emphasize that cultivating an openness to new *moral experience*, rather than rational thinking, is the most important antidote to dogmatism or habits of not-thinking. In practice, at least, few people are dissuaded from firmly held views by rational argument alone; the crucial difference is made by an experience that changes *the way they see things*, and thereby changes what arguments they are susceptible to, as well as the weight they give to various considerations.[19] The way to prevent indoctrination, then, from the point of view I defend here, is to emphasize the imperfect nature of any moral system and to keep drawing attention to that (response-demanding 'value') which should underlie moral values and principles but is at best imperfectly and partially embodied in them. Responsiveness to value – aided, of course, by critical thinking – is what enables people to transcend the limits of conventional morality, and what has inspired countless acts of conscientious objection and civil disobedience in the past.[20]

Hand distinguishes moral standards that are 'robustly justified' from standards about which there can be 'reasonable disagreement'; in the former case we should teach for 'full moral commitment' by means of 'directive moral

[18] Ibid., 10.

[19] The newspaper I read before I began writing this section offers a nice illustration: in a letter to the editor a reader tells us that she grew up in the country and that her father had a vegetable garden and free range chickens. When she was fourteen she went on a school excursion to a chicken 'farm', where she saw huge numbers of 'ééndagskuikens' (newborn chicks, literally 'one-day-chicks', that are usually shredded alive, often to serve as pet food) and adult chickens stuffed together in undersized cages. When she returned home she told her parents she wanted to become a vegetarian. Diena Wolters, 'Op het Kippenbedrijf Werd Ik Vegetariër', *Trouw*, 21 June 2019, 23.

[20] See Anders Schinkel, *Conscience and Conscientious Objections* (Amsterdam: Pallas Publications, 2007).

inquiry', whereas in the latter case we may only teach nondirectively with the aim to 'equip children to form their own considered views'.[21] From the alternative perspective I have outlined above, however, the distinction Hand makes is much harder to maintain. The distinction comes into (relatively) clear view because of the type of justification of morality and moral education Hand defends: some moral standards are clearly necessary for the more or less harmonious functioning of society, others are not. But when the justification of morality and moral education is tied to what in practice often motivates moral action and what I argue *should* motivate it, we find that (felt) moral obligations belonging to both of Hand's categories in fact share the same ground. There is no difference *in kind* between my belief that I should not kill (other) animals (for food or other purposes) and my belief that I should not kill other people (which is not to say that the strength of my inhibitions and feelings is the same in both cases, but such differences often have psychological grounds that lack moral justification); similarly, my belief that I ought to be kind to other people has no different foundation than my belief that I ought not to steal from them. Both stem from a response to the other, from an appreciation of their inherent worthiness of care, compassion, respect and protection.

Moral education, then, is again an instance of educating for 'heteronomy' in the sense explained in Chapter 3: the aim of education is that people are moved by the reasons there are for feeling, believing, and doing things; in other words, that people are world-oriented and world-responsive. In the moral realm this does not mean that we have to accept the idea that there are moral 'truths' out there the same way there is, say, a birch tree in my backyard; but it means that we cannot shake off the sense that morality involves responding to something that does not owe its reality to whether I 'see' it or not.

In the following section I explore wonder's moral potential at the hand of a number of authors (in particular Hepburn and Moore). These authors may not exactly share my view of morality, but Hepburn's and Moore's views certainly seem closer to that than to a view like Hand's, and nothing they say is incompatible with it. In the sections after that I explain my own view on wonder's moral (educational) importance, and this will be informed by the conception of morality and moral education sketched above.

[21] Hand, *A Theory of Moral Education*, 77, 80.

Wonder's Moral Potential

There are many ways in which wonder can be said to have moral importance. As Vasalou argues, to wonder is not – certainly not always – something that just happens to us; when we are confronted with something that disturbs our understanding of the world, and thus our sense of security, the question how we should respond to that disturbance can be seen as a moral one, in a broad sense of the term – a question pertaining to our character, who we want to be.[22] Wonder as the overcoming of fear can be seen as 'an ethical achievement'.[23] Furthermore, wonder can be seen as enriching our lives, at least subjectively: 'evoking the subjective sense that we have established a harmonious relationship with the widest possible range of human experience', as Fuller puts it.[24] It is also worth noting that wonder's moral importance can be located both on the *individual* and the *community* or *societal* level. If a community allows no space for (or to) wonder, we may be concerned that it might become blind to the intrinsic value of certain things, creatures, or people, and might – unwittingly – destroy or inhibit value and creativity.[25]

But more important for my purpose in this article are wonder's (potential) moral 'effects' on or in individuals, the moral attitudes it may foster, the moral awareness it may evoke, the values and commitments it may invite, and the insights it may support. Wonder has been said to lead to a revaluation, a new perspective on the importance of things in which the ego retreats into the background and the intrinsic value of the other-than-self is foregrounded. It has also been said to foster – also developmentally – empathy, love, and compassion, and to lure us towards a reverence for life. Wonder seems to be opposed to dogmatism and fanaticism, and associated with humility. It has been claimed to stimulate our search for higher (ultimate) values and meaning.[26] De Pascuale suggests that wonder may spark authentic existence: 'If attended to, the experience of wonder gives birth to self-examination and to a mindful awareness of the world. In time you come to know yourself as you have been and are – and this gives you the possibility of choosing *how* to be. Through the experience of wonder we become true individuals and true citizens of the

[22] Vasalou, *Wonder*, 68ff.
[23] Ibid., 71.
[24] Fuller, *Wonder*, 153. See also Carson, *The Sense of Wonder*, 100–1, and Hepburn, 'Wonder', 14.
[25] See Moore, 'The Truth of the Barnacles', and Ursula Goodenough's 'planetary ethic', mentioned in Fuller, *Wonder*, 128.
[26] Fuller, *Wonder*, ch. 7, on Carson.

universe'.[27] A related, though certainly not identical, point is that experiences of wonder can be epiphanic and morally (trans)formative. I will not attempt to discuss all of the items on this – undoubtedly far from exhaustive – list, but focus my attention on three of them: (1) wonder as leading to a reassessment of the importance of things, and as stimulating the transcendence of egocentrism; (2) wonder as fostering empathy, love and compassion; (3) wonder as morally (trans)formative experience.

Several authors on wonder have suggested that wonder can lead us – and sometimes it is suggested that it *does* lead us – beyond an egocentric concern with ourselves.[28] Why would this be so? As explained in Chapter 1, following Hepburn, it belongs to the phenomenology of wonder, to the structure and quality of the experience, that it is 'essentially *other-acknowledging*'.[29] Recall that Martha Nussbaum describes wonder as a noneudaimonistic, and therefore atypical, emotion. Although eudaimonistic emotions – emotions that have a connection with our well-being and the value of what we are perceiving for our well-being – are not at all necessarily egoistic or egocentric, wonder's noneudaimonistic nature does mean, according to Nussbaum, that it 'responds to the pull of the object, and (…) that in it the subject is maximally aware of the value of the object, and only minimally aware, if at all, of its relationship to her own plans'.[30]

27 Juan De Pascuale, 'A Wonder Full Life', *Notre Dame Magazine*, spring 2003, https://magazine.nd.edu/stories/a-wonder-full-life/, cited (from the print edition) in Fuller, *Wonder*, 43.

28 Fuller, *Wonder*, 95, 99; Hepburn, 'Wonder', 14–15; Moore, 'The Truth of the Barnacles', 269.

29 Hepburn, 'Wonder', 14. There may be exceptions to this; it is not clear that *all* forms of wonder are other-acknowledging, or that this always means the same thing. Some see the experience of the sublime as a form that wonder may take, for instance. But in the sublime it is ultimately the *subject*, not the object, of the experience that is 'wonderful': 'The powerful emotions aroused by spectacles of grandeur, thus processed, ultimately point away from their initial visual objects and return the gaze to the subject that holds these objects in his gaze. Kant (…) states that it is never truly external objects that are sublime, but rather the ground for the sublime is "merely one in ourselves" and the object only "serves for the presentation of a sublimity that can be found in the mind."' Vasalou, *Wonder*, 145–6; her references are to Immanuel Kant, *Critique of the Power of Judgment*, ed. Paul Guyer, trans. Paul Guyer and Eric Matthews (Cambridge: Cambridge University Press, 2000), 130 and 129 [§ 23]. Now, one could say that in the experience of the sublime the subject of the experience *becomes* the object, and that therefore in a sense the subject becomes an 'other' for itself; but this would drain the concept of being 'other-acknowledging' of much of its intended meaning, since that had to do with being drawn out of an ego-centric focus, and out of a concern with oneself. Of course the sublime's focus on the subject or the self could also be taken as a reason to reject seeing it as a form of wonder, but that response might moralize wonder too much. I am personally inclined to see the sublime as a type of experience that has strong similarities to what I call contemplative or deep wonder, especially at the 'start', but that as it develops in a particular instance collapses into something different, something more settled or decided (like awe), that has lost the openness and sense of mystery characteristic of wonder.

30 Nussbaum, *Upheavals of Thought*, 54–5, cited in Vasalou, *Wonder*, 15–16.

Try and think of a moment when you were 'wonderstruck' – at an amazing sunset, maybe, at the birth of a child, or at the improbability of existing, of being who you are, where you are, in the vastness of time and space. You will recognize, I expect, that when wonder strikes it sends into the background or (temporarily) makes you forget whatever thoughts and feelings you entertained (or occupied you) before. Moreover, such wonder comes with a powerful sense of deep importance and meaning, in light of which the things you were previously attending to – and the things that normally demand our attention – often seem petty, insignificant. One's perspective is widened, one's sense of the importance of things adjusted accordingly. Triggered by one's wonder-charged attention to a particular object or thought, one experiences a sense of zooming out: things that a moment ago appeared large and important now look small, unremarkable, much less significant. This effect is not tied to the *striking* of wonder either; it is equally inherent in an enduring, dispositional wonder, wonder as a more or less stable ingredient of one's cognitive–affective composition at any moment in time, that it is object-centred. Anything one might want of or with the object, any relation it may have to one's desires, plans or needs, is bracketed. Hence wonder also seems incompatible with exploitation; it is rather 'non-exploitative' and 'non-utilitarian'.[31]

In keeping with this, but with a stronger emphasis on the affective, wonder has also been said to inspire and nourish empathy, love and compassion and the development of such dispositions, and to foster a respectful and caring attitude towards all life. William James already wrote that 'ontological wonder' (like 'religious rapture, moral enthusiasm [and] cosmic emotion') is a 'unifying state of mind' in which 'the sand and grit of the selfhood incline to disappear, and tenderness to rule'.[32] Fuller observes: 'No other emotion so readily kindles a reverence for life'.[33] And Moore says that '[a] sense of wonder impels us to act respectfully in the world' and that '[a] sense of wonder that allows us to see life as a beautiful mystery forces us to see life as something to which we owe respect and care'.[34] Hepburn explains the connection between wonder and compassion as follows: 'Where a human life is the object of wonder, there can be a poignant realization of both potentiality and fragility. From that point of

[31] Hepburn, 'Wonder', 15. 'Non-utilitarian' means that questions of use do not arise; someone who wonders is not concerned with utility. But although wonder is opposed to exploitation, it is compatible with (respectful) use.

[32] James, *Varieties of Religious Experience*, 221.

[33] Fuller, *Wonder*, 158.

[34] Moore, 'The Truth of the Barnacles', 271, 273.

view of humanity compassion can readily flow'.[35] I know of no better illustration of this point than the poems of Wisława Szymborska, poems that breathe and breed wonder, always keeping a bemused distance,[36] yet always compassionate, never cynical. The poem *A contribution to statistics*, for example, presents the reader with human – but also humane – 'statistics':

Out of a hundred people

those who always know better
– fifty-two,

doubting every step
– nearly all the rest,

(…)

capable of happiness
– twenty-something tops,

(…)

righteous
– thirty-five, which is a lot,

righteous
and understanding,
– three,

worthy of compassion
– ninety-nine,

Mortal
– a hundred out of a hundred.
Thus far this figure still remains unchanged.[37]

Paradoxically, by zooming out from our human particulars, we become more human. The poem expresses exactly the 'poignant realization of potentiality and fragility' of which Hepburn spoke, though our potentiality is here seen as

35 Hepburn, 'Wonder', 15.

36 Remember that Parsons observed that wonder is characterized by 'an element of detachment or ideation, (…) a control of emotion that gives psychic distance to the event'; Parsons, 'A Philosophy of Wonder', 87.

37 Wisława Szymborska, *Poems: New and collected* (Orlando: Harcourt, 1998).

refracted by our fragility, our limitations and imperfections – a perspective from which compassion flows even more readily.[38]

When Hepburn says that compassion 'can readily flow' from 'that point of view of humanity' I take it he is not just making a psychological point, though that is important, too. Psychologically, emotionally, wonder has a close affinity with compassion, as well as with respect, gentleness and humility (as Hepburn also notes). But this affinity seems to be more than a contingent fact of our psychological make-up. It is not the same kind of connection as, say, that between exhaustion (after running a marathon) and emotional lability. Insofar as wonder is indeed 'other-acknowledging', implying a bracketing of one's own desires and interests and an openness towards the value of the other, the 'logic' of wonder prepares the way for compassion. But a rigid distinction between the logical and the psychological, the conceptual and the empirical, seems unsatisfactory here, for wonder – *some* kinds of wonder, at least – and compassion seem to be connected in their experiential natures. Both are other-oriented, attentive, receptive states, for instance; and both imply a certain humility, both moral and intellectual. (That is not to say, however, that the connection is logically or psychologically *necessary*, or that it holds for any type of wonder, a point to which I shall return below.)

Moving now to the third point I wish to discuss in this section, the combination of wonder's shock-potential – unsettling one's ordinary ways of viewing the world – and its affinity with moral emotions and dispositions explains why experiences of wonder can constitute 'Morally Formative Experiences'.[39] They can be morally formative in the 'everyday' sense of contributing something to our moral development, the way many of our experiences do, but a 'Morally Formative Experience' is a more striking or memorable experience that – in hindsight at least – stands out as an important, perhaps even crucial or pivotal, moment in one's moral development. There is a connection here with epiphanic experiences,[40] perhaps particularly of the Other, in Buber's sense:

38 For similar reasons Evans argues that wonder can be an important ethical source in the 'clinical encounter' between doctor and patient; wonder can help the doctor see the human being in the patient, and this may support the doctor in resisting the problem that patients and treatments become 'routine'; see Howell M. Evans, 'Wonder and the Clinical Encounter', *Theoretical Medicine and Bioethics* 33 (2012); also Howell M. Evans, 'Wonder and the Patient', *Journal of Medical Humanities* 36 (2015) and Howell M. Evans, 'Medicine, the Body and an Invitation to Wonder', *Medical Humanities* 42, no. 2 (2016).

39 I discuss this more fully in Anders Schinkel, 'Wonder as a Morally Formative Experience', unpublished manuscript.

40 See Kristján Kristjánsson, 'Epiphanic Moral Conversions: Going beyond Kohlberg and Aristotle', in *Self-Transcendence and Virtue: Perspectives from Philosophy, Psychology, and Theology*, eds. Jennifer A. Frey and Candace Vogler (London: Routledge, 2019), 15–38.

> In the eyes of him who takes his stand in love, and gazes out of it, men are cut free from their entanglement in bustling activity. Good people and evil, wise and foolish, beautiful and ugly, become successively real to him; that is, set free they step forth in their singleness, and confront him as *Thou*. In a wonderful way, from time to time, exclusiveness arises – and so he can be effective, helping, healing, educating, raising up, saving.[41]

This attitude, this relationship, cannot be maintained all the time, but must be re-established and renewed again and again; each time the Other is revealed once more as a *Thou* (and you are revealed as a different *I*, in relation to that *Thou*) – a repeated epiphany of what was already known, the same way wonder can make us see the familiar afresh.

Fuller presents three examples of lives decisively influenced by (experiences of) wonder, the lives of John Muir, Rachel Carson and William James. John Muir was highly prone to wonder from an early age, but after his family's emigration to the United States his immersion in 'American wilderness' profoundly influenced the person he was to become. Looking back on his time in rural Wisconsin, he wrote: 'This sudden plash into wilderness – baptism in Nature's warm heart – how utterly happy it made us! Nature streaming into us, wooingly teaching her wonderful glowing lessons'.[42] And the solitary years he spent in the Sierra Nevada mountains further transformed his perspective on the world, and his moral outlook, making him one of the fathers of the American conservation movement. Muir's life, as that of Carson and James, bears witness to wonder's (trans)formative power.

All in all, it seems undeniable that wonder *has* moral potential, that it can and sometimes, perhaps even often, does inspire and foster moral emotions, attitudes, dispositions, and commitments. But it is by no means clear yet that wonder necessarily has that effect or how strong that effect is, nor that any type of wonder has it, and in any person, under any circumstances. In short, we still know very little about wonder's moral importance and the role it could or should have in moral education. I now turn to an example that suggests that the relation between wonder and morality is not straightforward.

41 Buber, *I and Thou*, 19–20.

42 John Muir, *The Story of My Boyhood and Youth* (Boston: Houghton Mifflin, 1913), 31, cited in Fuller, *Wonder*, 46.

Disturbing Wonder

I began this chapter with a quotation from Rachel Carson. Immediately following those lines, Carson expressed the following wish – or prayer, almost:

> If I had influence with the good fairy who is supposed to preside over the christening of all children I should ask that her gift to each child in the world be a sense of wonder so indestructible that it would last throughout life, as an unfailing antidote against the boredom and disenchantments of later years, the sterile preoccupation with things that are artificial, the alienation from the sources of our strength.[43]

And a bit further on she suggests, for the parent 'who feels he has little nature lore at his disposal': 'And with your child you can ponder the mystery of a growing seed, even if it be only one planted in a pot of earth in the kitchen window.'[44] Now consider this example from Margarete Götz's work on the German elementary school in the Nazi era. Götz explains that according to government guidelines nature education in that period was to instil in children reverence for the Creator and joy at the life of nature. She illustrates the danger of such an 'emotionalized approach to nature' at the hand of an example from a late 1930s schoolbook by Fritz Vogt.[45] Vogt describes children's response to the flowering of a lily in the windowsill:

> All heads turn towards the happening, and bafflement and wonder seize the crowd with suggestive power. Questions spring up, answers are given. 'No human being can do this!' – 'This is the work of the good God!' A silent interval ensues. In quiet reverence large, clear children's eyes look upon the natural event. Then the suspense dissolves. The event has been made sense of, the riddle solved. All the while the teacher did not utter a word; but the children learned a lesson about the Creation, of a kind that the jewish legend of the creation of the world could not give.[46]

[43] Ibid.

[44] Ibid., 66.

[45] Fritz Vogt, Heimatkunde in der Grundschule. Nach den Hand des Lehrers (Berlin: Osterwieck, 1938), 46, quoted in Margarete Götz, Die Grundschule in der Zeit des Nationalsozialismus: Eine Untersuchung der inneren Ausgestaltung der vier unteren Jahrgänge der Volksschule auf der Grundlage amtlicher Maßnahmen (Bad Heilbrunn: Verlag Julius Klinkhardt, 1997), 212.

[46] My translation. It is not clear to me why Vogt saw a superior 'explanation' of the event in the idea that 'this is the work of the good God' than in the Jewish (and therefore biblical) 'creation legend' (other than that for him the fact that the latter was Jewish made it inferior); Götz does not comment on this either. Moreover, there is something odd about speaking of an 'explanation' that 'makes sense' of the event in the first place; as if acknowledging that something is God's work makes it any less mysterious. It would not be strange to think that this attitude (on Vogt's part) gives the wonder in his fictional example a different (perhaps lesser) moral quality than a wonder that does not do away with mystery, but, firstly, this cannot explain the difference between wonder that leads to a desire to protect or care for the object of wonder and wonder that does not lead to such a desire or caring attitude (since God's work would surely still be worth protecting), and secondly, to generalize from this example would give it too much weight.

The 'religion of nature' in Nazi Germany and the ecofascist movement have been well documented.[47] Important themes in this ideological movement were the alienation from nature in modern, urban life, and the need to reconnect with nature to overcome the weakness caused by civilization. In a book on German forestry of the same year, Franz Heske explains that 'German culture sprang from the forest':

> In the old forests, the present generation seeks to recapture that reverential awe which is the foundation of morality. The culture of the city, with its unceasing human turmoil and daily elbow-to-elbow struggle for bread and for preferment, moves the little Ego into the center and finally causes the whole world to be viewed from this minute observation post. The civilized countryside, with its flat fields, its innumerable boundaries, fences, hedges, and boundary stones, is everywhere a reminder of exclusiveness and segregation, of the ego and of the microcosm subservient thereto.
>
> Not so in the woods. Primordial depths, mysterious murmuring, and whispering surround the wanderer. Loneliness in the face of a gigantic Nature [sic] in which everything is large, everything is complex and yet unified, soon makes the little ego dissolve organically into the new totality. The egoistic soul expands and becomes like a transparent ball in which the organic streams of the universe flood back and forth. The armor falls, and man is free![48]

Wonder at a plant in a window, an instinct for what is awe-inspiring, clear-eyed children, alienation from nature and from the sources of our strength, reverential awe as the foundation of morality, a sense of mystery – the language of Carson's gentle and uplifting work and that of the Nazi-era literature cited above are almost interchangeable. (Almost, because of course one will not find any anti-Semitic or nationalist sentiments in the former.) Nature as drawing us out of selfish preoccupations to embrace a wider perspective, in which we are part of an organic whole – this, too, as we will see, is often said to be part of the moral import of wonder.

What must we make of this resemblance between national socialist writing on nature, awe, wonder, and education, embedded as it was in a morally repugnant ideology, and more recent work on these topics that it would be hard to find

[47] See, for instance, Robert A. Pois, *National Socialism and the Religion of Nature* (New York: St Martin's Press, 1986) and Joachim Radkau and Frank Uekötter, eds., *Naturschutz und Nationalsozialismus* (Frankfurt: Campus Verlag, 2003).

[48] Franz Heske, *German Forestry* (New Haven: Yale University Press, 1938), 180–1, cited in Robert G. Lee and Sabine Wilke, 'Forest as *Volk: Ewiger Wald* and the Religion of Nature in the Third Reich', *Journal of Social and Ecological Boundaries* 1, no. 1 (2005): 22.

fault with, morally speaking? Does it tell us something about wonder's moral importance and its possible role in moral education? The main message, I think, is that we should be careful to assume too readily that fostering children's sense of wonder will have (desirable) moral effects. As the above example shows, a sense of wonder (at nature) is compatible with antisemitism and more; it was part of a religion of nature that supported Nazism's rise to power. And the problem is not just that the Nazis' sense of wonder was only directed at nature, and not at the people they considered inferior to themselves; for, as I argue below, it is also not necessarily the case that we care for and wish to protect whatever we wonder at – this depends very much on the nature or quality of the wonder involved. But as I will also argue, the fact that the sense of wonder does not offer a guaranteed route to virtue is no reason whatsoever to retreat completely from the view that wonder is – generally speaking – a positive moral force and an ally of (positive) moral development.

Wonder's Moral Importance: An Evaluation

Some of Moore's formulations – 'wonder impels us', 'wonder forces us' (to, for instance, 'act respectfully in the world') – seem too strong; without qualification such claims are defeated by the examples presented above. *A* sense of wonder – *any* sense of wonder – does not possess this power. After discussing the association of wonder with an 'aesthetic spirituality' that emphasizes living in harmony with the universe and values that experience over doctrine Fuller mentions 'the life and thought of someone like Jonathan Edwards' as 'an excellent counterexample to the seeming symmetry between the experience of wonder and what we are calling aesthetic spirituality. (…) Jonathan Edwards – who almost surely had vivid experiences of wonder – resisted the cognitive tendencies usually associated with wonder and retained the conservative, doctrinally based religious orientation of his Puritan heritage'.[49] *Psychologically*, then, people can combine a deep sense of wonder with beliefs, behaviour, and dispositions that seem incongruous, even morally repugnant. As Nussbaum writes, though in a different context: 'We are capable of the most extraordinary feats of "doubling" – the term used by psychologist Robert Jay Lifton to describe

[49] Fuller, *Wonder*, 148.

Nazi doctors who carried out cruel experiments on Jews while living ethically decent family lives at home'.[50]

One problem with many claims about wonder and its moral importance is that they tend to be highly general, ignoring either the diversity 'within' wonder or the contextual nature of many experiences of wonder. Wonder may be 'essentially other-acknowledging' in one way or another, but when we think of what we might call *scientific* wonder, an active wonder that drives systematic investigation and analysis, it is not at all clear that this is necessarily or even in most cases associated with a non-exploitative or a caring and protective attitude. The wonder of the dissecting scientist may be directed at the parts, not the whole, at the inner workings of an animal, rather than its mind, personality, or unique life.

Even if wonder is indeed other-acknowledging, as seems to be true for many kinds of wonder at least, it is still important to distinguish single (however striking) experiences of wonder from an enduring sense of wonder that permanently informs and colours a person's perception of the world. It seems perfectly possible for someone to have a single or, spread over time, a number of strong experiences of wonder whose moral effects, if any, dwindle quickly once the ordinary has re-established its dominance. Deep experiences of wonder may be epiphanic or morally (trans)formative (in the strong sense used above), but it is unlikely that they will be if the ground is not prepared beforehand, and in the absence of favourable conditions. By the former I mean that cognitive restructuring is only possible if some conceptual framework is available to take the place of the old, or around which the new cognitive structure can crystallize.[51] 'Favourable' conditions might include such diverse things as a previously experienced lack of meaning in life, inspiring examples or friends that support one's development, and frequent contextual reminders of the experience and its perceived moral import. An *enduring* sense of wonder seems more promising, morally, though here we must once again acknowledge the possibility of 'doubling' or splitting – the mental gymnastics people are capable of – as well as raise the question of spillover effects.

[50] Martha C. Nussbaum, 'Animal Rights: The Need for a Theoretical Basis', *Harvard Law Review* 114, no. 5 (2001): 1506–49.

[51] The literature on (religious) conversion is relevant here. The interpretation of conversion experiences in terms of cognitive restructuring is one of various approaches to this phenomenon; see, for instance, C. Daniel Batson, Patricia Schoenrade, and W. Larry Ventis, *Religion and the Individual* (New York: Oxford University Press, 1993).

Hepburn admits that 'it is easy to exaggerate the reliability of carrying over attitudes and emotional responses from one domain to another, from the non-moral to the moral'.[52] He adduces the example of Wordsworth, deeply concerned with the fostering of wonder as well as with exploring 'affinities between attitudes to non-human nature and to persons in moral relationship'. But as Wordsworth scholar John Beer noted, 'even in his own case he could not be sure that the experiences of wonder had always led to the love of humanity: there was some evidence that, in his youth, cultivation of the wonderful in nature had led to an isolating aestheticism'.[53] Crudely put: experiences of wonder can be so rewarding in themselves that they become addictive, provoking an egocentric search for more.

In his wonder-brimming book *Landmarks* Robert MacFarlane says something that seems to contradict Hepburn's sobering remark; he writes that 'while writing about landscape often begins in the aesthetic, it must always tend to the ethical. [Author of *Arctic Dreams*] Lopez's intense attentiveness was (…) a form of moral gaze, born of his belief that if we attend more closely to something then we are less likely to act selfishly towards it'.[54] It is not fully clear with what kind of 'must' we are dealing here, however; if it is intended to imply inescapability, then it is plausible only if – and because – the writing and the gaze that informed it were never *purely* (never merely) aesthetic to begin with, but always already concerned in a way that was, if not yet fully moral, very close to it. Still, it is plausible enough that an aesthetic wonder provoked by a natural phenomenon will often go together with at least an inclination to protect it, even if partly for 'selfish' reasons: wanting to preserve what we find beautiful. It is important to note, though, that such an inclination need not at all be strong enough to override other, possibly utilitarian or exploitative, considerations. Not everyone capable of experiencing wonder at nature becomes a conservationist.

Spillover effects might occur between the non-moral and the moral (i.e. between domains), but also from one object of wonder to another. This may actually be the more difficult transfer. The national socialist's wonder at nature may well have a strong moral dimension, his attitude with regard to nature may well be caring, protective and humble, but this does not mean his attitude towards all other human beings will partake of the same qualities. Nor need the

[52] Hepburn, 'Wonder', 14.

[53] John Beer, *Wordsworth and the Human Heart* (Houndmills: Macmillan, 1978), 188, cited in Hepburn, 'Wonder', 15.

[54] Robert Macfarlane, *Landmarks* (London: Penguin Books, 2016), 211.

scientist's (non-moral) wonder at the intricate machinery of the cell spill over to the whole organism of which the cell is a minute part.

None of this wholly discredits the claims about the moral importance of wonder discussed above; and of course the real test of its actual importance – once we are agreed on the conceptual and normative issues, i.e. on the definition of wonder and on what counts as moral importance – is empirical. It would be great if we could do more than speculate and reason about the moral effects of (experiences of) wonder and the relations between a sense of wonder (and its various objects) and moral emotions, dispositions, and beliefs. In the absence of such data – that are very difficult to gather – it seems better to think about wonder's moral importance in terms of affective and cognitive *coherence*, mutually supporting emotions and attitudes, et cetera, than in terms of more or less guaranteed moral effects of wonder.[55] It would seem more *coherent* to combine a deep sense of wonder about nature or existence as such – including the openness, humility, awareness of the limits of one's understanding and so on, that accompanies such wonder – with at least an open, if not a gentle, caring, and forgiving attitude towards other human beings, than with racist sentiments, anti-Semitic prejudice, or indifference in the face of injustice. To be capable of wonder is to be capable of adopting a receptive attitude of appreciation of something for its own sake, apart from any reference to one's own desires, preferences, or plans. To adopt such an attitude usually leads to a reassessment of one's own importance 'sub specie aeternitatis'; it seems incoherent to simply abandon that attitude and reassert one's own (relative) importance in reaction to particular things or beings.

But perhaps if we are honest 'incoherence' is still too strong a word, since it presupposes a narrative in which some elements do not fit well together – a narrative, however, that the wondering national socialist (for instance) need not accept and may well want to, and be able to, substitute with another, in which those elements *do* fit, in however complicated a way.

At this point it might be tempting to interject that the wonder described and experienced by national socialists in Nazi Germany (or any other wonder combined with or embedded in a perverse ideology) is not, *cannot* be, *real* wonder and therefore cannot disprove the connection between wonder and morality, a connection that is actually tight and unambiguous. Put this strongly

[55] Much of the research undertaken in the research project in the context of which I have written this book is in fact empirical, and some of the data gathered will hopefully shed *some* light on the empirical connections between wonder and moral emotions, dispositions and beliefs.

this is, in my view, wishful thinking. A Nazi's wonder at nature was as real as any other's, even though it was differently toned, ideologically. To say otherwise is merely to introduce a persuasive definition of wonder that allows one to exclude anything that is not to one's liking.

Admittedly, there is *something* in this intuition that may tempt us towards adopting such a definition, and this has to do with the link between wonder and openness: to follow the 'logic' of wonder to its most radical conclusion would mean to abandon any preconceived notions of the meaning and value of things and people. This would be a Cartesian wonder, wonder as 'the first of all the passions', among other reasons 'because unlike the other emotions, it is prior to judgment and comparison'.[56] But that still does not deliver the desired result, because then we would also lose our grip on the sense of value and importance inherent in the experience of wonder; we may be left with a hint of it, but not enough to support firm conclusions. *Pace* Kathleen Moore, wonder alone does not close the gap between is and ought; we need to bring something to it to tip wonder over to the value-affirmative side.[57] As Vasalou writes in commenting on Schopenhauer's description of the star-filled sky – a description involving reference to 'the infinite greatness of the universe in space and time' and 'innumerable worlds' –

> [W]hat we behold when we lift our eyes to the nighttime sky are not 'innumerable worlds,' not a greatness that we could describe as 'infinite' on the basis of what we see (...). What we see, at most, are spots of light which require to be read in thicker terms, relying on a richer kind of activity, in order to move us to awe or wonder. (...) Standing before the nighttime sky, its grandeur and thus its sublimity would be inaccessible to us without a more reflective or imaginative engagement with the seen.[58]

Without interpretative schemes that tip wonder over towards awe, reverence, or respect, it may also collapse into fear or other 'negative' states; and the more we see wonder as in itself open, prejudgmental, neutral (so not already morally charged), the stronger this holds. Hence for Descartes wonder could be followed either by esteem or by disdain or scorn.[59]

[56] Marguerite La Caze, 'The Encounter between Wonder and Generosity', *Hypatia* 17, no. 3 (2002): 2.

[57] Moore, 'The Truth of the Barnacles', 267. La Caze, 'Encounter', 9, reaches a similar conclusion in her discussion of Irigaray's account of wonder and its role in an 'ethics of sexual difference': 'Wonder (...) cannot both be prior to judgment *and* involve an attraction to and respect for the other'.

[58] Vasalou, *Wonder*, 152–3.

[59] La Caze, 'Encounter', 11.

An alternative objection might be that the problem with the Nazis' wonder was that it was only directed at certain objects, that it should also have been directed at other people, including those they despised and murdered. But this is to say that the Nazis' sense of wonder *should have* extended to those people as well, and thus to introduce – to presuppose – a moral judgement – morality here directs wonder, not the other way around. And again, if the claim is that *had* the Nazi's wonder been directed at all other people as well, they would not have been able to despise and kill them, this claim assumes *a particular kind of* (morally charged) wonder. Terrible as it may sound, it is perfectly conceivable that some Nazis did experience (deep) wonder at 'inferior' people, at how strange it was that human beings could come in such different forms and levels of (im)perfection, and at how remarkably similar to 'Aryan' people they could superficially look.

To have moral importance, then, wonder cannot be divorced from interpretative schemes that make sense of what we perceive – even if not in the moment of wonder itself – and of our wonder itself. Wonder's moral importance largely depends on what we, consciously or unconsciously, take that wonder to mean.

Wonder and 'Otherness'

In the movie *The Shape of Water* Sally Hawkins plays a lonely janitor, Eliza Esposito, who works in a military government facility where secret operations go on. (This is in the 1960s, in the Cold War era.) Eliza is unable to speak; a scar consisting of three parallel lines in her neck suggest that her vocal chords were cut when she was a baby. She is an orphan, and she was found near water. One day she accidentally discovers that an alien amphibian creature, a fishlike man, has been brought into the facility by Colonel Strickland, who caught him in the Amazon River. Strickland abuses and tortures him, wants to use and exploit him, hoping that it will give America an advantage in the space race with the Soviets, but has no interest in the creature as such, let alone any empathy or compassion. But Eliza connects with him and vice versa. They both can't speak except in sign language, gestures, body language, and facial expressions. They see and understand each other. When the military decides to kill the creature in order to vivisect it, Eliza helps it (or him) escape with the help of her friend and neighbour, a co-worker, and a scientist working in the facility who is actually a Russian agent. The creature stays with her for some time, and a love relationship develops between them. When the autumn rains have come she and her neighbour bring the creature to water that connects with the ocean, but Colonel Strickland has tracked them down and shoots the creature, then Eliza. The creature self-heals, kills Strickland, takes Eliza into his arms, and jumps into the water, where her scars become gills.

Wonder figures prominently in this film: Eliza views the creature in wonder, is open, curious, respectful and caring. Being 'strange', 'other', herself, she is interested in this 'alien'. Her wonder grows into love. The Russian scientist's wonder is more inquisitive, but also includes an appreciation of the beauty of the creature and inspires a desire to protect it. 'Otherness' (in the sense of differing from the norm set by the dominant social category: able-bodied white men) plays a central role in the film: being unable to speak (and thus 'disabled'), being a woman, being black, being old, being non-human. The opposite of wonder – cynical indifference and closed-mindedness – is embodied by the creature's captor, Colonel Strickland, and an army general. Strickland seems incapable of wonder, and in particular of the kind of wonder that involves seeing something or someone as remarkable, not in view of its unusual characteristics of achievements, but as such, as being-what-and-how-it-is. He suffers from what we might call a moral failing, a blindness – a metaphor that is apt, but in this context at the same time somewhat unfortunate – to the extraordinary that leads him to devalue everything to a status of ordinariness and indifference.

This example can help us to get a better understanding of wonder's relation to 'otherness', for on closer inspection this is far from simple. Any experience of wonder (whether inquisitive or contemplative) involves, or is a response to, 'otherness' in the sense that what one wonders at or about is experienced as in some way strange, mysterious, puzzling, beyond one's understanding. But this is not yet what Hepburn meant when he said that wonder is other-*acknowledging*, for this has to do, firstly, with not being 'shut up in self-concern or quasi-solipsistic withdrawal', and secondly, with the fact that wonder 'does not see its objects possessively: they remain "other" and un-mastered'.[60] So there is a twofold moral quality to such wonder: it is non-egocentric, as one's attention is directed at the other; and it 'lets the other be', it refrains from the violence involved in objectification, in reducing the other to one's conception of the other in order to add it, her, or him to one's stock of knowledge or gain some form of power over the other.

60 Hepburn, 'Wonder', 14 and 4.

Now, imagine a European primary school classroom filled with 'white' children in a time and place where 'black' people are merely heard of, and where, at the start of a new school year, a new boy sits amongst them. His skin is deep dark brown, for his family immigrated from the Congo. His classmates stare (gape) at him in wonder – a wonder at his 'otherness'. But this wonder most likely does not have the moral quality that Hepburn was after, for this is (or is likely to be), quite literally, a *superficial* kind of wonder, caused, we might say, by a flawed sense of normality. This kind of wonder may well go hand in hand with 'Othering', a reductive and exclusionary viewing and categorizing of other persons as different from and (therefore) inferior to the norm(al), i.e. oneself and one's social group. The other is seen as odd, deviant, a marginal phenomenon.[61] For Colonel Strickland in *The shape of water* the creature is other in this sense, it is totally other in a way that places it outside of the scope of moral consideration. For Eliza and the Russian scientist, on the other hand, the creature is both other *and* same, and thus they are able to establish a *relationship* with the creature. They can see through the otherness towards the sameness, and they can see the sameness without losing sight of the creature's otherness.[62] The recognition of otherness here has its basis in, on the one hand, the ultimate mystery of the being (the existence, the that-ness which is at the same time a thus-ness) of any 'being', and on the other hand, the infinite complexity of any particular being, which brings with it the ineliminable incompleteness and distortiveness of all knowledge about, understanding of, and perspectives on that being.

The children's wonder at the dark-skinned boy is likely to involve 'Othering'; but it is worth noting that this need not be the case. We can also imagine that their confrontation with a dark-skinned human being suddenly 'brought

[61] Iris Marion Young pointed out similar dangers in response to Luce Irigaray's account of wonder: 'This concept of wonder is dangerous. It would not be difficult to use it to imagine the other person as exotic. (…) Or wonder can become a kind of prurient curiosity. (…) Both stances convert the openness of wonder into a dominative desire to know and master the other person'. Iris Marion Young, 'Asymmetrical Reciprocity: On Moral Respect, Wonder, and Enlarged Thought', in *Intersecting Voices: Dilemmas of Gender, Political Philosophy, and Policy* (Princeton: Princeton University Press, 1997), 56, cited in La Caze, 'Encounter', 10.

[62] In her inaugural lecture at her instalment as Professor of Education at the University for Humanistic Studies in Utrecht (28 May 2019) Doret de Ruyter proposed that moral citizenship education should entail that students learn to view each other with a 'double gaze', seeing each other as both (simply) a human being and a unique person at the same time. Eliza and the Russian scientist view the creature with a double gaze that is quite similar; only where De Ruyter speaks of a 'unique person' in the sense of a human being with a unique constellation of traits, talents, interests, identities or identity aspects, and so on, the otherness that Eliza and the scientist see and respect has more to do with a recognition that they cannot claim to know the creature, so with the non-possessiveness of which Hepburn speaks. See Doret J. de Ruyter, *De Betekenis van Educatie: De Bijdrage aan Menselijk Floreren in een Diverse Samenleving* (Utrecht: Universiteit voor Humanistiek, 2019).

to [their] attention the very fact of encounter', something that happens more easily, as Jeff Malpas notes, when we encounter something beautiful, sublime, or otherwise extraordinary – these things 'call attention, most immediately and most directly, to their own appearing, to the fact of their being encountered'.[63] In that case, the appearance of a dark-skinned human being becomes an occasion for wonder at human being, at being as such as something we are inexplicably part of and witnesses to.

Extending the example we can imagine that the children have been brought up with certain prejudices about 'coloured people' or 'foreigners', and that they experience wonder when they see that actually, this boy is not really different from them at all. In a way this is what one would hope to occur in such a situation. Yet this wonder also does not feel right (imagine being at the 'receiving' end of such wonder); *ideally*, seeing that other people are actually also just people *should not* arouse wonder in anyone. Such wonder at sameness can only occur on the basis of an initial, mistaken, assumption of otherness – an assumption that presumably had not been (sufficiently) exposed to critical reflection. This raises the problem of 'foolish wonder', defined by Hepburn as 'wonder that is purely a function of our ignorance'.[64] Presumably, Hepburn intended 'foolish wonder' to cover cases where a person's wonder attaches purely to the inexplicability of something, and where our ignorance is to blame for this inexplicability, since there is a perfectly satisfactory explanation for the phenomenon in question. We might also call this 'misplaced wonder', wonder at or about something that is in no way worthy of wonder, or – to be more precise – wonder that is 'wrongly motivated', in the sense that it is aroused by something for the wrong reason. (Anything can be said to be 'wondrous' because of the fact that and how it exists, but it may arouse wonder not for this, but for a 'foolish' reason.) It is hard to say how often 'foolish wonder' occurs, but it seems plausible that it does sometimes occur. 'Ignorance' plays a large role in children's wonder, and especially of course in inquisitive wonder; but as I noted in Chapter 1, inquisitive wonder may be interested in pushing back the mystery experienced in wonder-encounters, but it is not entirely insensitive to mystery – it is also in that respect still clearly different from (what we usually express in terms of) curiosity.

[63] Malpas, 'Beginning in Wonder'.

[64] Hepburn, 'Wonder', 2.

Wonder at sameness that stems from a mistaken assumption of otherness can be described as 'foolish wonder', and therefore as not *intrinsically* valuable, but that does not make it *educationally* useless.[65] It may, especially with the right guidance, lead to wonder about one's own wonder; it may lead someone to ask: 'Why am I surprised, why does it amaze me that these people are essentially like me?' And this can plant the seeds of a deepened, more refined, conception of otherness that is always an appropriate 'object' of wonder, and in that way prove a fertile ground for moral education.

The Potential Role of Wonder in Moral Education

Does Wonder Reveal Value?

Vasalou notes that our wonder often needs 'to be invited through another's bid to guide our gaze', and that this fact may remind us of something 'more basic': 'our profound dependence on others to educate our attention and to orient it to what is worthy of remark'.[66] Wonder implies attention to something 'worthy of remark', and as such educators may deliberately try to evoke wonder, and to sustain and cultivate children's sense of wonder, in order to direct their attention to what is (deemed) important and valuable.

An important question here, a crucial one in fact with respect to wonder's potential role in moral education – and one that Vasalou takes head-on – is a specific version of the question addressed in Chapter 2, namely whether wonder actually *tells us something* about its object, whether it *reveals value*. Tobia is quite clear in his answer to this question: '[the concept of] wonder requires its object to *seem* valuable, but whether the object is *in fact* valuable remains an open question. Wonder enraptures us with objects that might be of true *or* merely illusory value'.[67] In Chapter 2 I broached this issue in the form of the more general question whether wonder is (sometimes) an *appropriate*, fitting, even *required* response to the world – a world that would then (in some respect) *be* 'wonderful' and 'demand' to be perceived as such. Hepburn's reply was a bit more cautious than Tobia's, but he still concluded that

[65] This does not mean, to be sure, that any wonder-charged realization of sameness (of human beings) is an instance of what Hepburn called 'foolish wonder'; for quite often such wonder is not born of ignorance but of a shift in perspective much like the shift, in Buber's terms, from an I–it mode of perception to an I-Thou relation.

[66] Vasalou, *Wonder*, 104.

[67] Tobia, 'Wonder and Value', 960.

> [N]o transcendental argument seems feasible to show that wonder is rationally demanded towards the world; and on the other hand not even the dysteleological elements seem to rule it out as inept. But I see no way of decisively excluding a wide range of alternative responses to the basic cosmic situation in relation to man: sardonic or ironical or depressive (…). 'Nausea' and dread are others.[68]

Contemplating the mystery of (our) existence in the vastness of time and space may induce nausea or dread as soon as wonder, and with no obviously inferior 'justification', from a strictly rational point of view, so Hepburn suggests. Vasalou, unsatisfied with this result, seeks 'a deeper normative muscle (…) that we can feel moving', a justification of wonder, too, that is grounded in its object rather than just forward-looking to the mode of living it makes possible. (Which is not to say that such a forward-looking justification is to be scoffed at, of course; if wonder enables a richer, more fulfilling and more virtuous life – if wonder is 'life-enhancing', as Hepburn put it –, that is surely a good reason to promote it.[69]) She finds it in wonder's other-acknowledging nature, its non-exploitative stance, the recognition that the world does not exist for us, 'but precedes and outlives us and exists in its separate being, which demands to be honored as such'. This recognition leads to a sense of indebtedness, and to piety and reverence.[70]

I am sorely tempted to accept this reply, but I think it is a temptation that should be resisted. For what Vasalou says here cannot *show* wonder to be a fitting or required response to the world; rather, it *requires* a wondering gaze to see the world this way, or if not yet a wondering gaze than at least a particular moral outlook that in turn demands justification – and at some point the justifications will inevitably run out and all that will be left to us is to say: 'Here, look! Listen!' In the end, wonder cannot be justified – to those who do not yet wonder, or do not wonder in the same way, at the same things – without circularity or question-begging.

Cultivating a Morally Educational Kind of Wonder

The important point to take away from the above with regard to moral education is that wonder *in general*, and *by itself*, cannot be seen as a 'morally educational' experience. We need to acknowledge that wonder requires a narrative context, a further cognitive and emotional context, if it is to fulfil its

[68] Hepburn, 'Wonder', 13–14.
[69] Ibid., 14.
[70] Vasalou, *Wonder*, 203, 206, 207.

moral (educational) potential, the quality of which depends on that context. It is not enough to stimulate any kind of wonder. Rather, if we wish to give wonder a place in moral education (and I think we should), we should stimulate *a particular kind of wonder*, a wonder that leans towards the affirmation of the intrinsic value of the other, and that is supported by and embedded in a coherent and consistent moral outlook on the world. It is inconsistent, for instance, to encourage children to explore all the natural and cultural wonders of the world for themselves, to go and see them with their own eyes, wherever they are, in an effort to make them want to preserve and protect those wonders; for such behaviour – flying from one side of the globe to the other and back – is simply not sustainable. The challenge is to see the wonderful in the familiar. This is not to say that it is *easy* to experience wonder at the strange; seeing the Grand Canyon for the first time may simply be overwhelming, enormously impressive, so much so that there is no room for wonder. But familiarity is the greater obstacle to wonder, which is always more easily aroused by the new and the strange.

A related but different point is that we should try to cultivate an *enduring* sense of wonder, rather than a 'thrill-seeking' wonder; the latter is much more likely to become an end in itself. If wonder is to influence our moral dispositions it needs to become dispositional in itself, and not just in the sense that one is disposed to experience wonder on specific, rare occasions, but in the sense that it becomes woven in the texture of one's awareness of the world – not as a full-blown continuous presence, but as a permanent tone in the background, always ready to come to the fore. We should try, in words that emphasize the 'objective' side of the encounter more, to cultivate children's *sense of wonder*, an antenna for, a sensitivity to, the wonder to be experienced if only we are attentive enough to the world that we are part of.

With regard to interpersonal morality, we may try to stimulate experiences of deep wonder that, if not yet moral in themselves, lean towards the moral: with wonder at the otherness of another person – an otherness that belongs to us all, and that means that we are never fully 'known' by anyone, including ourselves –, and at the mystery of her existence – an individual, fragile, finite creature allotted a brief window of existence in eternity – the sense of 'value', of 'preciousness' is just around the corner, or perhaps already in background, though not yet in focal awareness. This requires a cultivation of a specific kind of *attention* that goes to the heart of moral education, and that has also been described as central to spiritual education:

> This awareness is neither that of a detached observer, nor of an emotionally involved participant. It holds together the impartiality for which the 'objective' observer strives and the aspect of encounter which is an element within passionate subjectivity. Attention of this kind embodies and fosters a respect for the other as it is in itself, letting the other be and making oneself available to its disclosure of what it is on its own terms.[71]

But again it is not attention *by itself* which leads to a moral response. Attention not only 'fosters' but also already 'embodies' a respect for the other; i.e. it is *morally informed* attention. This is not to say that value is in the end something we *project* onto the world, but rather to admit that the view that value can be *encountered* and *discovered* in the world – a view I subscribe to – ultimately falls short of a complete rational justification, and yet decisively influences what we think of when we think of 'attending' to someone or something in the way described above.

Wonder can be an element in – and an instrument of – deeply desirable as well as profoundly disturbing kinds of moral education. (I use 'moral' here in the descriptive rather than the normative sense in which I have been using it throughout this chapter and also use it below.) It may not be the most 'natural' ally of many kinds of immorality, and in many cases to cultivate wonder will mean inadvertently or consciously to foster empathy, humility, respect and a suspicion of dogmatism at the same time, but it requires the support of a moral outlook. Seen from the other end, it is doubtful whether a moral education that does *not* include wonder can be regarded as complete. It is difficult to see how a deep sense of the preciousness of another (human) being or an attitude of appreciation and respect for the natural world can be attained and sustained without it. If we think these are important things to foster in moral education, we have a further reason to promote children's sense of wonder.

Wonder and Moral Obligations

Near the beginning of this chapter I compared and contrasted my view of morality and moral education with Michael Hand's. From his point of view moral education can do very well without wonder, since it is not necessary to learn what my moral obligations towards others are and to (learn to) meet

71 Alex Rodger, 'The Spiritual in Values Education', *Journal of Moral Education* 29, no. 4 (2000): 474.

them.[72] This objection obviously rests on his particular – and in my view narrow – understanding of 'morality'. For Hand a standard is moral 'when a person's subscription to it is both universally-enlisting and penalty-endorsing; that is, when she wants and expects everyone to comply with it and supports some kind of punishment for non-compliance'.[73] He notes that the same standard may be moral for one person and non-moral for another, but also argues that there is a robust justification (beyond reasonable disagreement) for certain basic moral standards that virtually everyone recognizes. I take it that these standards (prohibitions against lying, stealing, harming, et cetera) are what he has in mind when he speaks of moral obligations towards others. So his claim is that wonder is not needed to educate children about these obligations. Responding to this claim will help me flesh out my view of the potential role of wonder in moral education somewhat further.

Firstly, moral education, as Hand also argues, involves not just making children adhere to moral standards but also making them understand why they should do so. But as I explained before, our answers to this why-question differ. My view is that any understanding of (the justificatory ground of) moral standards that does not involve a felt appreciation of the inherent value, preciousness, or respect-worthiness of other beings is incomplete, and misses the ultimate point. (Note that such an appreciation need not involve any explicit thoughts in such terms.) Moral behaviour is certainly possible without it, just as a lot of people are able to deal with all kinds of mathematical problems without fully understanding why they are doing what they are doing and without experiencing the self-evidence that comes with an intuitive (and not merely cognitive) understanding of why the operations they perform are valid.[74] A contractarian justification of morality, from this perspective, is like a mathematical trick one could ideally do without; it may be helpful, but it is second-best to an understanding that goes all the way down.[75] Fortunately, unlike in mathematics, in morality such an understanding is not reserved for a lucky few, but in principle attainable by everyone. And one reason why this is so is that there is probably no-one entirely

72 Hand put this challenge to me in his aforementioned response to my article on which this chapter is based, admitting that 'wonder is a vital feature of rich and rounded human lives' (and therefore 'ethically' important) but denying that it is *morally* important; Hand, 'Wonder and Moral Education'.

73 Hand, *A Theory of Moral Education*, 22.

74 This comparison should not be taken to mean that I believe morality and mathematics to be completely comparable from an epistemological perspective; this is an issue on which I have no developed position yet.

75 Note that I take a first-person perspective here; it is another question which type of justification of morality is preferable from a political point of view. Hand's justification is arguably more plausible on that level, at least, than on the individual level and in the educational domain.

incapable of wonder, including the type of wonder in which others appear to us as remarkable, precious creatures. Such wonder need not be the foundation on which children's moral character is (initially) built, but it can become part of that foundation, or add a deeper layer to it, as it changes the quality of their moral outlook. This might not even change a person's moral norms and values, but it would involve a reinterpretation of their meaning and justification. Wonder, as I have noted elsewhere, 'changes the ground under one's feet'.[76]

Secondly, regardless of where one stands with regard to the justification of morality, and even if we accept a narrow interpretation of 'moral obligations', wonder can play an important role in moral education. Experiences of wonder of the kind described above can change and strengthen our moral motivation to meet our obligations. They can also change the *way* in which we meet our obligations – with more grace, perhaps, or with a different sense of obligation (one less opposed to the rest of our motivational make-up). Experiences of wonder may also support the exercise of virtues like care and attentiveness and our resolve to cultivate these; and with increased attentiveness may come increased moral sensitivity, including a feeling for what our obligations are in a particular situation. This is another way in which wonder may help us meet our moral obligations – not by strengthening our motivation to do so, but by helping us find out what our obligations are. Such practical wisdom depends on a sense of wonder in two ways: wonder *at morality* or at particular moral views defamiliarizes the familiar (including conventional morality), opening up space for alternatives (this is its critical moment); and the kind of *other-acknowledging* wonder that involves or may lead to the fundamental ethical experience of the value of other beings not only enables us to break out of constricting moral views, but also leads us to the source that inspires the construction of new moral points of view, from which we may reassess our moral obligations. Arguably, a 'mature' morality includes the ability to wonder *at* morality, even at the institution as such, and even to have doubts about its sense and justification; and a 'moral' wonder at the other may help to pull us back from such doubt before it overwhelms us.

Wonder and Love

In an article on the educational importance of deep wonder I suggested that there is a close affinity between deep or contemplative wonder and love, an

[76] Schinkel, 'Educational Importance of Deep Wonder', 543.

affinity that might be 'explained, in part, by their "erotic" nature, the longing that characterises them; wonder is the beginning of philosophy, the love of wisdom (...). At the very least, wonder implies a longing for meaning; but in many cases especially deep wonder borders on and may lead to a love of the world'.[77] I explored this idea using John Williams' novel *Stoner*, in which the protagonist 'falls in love' with literature, and the example of love between persons in intimate relationships. But my emphasis lay not so much on the romantic aspect of such relationships as on love for the other as 'other', on attentiveness to the mystery of the other – a mystery that is irreducible, that resists complete understanding – and its connection with a love for the world.[78] That there is a world is another irreducible mystery, and although in wonder we often experience an intimation of meaning, that meaning is forever elusive, and this may nourish our love for the world.[79]

If wonder is (in important respects) like love, does this mean that, like love, it entails an 'overvaluation' of things and that wonder is for that reason problematic?[80] I think this is true for falling in love and being in love (romantically) and thus for forms of wonder that resemble this, but not for love and wonder as such. In fact, I would argue that without love and wonder – and therefore most of the time – we undervalue things, because we do not give them the loving attention necessary to do them justice. Most of the time our attention is limited, short-lived, superficial; the sense of wonder is one of the things that makes us stop and look, listen, feel sometimes, and thereby counters our ordinary 'ignorance' and 'forgetfulness'.

In ethics words like 'love' and 'wonder' (but also 'respect', depending on how this is used) have an advantage over terms like 'human dignity' and 'human rights' that makes them important complements to such terms: they do not express too much confidence in knowing what it is about others that makes them 'valuable', worth protecting or saving from harm.[81] Terms like 'intrinsic value', 'inherent value' or 'preciousness' have the advantage of being general value terms that do not aim to pinpoint the 'source' of value, but also the disadvantage,

[77] Ibid., 549.

[78] At the aforementioned conference (see footnote 5) Genevieve Lloyd also suggested that wonder at the other (in the sense in which I have spoken of this in this chapter) might be comparable to love – but not romantic love, which would be more like being wonder-struck by another. I agree that the kind of wonder at the other worth cultivating has close affinities with *agapeic* love rather than romantic love, but I would not want to lose sight of the touch of longing implicit in wonder.

[79] See Carson, *The Edge of the Sea*, 7, cited in Moore, 'The Truth of the Barnacles', 271.

[80] This question was put to me by Laura D'Olimpio at the conference mentioned in footnote 5.

[81] This paragraph was prompted by a comment by Sophia Vasalou at the same conference.

compared to, for instance, 'dignity', of being emotionally rather sterile (though preciousness does better than the other two in this regard). 'Wonder' – in the sense of 'moral' wonder – combines the benefits of both, and extends the former benefit by making more explicit that we are faced with a mystery that asks for restraint, caution, and respect.

Conclusion

I hope to have shown in this chapter that wonder has close affinities with moral emotions and attitudes, but that we must be cautious in our thinking about this. Not every kind or instance of wonder leads naturally to desirable moral sentiments. Still, there are good reasons to believe that wonder should play a role in moral education. An other-acknowledging wonder that helps us appreciate the preciousness of other beings can inform our understanding of our own morality and inspire us to live in a morally responsible and responsive way. There are also intimate connections between wonder at and love for the world. At the same time there is a danger in making wonder's role in moral education too dependent on wonder's affinity with love for the world; for not only can a more 'neutral' form of contemplative wonder play an important critical role in moral thinking ('wonder at morality'), we should also be aware that the world is in many ways not a 'lovely' or loveable place – and for some people less than others. In some cases to ask a child to develop a 'love for the world' may be to ask too much; it may be theoretically possible, but psychologically impossible. This inequality that characterizes – even structures – the human world is one reason to ask whether wonder has a role to play in *political* education as well; this is the topic of the next chapter.

5

Wonder and Political Education

Politics and the political are not the same thing. With many people in the UK, I presume, the term 'politics' will immediately evoke 'London' and 'Brussels' as the places *par excellence* where politics happens. In my own country, the Netherlands, people will think of The Hague (and perhaps also Brussels). But most people will readily acknowledge that politics goes on in other places and on both smaller and larger scales as well: the office, the football club, the United Nations – wherever people meet to order some aspect of human living together. Yet 'the political' as a dimension of the social, of human living together, is not exhaustively defined in terms of some designated spaces where political activity happens. Rather, what makes this activity political is that it is in every instance concerned, in one way or another, with a fundamental aspect of the human condition: the problem of order. Human beings (like other primates) live in groups, and life in these groups requires coordination and the making of decisions that affect and concern all group members.[1] Since human beings are not necessarily of the same mind, and their interests do not coincide or harmonize perfectly, conflicts will need to be regulated, and this occurs at least in part – and in complex societies it is the greater part – through persuasion, power, and authority. Moreover, as political theorist Chantal Mouffe points out, because any existing social order is contingent in the sense that it is not natural or inevitable and could always be otherwise, and therefore 'is predicated on the exclusion of other possibilities', any social order can also be called a 'political' order, 'since it is the expression of a particular structure of power relations'.[2] 'The

[1] For other primates see Frans de Waal, *Chimpanzee Politics: Power and Sex among Apes*, revised ed. (Baltimore: Johns Hopkins University Press, 1998).

[2] Chantal Mouffe, *On the Political* (London and New York: Routledge, 2005), 18.

political' is that aspect of human living together that we tend to express in terms like 'power', 'authority', 'conflict' and 'order', in 'political' language.[3]

Mouffe makes the distinction as follows: 'by "the political" I mean the dimension of antagonism which I take to be constitutive of human societies, while by "politics" I mean the set of practices and institutions through which an order is created, organizing human coexistence in the context of conflictuality provided by the political.'[4] We could also say, with a little less emphasis on conflict alone, that whereas politics is concerned with handling conflicts, coordination problems, and collective decision-making within the context of a particular order that it helps to reproduce, the political concerns the problem of order as such, the constitutive elements and the conditions of (im)possibility of any political order.[5] The value of the distinction between politics and the political lies (among other things) in creating space for political thinking and political activity outside of the conventional framework of political institutions and their ideological and philosophical legitimations. Mouffe argues that liberalism, due to its individualism and rationalism, is constitutively unable to address or even see the political, since it can neither deal with the importance of collective identities nor with the reality of antagonism, of radical decisions unsolvable by reason, as lying at the heart of the political.[6] (In Hannah Arendt's terms, referred to in Chapter 3, the problem would be the failure to recognize *plurality* as the condition of human action, as the *sine qua non* of political life.) Hence the dominance of liberalism comes to expression in the depoliticization of political problems, i.e. their reduction to issues to be solved through consensus, or expert knowledge, or the market. In this connection Sheldon Wolin speaks of the 'inverted totalitarianism' embodied in 'a new but still tentative regime, Superpower', 'an expansive system of powers that accepts no limits other than those it chooses to impose on itself' and that 'blends the political authority of the "democratic" state, *de jure* power, with the powers represented by the complex of modern science-technology and corporate capital.'[7] Whereas earlier forms of totalitarianism (such as Nazi totalitarianism)

[3] Sheldon Wolin, *Politics and Vision: Continuity and Innovation in Western Political Thought*, expanded ed. (Princeton and Oxford: Princeton University Press, 2004), Chapter 1.

[4] Mouffe, *On the Political*, 9. She notes that in philosophical (more specifically, Heideggerian) terms 'politics' might be seen as belonging to the ontic level, 'the political' to the ontological.

[5] The understanding of 'politics' and what counts as 'political' in the ordinary sense of the word naturally changes depending on the historical and political context; Wolin, *Politics and Vision*, 5–7. It is worth noting that the term itself arose only in the thirteenth century, with the rise of the concept of the state; Walter Ullman, *Medieval Political Thought* (Harmondsworth: Penguin Books, 1975), 17.

[6] Mouffe, *On the Political*, 11–12.

[7] Wolin, *Politics and Vision*, xvi.

mobilized citizens, inverted totalitarianism *depoliticizes* them; it promotes not 'a sense of collective power and confidence' but 'a sense of weakness, collective futility that culminates in the erosion of the democratic faith, in political apathy and the privatization of the self'.[8]

While I cannot go into the above analyses in more detail here, let alone defend them against possible criticisms, I take it that the observation they have in common is fundamentally correct, namely that depoliticization is an important characteristic of contemporary political systems in 'liberal democracies'.[9] This situation is mirrored in political education in these same countries. Political education tends to forget the distinction between politics and the political, and this reduces its interest and its potential to promote genuine critical thinking. Political education mostly goes by the name 'civic education' or 'citizenship education', or something similar (possibly precisely because it sounds less 'political'), and its purpose, as Michael Merry writes, is generally conceived as producing 'good citizens', 'ensuring that when children grow up and leave school, and perhaps even before, they are prepared (even if not necessarily inclined) to practise the civic virtues most valued in their respective societies'.[10] Merry argues that although many liberal theorists place great emphasis on the cultivation of critical capacities and autonomous thinking, liberal political educational theory in fact leaves little room for real dissent. He also notes that the empirical evidence on existing rather than idealized citizenship education provides no ground for optimism about schools' potential to produce anything other, on average, than either political disinterest or conformism.[11] Similarly, Jason Brennan sums up decades worth of empirical evidence that 'deliberative democracy', the liberal idea(l) of a democracy in which citizens deliberate with each other in a reasonable, open-minded way to reach a well-informed consensus, and these citizens become better persons in the process, does not exist in practice. In practice, deliberation tends to make people worse in various

[8] Ibid., 591–2.

[9] Depoliticization works in many ways – through naturalizing, essentializing or individualizing discourses that frame social or political issues such as integration and socioeconomic or gender inequality as reducible to individual traits and decisions, cultural characteristics or innate differences. See Willem Schinkel, *Imagined Societies: A Critique of Immigrant Integration in Western Europe* (Cambridge: Cambridge University Press, 2017), 152ff.

[10] Michael Merry, 'Can Schools Teach Citizenship?' *Discourse: Studies in the Cultural Politics of Education* (2018). https://doi.org/10.1080/01596306.2018.1488242.

[11] See also Isolde de Groot and Wiel Veugelers, 'Why We Need to Question the Democratic Engagement of Adolescents in Europe', *Journal of Social Science Education* 14, no. 4 (2015), who observe that very few adolescents develop a 'thick' form of democratic engagement, whereas the majority develop a 'passive' or 'thin' type of engagement.

ways – more extreme, or nihilistic or apathetic – and it often leads to more deeply entrenched conflict rather than consensus.[12]

It is worth noting that such observations are far from new. Close to forty years ago, even in the Cold War era, Tom Brennan, commenting on political education in Britain, observed that 'its effect has been to produce from the bulk of the nation's children a conformist citizenry playing minimal political roles'.[13] Margaret Thatcher was prime minister of the UK at that time, for the Conservative Party. Her famous slogan 'There Is No Alternative' (often abbreviated TINA), by which she expressed her conviction that there was no viable alternative to capitalism and the distribution of goods through free trade and the market economy, is a poignant example of depoliticization in action. Any political education worth the name should foster resistance to such ideas. The purpose of this chapter is to argue that, however modest our expectations about political education must be, wonder can play a role in (genuine) political education – among other things, as an antidote to TINA. The importance of *political*, as distinct from civic, education, has arguably rarely been as great as today. The ecological crisis means that the problem of order has taken on unprecedented dimensions; for the first time since our species spread across the globe we are faced with the very real possibility of the worldwide break-down, in the near future, of human 'civilization' (not to mention the sixth major extinction of non-human life).[14] Scientific knowledge and understanding of the problem – of the causes of our ecological predicament – are not lacking, but rational argument, however well informed, has so far proven powerless to change anything, because reason alone does not move anyone or anything. Not the balance of argument is decisive (as deliberative democrats would have it), but the balance of caring. What we need, therefore, as Kingsnorth writes, are new stories, because stories have the power to change what we care about:

> If we are indeed teetering on the edge of a massive change in how we live, in how human society itself is constructed, and in how we relate to the rest of the world, then we were led to this point by the stories we have told ourselves – above all, by the story of civilization. (…) Words and images can change minds, hearts, even

[12] Jason Brennan, *Against Democracy* (Princeton and Oxford: Princeton University Press, 2017), Chapter 3.

[13] Tom Brennan, *Political Education and Democracy* (Cambridge and New York: Cambridge University Press, 1981), 5.

[14] See David Wallace-Wells, *The Uninhabitable Earth: A Story of the Future* (n.p.: Penguin Books, 2019) and Elizabeth Kolbert, *The Sixth Extinction: An Unnatural History* (London: Bloomsbury, 2015).

> the course of history. (…) It is time to pick up the threads and make the stories new, as they must always be made new, starting from where we are.[15]

We need to imagine and to feel – we need imaginative political education – and therefore wonder is a good place to start.[16]

And for that same reason this is a somewhat unusual chapter: an essay in two parts, or a chapter in two essays, two approaches to the same end. The first offers a story about the importance of wonder in political education, a story that certainly includes argument but does not prioritize it over (hopefully) more evocative narrative and imagery.[17] The second takes a more conventional form in giving more prominence to argument – but it inevitably also remains a story.

Essay 1

As I write this I am on my way back from England to the Netherlands.

I will cross three borders.

I am allowed to do so because I carry a certain object, a hybrid of paper and plastic – that is, of tree and oil, of recent and ancient flora – that identifies me as a Dutch citizen, a member of a nation state recognized by other nation states.

The customs officers did not recognize me, of course (they don't know me), yet they recognized me, or rather the polity I belong to.

[15] Kingsnorth, *Confessions of a Recovering Environmentalist*, 270, 272 See also Tokarczuk, 'The Tender Narrator', 20: 'Could there be a story that would go beyond the uncommunicative prison of one's own self, revealing a greater range of reality and showing the mutual connections? That would be able to keep its distance from the well-trodden, obvious and unoriginal center point of commonly shared opinions, and manage to look at things *ex*-centrically, away from the center?' Tokarczuk seems to be asking for a story written in the mode of wonder here.

[16] 'Imaginative Education' (IE) is a term for an approach to teaching and learning developed by Kieran Egan, Gillian Judson, and others, that assigns a central role to engaging students' imaginations, and thereby to consideration of the possible rather than (just) the actual, to what might be instead of only what is actually the case. It is because of this latter feature that I use the term here, but it is worth noting that IE encompasses much more; among others a commitment to education that is meaningful to the students and, in connection with this, the effort to teach in ways that are sensitive to ways in which children at different stages in their cognitive development understand the world. See https://ierg.ca/about-us/what-is-imaginative-education/; Egan, *Imagination*; Kieran Egan and Gillian Judson, *Imagination and the Engaged Learner: Cognitive Tools for the Classroom* (New York: Teachers' College Press, 2016); Egan, Cant, and Judson, *Wonder-full Education*. One application of IE is in 'imaginative ecological education'; see Gillian Judson, *Imaginative Ecological Education* (PhD diss., Simon Fraser University, 2008), Gillian Judson, *Engaging Imagination in Ecological Education: Practical Strategies for Teaching* (Vancouver: Pacific Educational press, 2015), and Gillian Judson, *A Walking Curriculum: Walking, Wonder, & Sense of Place (K-12)* (n.p.: 2018).

[17] This essay was also presented at the LEARN! Conference held at Vrije Universiteit, Amsterdam, the Netherlands, on 17 September 2019.

My passport doesn't mention this, but I am a *Homo sapiens*–Neanderthal hybrid. My hybrid ancestors have roamed the part of the earth we now call Europe for 40,000 years without encountering any borders – without even having the *concept* of borders. My *Homo sapiens* ancestors roamed even more widely, for 200,000 years; and Neanderthals moved freely over the surface of the earth for at least 200 millennia more.

Borders of a kind weren't invented until a mere 10 millennia ago, by the first sedentary people (who slowly but surely replaced our mobile *Homo sapiens*–Neanderthal ancestors); and borders that envelop the earth like an irregular spider's web, forbidding human beings from walking their planet of birth unhindered, have existed for just a few centuries. Sedentary people distrust their mobile kin. Those who sit on their comfortable backsides now routinely decide whether or not they are willing to make an exception for a particular mobile human being, whether they have a special category for this mobile person: refugee prepared not to remain seated, or useful migrant worker willing to sit down.

Borders are real, but not as real as we think. It is strange to think that the earth's surface was once just what it was – presenting natural obstacles, perhaps, but no artificial ones. It makes one wonder.

Wonder tends to be too readily associated with a childlike, if not childish, attitude; with learning and wanting to learn, but implicitly also with still *having* to learn; with naivety and a rose-tinted view of the world. But this view ignores other types of wonder, that are not simply a product of unfamiliarity, of the novelty of the world to the person taking it in.

Moreover, in the same stroke it turns wonder into something naive, innocent, harmless; and it denies the seriousness of wonder and the very real relation it has to the world.[18]

It ignores also the crucial role wonder has – or can and ideally should have – in adults' (not least educators') lives.

With my opening example I attempted to evoke – or at least sensitize you to – a type of wonder that has a much less immediate connection with education than children's inquisitive wonder. (Which is not to say that children's wonder is always of the inquisitive type.) This other type of wonder may have no connection with the novelty of the object of attention at all; just as often it is something so familiar that we barely notice it and rarely if ever think about

[18] This point is also stressed by Verhoeven, *Inleiding tot de Verwondering*, 32.

it. But then, suddenly, and often for no discernible reason, this familiar thing strikes us as utterly strange, as mysterious even.

Perhaps we feel the warmth of the sun on our skin and suddenly realize that this pleasant warmth derives from a sun – not just 'the sun', but *a* sun, a particular type of object in the galaxy, the centre of our solar system, a seething ball of burning gas, on average ca. 150 million kilometres away from our planet, from you. Or perhaps we zoom in on our skin, magnifying our cells so much that we can perceive the effect of the sun's radiation on the microorganisms that are at home there. We are not – or not just – individuals; we are ecosystems. How can it be that *you* are implicated in things on these scales? That one way in which the organization of the universe manifests itself is as your sensuous pleasure? That you are an environment within in environment?

These are not ordinary questions, of course, not questions that need answering. We know the answer, or think we do, or at any rate assume that the question lies firmly within the realm of answerable questions, in which case it doesn't even matter if we know the answer or not – we are not wondering *about* this connection between ourselves and the sun, we are wondering *at* it. Our questions merely *look like* 'normal', (in principle) answerable, questions, simply because that is the form puzzlement tends to take.

Wonder *at*, deep wonder, or contemplative wonder, is a response to mystery; and it foregrounds, makes us acutely aware of, the mysteriousness of things, which persists despite knowledge, despite all the answers we can think of. As Ronald Hepburn writes, there are various forms of wonder that are immune to dissolution by causal explanation: 'the persistence of the "fragile," living beings (…), on the thin habitable zone of the earth's surface, surrounded by enormous airless spaces', for instance, may evoke wonder; and while this may partly be dissolved by causal explanations that reduce the 'surprise-element' of wonder, what remains is 'the contrast for perception and imagination between living beings and their cosmic environment, between their sensitivity, sentience, internal complexity, vulnerability and the indifferent and mindless regions around them. This contrast, and the wonder it can evoke, survive the acceptance of a causal account'.[19] Causal explanations ultimately run up against the totality, against the mystery of being as such, why there is something rather than nothing. And wonder at any particular thing – a snowflake, DNA, the 'miracle of birth' – receives its charges from the wonder appropriate to the whole. When

[19] Hepburn, 'Wonder', 7–8.

we perceive them, not analytically, but as wholes, they exceed our senses and our comprehension. The being of any particular being can never be grasped in its fullness. Deep wonder therefore renders us speechless; we have run up against the limits of understanding, the limits of what we can say. William James said that children are born into a state of 'aboriginal sensible muchness'; in wonder we do not exactly return to such a state, but experience something similar, though with much more cognitive content: the excessiveness of the world, the fact that it spills over any categorization and conceptualization.[20]

A pragmatic question may arise: what use is such an attitude, or such a mode of consciousness, in our lives and (therefore) in education, oriented as it is to the irreducible mystery of existence, and with its tendency to view everyday life from a cosmic or a microscopic – but at any rate a *remote* – perspective? A form of awareness that silences us and dissolves all opinions, all points of view? What use is it, more specifically, in *political* education?

Isn't wonder – this type of wonder – rather an apolitical, or even antipolitical, sentiment or attitude? Isn't it the state of mind that one gets lost in, that dreamers hide in to escape from the world? That was Hannah Arendt's criticism of Heidegger; as Mary-Jane Rubenstein notes, Arendt attributes Heidegger's decision in 1933 to accept the rectorship of the Nazified University of Freiburg (which implied an endorsement of National Socialism) to 'an excess of wonder'. According to Arendt the problem lay with Heidegger's 'taking up and accepting this faculty of wonder as [his] abode'.[21] Arendt's concern was that wonder could make one withdraw from the world and thereby from any sense of obligation towards the world. It is an understandable concern, but like Rubenstein I believe wonder nevertheless has significant political potential.

Deep wonder is a mode of consciousness in which we are attuned to the world in a way that differs markedly from our ordinary awareness of the world: our attention is arrested by something that eludes our grasp and yet seems important. The 'object' of attention is central in our experience, we forget about ourselves and any relation the object might have to our desires or intentions. Wonder is a receptive mode of consciousness, rather than an actively seeking or grasping one, it is open to the world – and open also in the sense that the attitude to take towards the object of wonder is as yet not (wholly) decided; hence puzzlement is an important part of the subjective form of wonder. In wonder we (first)

[20] James, *Some Problems of Philosophy*, 50, cited in Horowitz, *On Looking*, 26.

[21] Hannah Arendt, 'Martin Heidegger at Eighty', in *Heidegger and Modern Philosophy*, ed. Michael Murray (New Haven: Yale University Press, 1978), 299, cited in Rubenstein, *Strange Wonder*, 20.

experience a breakdown of meaning – the everyday meaning of things falls away, and our frameworks of interpretation give out – but often also a hint of a deeper or more encompassing meaning, which wonder may inspire us to seek.

This brief phenomenological description of wonder contains a number of features that argue against the idea of wonder's supposedly a- or antipolitical nature. Firstly, wonder is characterized by an essential *openness* towards the world, and the experience of wonder can revive or help sustain our interest in the world. It is world-oriented and world-affirming.

Secondly, wonder is anti-dogmatic and anti-conformist. As Mario Di Paolontonio argued (interestingly also with Arendt), wonder guards against 'thoughtlessness', against uncritical conformism.[22]

Thirdly, due to the breakdown of meaning we experience in wonder, wonder makes us acutely aware of the abnormality of the normal. In Jeremy Bendik-Keymer's words it 'throws a margin of doubt around the normal'.[23] As adults we sometimes wonder at something and then simply get on with our day and immerse ourselves in the normal order of things. To take wonder seriously means to refuse to 'simply' get on with our day. There is nothing normal, nothing ordinary about ordinary life, and to pretend otherwise is an act of violence against reality – and against very real others. Doubt about the normal and awareness of the contingency of the current order are crucial to a healthy political sphere.

Fourthly, and relatedly, wonder is a phenomenon of the limit – we have reached the limits of understanding, and the limits of what we can say – but this limit is also a threshold: beyond it lies the world, with its 'muchness', its excessiveness, and this presents itself as a space of possibility. The world is always more, always other than what we make of it. And this means that *our* world can always be other than it is. Wonder is the denial of Margaret Thatcher's TINA ('there is no alternative'), because it shows us that there are *always* alternatives, and stimulates our political imagination.

Fifthly, wonder is other-acknowledging, and in its more affirmative, morally toned, form, this means that it is non-egocentric and non-reductionist: to perceive another person or another being with wonder means not to objectify it, but to be appreciative of its unique nature and acutely aware of one's inability to grasp the other entirely. This type of wonder at otherness is an important part of the moral sensibility necessary for a maximally respectful and caring

[22] Di Paolantonio, 'Wonder'.
[23] Bendik-Keymer, 'The Reasonableness of Wonder', 344.

politics. Jeremy Bendik-Keymer (interpreting and developing work by Martha Nussbaum) asked a version of the pragmatic question I asked just now: what use is biocentric wonder – wonder at life in all its forms – in the human political sphere? His answer is that biocentric wonder, because it is open to considering other kinds of lives, is helpful to considering the lives of others. Moreover, biocentric wonder that sees our form of striving as one type among many others means that we abstract from particular conceptions of striving (for a good life), and it puts us in a position to consider what is good for all, and in a better position to reason with others.

So wonder – even and perhaps especially deep or contemplative wonder – has political importance. If so, then it stands to reason that it is important for political *education*, too. I think that is indeed the case. As argued in Chapter 3, there are strong intrinsic connections between wonder and education; if anything, education should open up the world to children (and adults), and wonder is probably the purest form of openness to the world that we can experience.

More practically, political education – usually (and revealingly) called 'civic education' or 'citizenship education' – still tends to be mostly political *socialization*, making children acquainted with the ways of our political world and adjusting them to it. But *education*, if it wants to be worthy of the name, is inversely related to the extent to which we take things for granted or accept them on authority. Thus it requires wonder, among other things, to defamiliarize the familiar. Common political education, however, does nothing to diminish the apparent 'naturalness' of things; insofar as it aims at understanding of why the current order is the way it is, it does so in a way that shores up its inevitability.

Political *education* would begin by making the phenomena of political order and of politics as such objects of wonder, and one way to do so could be by highlighting their recent (in evolutionary terms) appearance on the face of the earth.

I will conclude with another example to show the value of taking wonder's wide perspective – an example which at the same time suggests there's an important role for parents here, not just schools. One of today's major concerns is, or should be, climate change. That anthropogenic climate change is going on is something that has been known for at least half a century (and some realized it much sooner than that), but both collective and individual action have been slow. This is in part because of the immensity of the problem, the pure scale at which we are required to think. We cannot perceive climate change directly, we can only experience weather, here and now, and to supplement this we have some memory (the reliability of which is questionable) of weather patterns in our past. Furthermore, so long as we remain within our everyday frame of mind our imagination is highly taxed when we ask it to project an image of what our planet might look like a hundred or a thousand, let alone a hundred thousand years from now.

Wonder – triggered by the knowledge of carrying a few percent of Neanderthal DNA, for instance – is a mode of consciousness that is supremely helpful in this regard. It helps us take the perspective of the deep history of the earth and life on earth, a perspective from which it is much easier to ask – that even *prompts* us to ask: what strange creatures are we? *And what on earth are we doing?*

Essay 2

Political education opens up the world in its political aspect. It does not just inform children about 'politics', what political parties there are in their country and which ideas (and/or interests) these represent, the way the political system of their country is organized, and what international political institutions there are. Adding a dispositional component – the aim that students develop an interest in politics in combination with certain attitudes and civic virtues – still does not make for political education in the sense I am interested in. The problem is that both are compatible with an 'opening up' of the world in the barest, most minimal sense, where the experience of a full awareness of some aspect of the world never occurs, where the experienced world is in no way transformed, where one's outlook on the world remains essentially the same. The 'political education' that actually occurs in schools today is in most cases just an expansion of the sphere of normality and familiarity, the sphere in which one thoughtlessly goes about one's business. If we value education – in the sense discussed in Chapter 3 – and if we are not content with TINA as a justification of the political course taken by governments, we should value political education as a form of education that does not merely expand into new territory, but changes the ground under students' feet, that changes the way they look at their world, that makes them 'see' their world as if for the first time – a form of education in which there is an important role for wonder.

Clearly, political education in this sense – like education as understood in this book – is an ideal and in practice a rare thing. Yet it is a more realistic ideal than that of deliberative democracy, because, firstly, unlike perfect deliberation wonder is a real phenomenon and education – the breakthrough of understanding and awareness, the (sudden or gradual) transformation of outlook – actually happens, however rare it may be and however incomplete it always is. And secondly, in making the case for the importance of wonder in political education I acknowledge the importance of stories and of emotion in the political sphere; any political ideal that ignores or downplays this (as the ideal of deliberative democracy does) is too far removed from reality to be meaningful. In fact, political education is unthinkable without the education of moral–political emotions such as indignation and anger, respect, and compassion. Justice and injustice, conflict and its resolution, freedom and solidarity, and any other major political issues cannot be fully understood without the ability to experience the emotions appropriate to them. Also, desire, passion, and emotional identification are simply ineliminable aspects of human living together, so any realistic political theory and conception of political education will have to take these into account.[24]

Is Wonder Antipolitical?

Perhaps you will think: 'Emotions, sure – but wonder? Isn't wonder a rather apolitical, or even antipolitical, sentiment or state of mind?' It is a fair question, and the intuition may explain why so far very little has been written about the political (educational) importance of wonder. The 'risk' that wonder moves a person to withdraw from *politics*, at least, is real. I can testify on the basis of my own experience that wonder can offer relief from a certain fatigue with (hearing about, thinking about) politics; though at the same time I sometimes find myself almost forced out of direct engagement with political matters and into a more distant point of view that often gives rise to wonder – not just to find a temporary reprieve from politics but, it seems to me, because there is something to be gained from this, something with political importance. Still, the shift of perspective that occurs in wonder and the 'revaluation' this often brings with it – a revaluation that may puncture an inflated sense of self-importance or of the importance of petty concerns – may in the same move belittle the importance of almost any problem in everyday life, including political concerns, and for that reason wonder can offer relief from politics, a space to escape to.

The concern that wonder is (or can be) not just apolitical but even antipolitical was explicitly expressed by Hannah Arendt, who criticized Martin Heidegger for his decision, in 1933, to accept the rectorship of the Nazified

[24] See Michael Walzer, 'Passion and Politics', *Philosophy & Social Criticism* 28, no. 6 (2002); and Mouffe, *On the Political*, 28.

University of Freiburg. By this decision he implicitly endorsed National Socialism, and therefore closed his eyes to the political reality in Germany at that time. Arendt attributed Heidegger's decision to his 'taking up and accepting this faculty of wonder as [his] abode'.[25] Arendt felt that wonder offered an escape from reality and thus from any sense of political obligation; that it could render one vulnerable to being swept away unthinkingly by charismatic leaders or political movements; that it could alienate philosophers from the world around them; and that it would render them incapable of forming opinions or making decisions.[26] This danger applies in particular to wonder as I speak of it here – to deep or contemplative wonder – since, as Di Paolantonio explains, 'Arendt distinguishes between *thinking* and *pure contemplation*, and considers that the latter can become a way of disregarding the world in front of us, thereby hindering a true, grounded, and thorough way of thinking'.[27] Still, although we must acknowledge this possibility, I will argue that deep wonder has a unique political (educational) importance.

Wonder Is World-oriented and World-interested

Arendt saw this, too. As Di Paolantonio explains, there are two strands in Arendt's thinking on wonder. While on the one hand she saw wonder as 'limiting', on the other she recognized that wonder could also be 'enabling' from a political point of view. Wonder is a pathos that gives us pause, which makes us attend to things with care, and in a non-instrumental manner, not even with the aim of conquering ignorance. At a fundamental level the world escapes our conceptual grasp, and in wonder we become aware of this and endure it. Wonder, Di Paolantonio says, 'lights up a world through the *admiration* and *care* that we are able to broach, and through the questions that we share with each other when we wonder about those ungraspable things that give pause between us'. It is based on a 'sensed relation with the world' (and therefore can save us from philosophy's cold abstractions, its 'alienated non-thinking'), grounded in gratitude 'with the always more of the world that arches back towards us, impinging and pushing us to express ourselves to others in speech'.[28] Di Paolantonio here draws attention to the 'admiring wonder' Arendt speaks of in *The Life of the Mind*, a pathos that

[25] Arendt, 'Martin Heidegger at Eighty', 299, cited in Rubenstein, *Strange Wonder*, 20. See also Di Paolantonio, 'Wonder', 216.
[26] Rubenstein, *Strange Wonder*, 21.
[27] Di Paolantonio, 'Wonder', 215.
[28] Ibid., 221.

compels us to speak; we might say that as a form of the sense of importance it urges towards expression (the way a child *must* speak about things that are important in her experience). And because it 'breaks into speech towards others', makes us articulate our experience in words, it 'forges a community of sense'.[29] For Arendt Socrates is the best example of this – a philosopher whose wonder compels him to enter into dialogue with others, and who is motivated by a deep awareness of his not-knowing. Socrates' interest was less in knowledge than in *thinking*, in attending carefully to the world and to one's thoughts about the world in order to put these to the test. Wonder is thus (in this strand of Arendt's thought), Di Paolantonio argues, an antidote against thoughtlessness – against inattentiveness to the world and to the meaning and consequences of one's actions, and of this very inattentiveness itself for others. As such, wonder can help prevent various forms of evil – the evil that emerges from cultivated thoughtlessness.[30] In the educational context, for instance, it can prevent teachers from presuming they *know* their students, in a sense that precludes acknowledgment of the possibility of being surprised by them – by previously unseen aspects of them as persons, or by unsuspected abilities. Keeping a sense of wonder alive helps teachers remain attentive to their students as individuals.

There are a few aspects of Di Paolantonio's (and to some extent Arendt's) argument I find less convincing, but overall I think it succeeds in establishing that wonder *can* be politically and educationally important. To begin with the former, to speak of 'admiring' wonder grounded in gratitude narrows the concept of wonder considerably. It is intuitively plausible that this specific type of wonder – or a wonder that takes this subjective form – has a particular political importance, but less morally charged forms of wonder may still be (and in my view *are*) also politically important. Secondly, although it is conceivable that wonder may compel someone to express herself towards others, it is equally plausible – even for admiring wonder – that this does not happen. Wonder does not necessarily 'isolate us in some fanciful solo flight towards the heavens', but neither does it necessarily or naturally build communities.[31]

Still, it is clear that wonder need not be conceived as drawing us *out* of the world; it can also turn our attention *towards* the world – and away from our taken-for-granted constructions of it, our unthinking thinking. In fact, from a phenomenological perspective this is part of the 'essence' of wonder: that it is

[29] Ibid., 222.
[30] Ibid., 221.
[31] Ibid., 220.

world-oriented. By showing us the ordinary as extraordinary wonder sustains (or revives) our interest in the world. Counterintuitively, perhaps, wonder can therefore be a *grounding* experience; we were lost in ourselves, lost in thought(lessness), and are drawn back down to the world – 'Look! This is real. Are you sure what it means?'

Wonder Opens Up Space to Consider Alternative Possibilities

In Chapter 1 I distinguished deep or contemplative wonder from inquisitive wonder, the latter being (somewhat) closer to curiosity and characterized by an intense, focused searching for explanations. The 'what', 'why', and 'how' questions asked in inquisitive wonder are 'real'; they are (thought of as) in principle answerable questions. In deep wonder we often (silently) ask similar-sounding questions, but we do not expect answers, because we know we are confronted with something that lies beyond understanding. I also observed that deep wonder often renders us speechless, lost for words. This makes it sound very different from Arendt's admiring wonder, but this difference is merely apparent, not real. 'Admiring wonder' is a mode of consciousness characterized by an attunement to mystery, by an attentiveness without purpose, without a desire to know. As such, it is much closer to deep or contemplative wonder than to inquisitive wonder. And though I do not think that wonder *necessarily* breaks out into speech the state of being lost for words is often one from which words flow – most often in the form of poetry or philosophy. It is also not the case that (deep) wonder cannot *lead to* questions and questioning activity; but unlike inquisitive wonder it is not itself caught up in such activity, but constitutes, as Genevieve Lloyd also stresses (with Plato, Aristotle, and Spinoza), a 'pause in thought'.[32] This is a productive pause that can be 'the beginnings of political awareness'.[33] Lloyd explains that Spinoza understood wonder through the concept of *singularity*. Spinoza assigns an important role to the imagination in his account of knowledge; the imagination enables us to hold several things in our mind in order to compare them with each other. Wonder arises when we are confronted with a thing that we cannot connect with anything else, something without comparison, something unprecedented – a singularity. The imagination is brought to a halt, but only temporarily: 'Given that the mind of its nature – its *conatus* – strives to persist in understanding, the blocked pathway becomes

[32] Lloyd, *Reclaiming Wonder*, 41.
[33] Ibid., 18.

an impetus to finding alternative ways forward'.[34] It thus acts as a spur to the imagination, and it can do so in the political realm as well.

For instance, Lloyd discusses the ways in which the issue of mass movements and migrations of 'asylum seekers' and 'refugees' is discursively framed, and the role which the 'reiteration of spurious certainties' plays in debates about this issue (or complex of issues).[35] It is common pub and party talk as well, to say that 'of course we cannot let them all in', or that 'we should only take in *real* refugees' – suggesting that there is a clear-cut distinction between 'real' refugees and people who just pretend to be refugees, but who are actually just 'fortune seekers' (or in more official terms 'economic migrants'). These supposedly self-evident certainties suggest that there are no viable alternatives to current policies, or at any rate they serve to close down discussion about possible alternatives and allow us to close our eyes to the human (but blatantly inhumane) consequences of our policies. They are self-reproducing expressions of cultivated thoughtlessness.

There are at least two ways in which wonder can play a productive role here. One is by making us attentive to the 'considerability' of the people behind the labels 'asylum seekers' and 'refugees'. I will discuss this idea, that Jeremy Bendik-Keymer explores, in the next section. The other involves the notion of contrast. Wonder is often evoked by contrasts – for instance, the contrast mentioned in the previous essay between 'the persistence of the "fragile" living beings (…) on the thin habitable zone of the earth's surface' and the 'enormous airless spaces' that surround them, 'between living beings and their cosmic environment'.[36] A productive contrast in the context of the example of the refugee crisis might be that between the moral values and principles (including human rights) we subscribe to individually and as 'Western' countries and the harsh reality of – over the years – thousands of people drowning in the Mediterranean Sea, in touching distance of a Europe that has closed its borders and its eyes, ears, and hearts to them. The wonder this contrast may give rise to – at human hypocrisy, even at our capacity to absorb the very same cognitive dissonance produced by the contrast – can in turn be productive because it places us at some distance from 'the normal'. It pierces the veil of inevitability that shrouds established policies; it removes the taken-for-grantedness that shores them up. Furthermore, by showing us the 'ordinary' as 'extraordinary' (in this case not in

34 Ibid., 43. For a discussion of the educational implications of Spinoza's thinking on wonder see Lloyd, 'Wonder and Education'.

35 Ibid., 177.

36 Hepburn, 'Wonder', 7.

a positive sense), by defamiliarizing it in this way, it presents it as no more than a contingent possibility, as a state of affairs that could be different. Wonder thus opens up space to consider alternative possibilities.

Wonder's potential to do this can be explained in terms of its double relationship with meaning, the fact that experiences of wonder include both a deconstructive and a constructive moment. On the one hand, we experience a breakdown of meaning – our usual frames of interpretation no longer apply – but on the other hand experiences of wonder often suggest the possibility of a new, more encompassing, or deeper meaning, and it therefore motivates a search for new ways to understand the world. Amelie Rorty points out that handbooks on critical reasoning typically distinguish 'critical' and 'constructive or generative' functions of practical reasoning. She suggests that these are in fact 'two aspects of the same process of hypothetical and counter-factual thinking', and argues that 'imaginative thinking is an essential ingredient within practical reasoning'.[37] I would say that wonder can play a role in both; its critical aspect is not like critical reasoning, but works through defamiliarization – creating *space* for critical reasoning – and in stronger cases through *alienation*, i.e. by creating emotional distance between ourselves and a formerly taken-for-granted view of the world we now perceive as undeserving of that status. Its constructive role lies in motivating the search for alternatives, spurring us on to *imagine* alternatives, and to do both of these things in a way that is informed by an affective connection with a world we wish to do justice to.[38]

Wonder opens up space to consider alternatives in two ways: firstly, by opening up *internal* space – because wonder is an anti-dogmatic stance that, as long as it is endured (but this is a psychological challenge), is incompatible with the fixation of beliefs and meanings. Secondly, by shaking up one's sense of what is possible – that is, by opening up *external* space. Contemplated in a state of wonder, any form of order realized by particular groups of people at a particular point in time will appear as merely one of potentially infinite possibilities. This appearance may be illusory in a sense, because not anything is possible in concrete historical circumstances – but it is a productive illusion, because concrete circumstances always allow for more than one option. If wonder undermines the aura of inevitability that surrounds the status quo, that

[37] Amelie Rorty, 'Educating the Practical Imagination: A Prolegomenon', in *The Oxford Handbook of Philosophy of Education*, ed. Harvey Siegel (Oxford: Oxford University Press, 2018), DOI: 10.1093/oxfordhb/9780195312881.003.0012.

[38] Wolin emphasizes the role of the imagination in political thinking; the imagination is not only necessary in order to construct models of the political world, but also to construct visions of possible future orders; Wolin, *Politics and Vision*, 19–20.

is in principle a good thing; it means that wonder can indeed function as an antidote to TINA. The important work wonder does (or that comes to awareness in wonder) is to show us the present order, the way things are now, as *contingent*, as one way things can be, while they could be (and could have been) different. Living in a relatively stable political country like the Netherlands, for instance, it comes to appear as unchangeable, in a way – as if it has always been this way and will always remain so. But a brief look at history, or at places in the world that are currently in turmoil, places that have not 'solidified' yet, changes that perception and may induce a state of wonder in which 'the normal' is bracketed – both cognitively and affectively – and the present is 'seen' as if for the first time, in full awareness.[39]

Wonder and Considering Others

As noted by a number of authors and explained in Chapters 1 and 4, wonder is 'other-acknowledging'; and at least sometimes this takes the moral form of recognition of an 'other' as a person or being with a life of its own, a bearer of inherent value, a limit to one's will. As an ethical possibility (with obvious political importance) this was discussed by Luce Irigaray, who explored the relation between wonder and non-domination in the relation between the sexes. The emphasis here lay on the impossibility of knowing the other, of taking the other's perspective.[40] In a recent article Jeremy Bendik-Keymer explored an alternative political potential of wonder, one that centres rather on wonder's ability to sensitize us to the perspective, the interiority, even the specific form of life of other persons and beings.[41] Though not opposed to Irigaray's view – Bendik-Keymer does not claim that wonder enables us to (fully) know others – this view emphasizes the positive contribution wonder can offer to our willingness

[39] I thank my wife, Eva Moraal, for this example. Shortly after we had both read a book about lost, forgotten, feral and other places in the world – Alastair Bonnett, *Off the Map: Lost Spaces, Invisible Cities, Forgotten Islands, Feral Places, and What They Tell Us about the World* (London: Aurum Press, 2015) – we visited an exhibition about the Eighty Years' War (or the Dutch War of Independence against Spain, 1568–1648), which evoked in her a sense of the fluid state that 'The Netherlands' were once in, much like many places in the world today – a fluidity that is of course not gone at all, only less visible at the moment.

[40] See Luce Irigaray, *An Ethics of Sexual Difference*, trans. Carolyn Burke and Gillian C. Gill (Ithaca: Cornell University Press, 1993), and the discussion of Irigaray's thoughts on wonder in La Caze, 'Encounter' and Young, 'Asymmetrical Reciprocity'.

[41] Bendik-Keymer, 'The Reasonableness of Wonder'. At the workshop 'The Politics of Wonder', held at Exeter University on 12 September 2019 and organized by Jack Owen Griffiths, the organizer, Amy Lynch, Christopher Gill, and Urszula Lisowska responded to Bendik-Keymer's paper and offered their own reflections on the politics of wonder; and Bendik-Keymer contributed a reflection on the importance of 'being lost in wonder'.

and capacity to 'consider' others. He plausibly suggests that wonder challenges the self-interested starting point of liberalism and opens up space to challenge the distinction between the human and the non-human, as well as between the 'normal' and the 'abnormal'. Bendik-Keymer uses and develops Nussbaum's concept of wonder, which he takes to be biocentric, i.e. it is a form of wonder 'attuned to *living form* as such'.[42] It involves an appreciation of the various forms of life (or, in Aristotelian language, forms of striving) that inhabit this earth. Each form of life is understood as having and striving for its own good, and biocentric wonder sensitizes us to this, and to the beauty and considerability of each of these forms of striving. Bendik-Keymer then connects this notion of wonder with John Rawls' theory of justice, arguing that biocentric wonder can play a helpful role in Rawls' legitimation of the principles of justice he takes to be central to liberal democracies. Famously, Rawls justified these principles through a thought experiment, 'the Original Position', in which we imagine that the people who are to live together choose the basic principles that would regulate their living together under a 'veil of ignorance', i.e. not knowing what position they will have in society, whether they will be male or female, black or white, rich or poor, and so on. Bendik-Keymer argues that, since people in this situation would have to imagine what it would be like to be any kind of person, living any kind of life, biocentric wonder can be helpful here. 'Wonder would be helpful in the original position, because it would put us in a better position to see ourselves in our specific form of striving alongside other living forms.'[43] And this, Bendik-Keymer, would also benefit our ability to consider different human forms of striving, and to appreciate their considerability; this in turn means that wonder helps to open up 'the space of consideration', political space for people to speak, to have a voice and be listened to.[44]

Bendik-Keymer remarks on the demandingness of Rawls' exposition of the epistemic and rational conditions to be satisfied by public reasoning; people are expected to reason together 'in highly logical and empirically grounded ways' – something, as noted before, that people are not terribly good at.[45] But wonder, Bendik-Keymer says, is much more widely available than that. '[C]hildren commonly have it. All one needs for wonder is a sense that life is morally or ethically considerable and some imagination. Then, in that mental space, one

[42] Ibid., 340. See Willmott, *Reading for Wonder*, 51, for a similar, but even more encompassing (ecological) perspective.
[43] Ibid., 346.
[44] Ibid., 347.
[45] Ibid., 349.

can begin to consider striving from many different angles, curiously, appreciating the strangeness and even novelty of its facts.'[46] The observation that wonder is more widely available than well-informed, logically rigorous reasoning is worth emphasizing, I think, but it also needs some qualification. I take it to be true that everyone without specific mental impairments is in principle capable of wonder; it does not require that a person is well informed or capable of reasoning that meets demanding logical standards. I also think that this makes wonder a more plausible candidate for cultivation as a helpful political capacity than such reasoning abilities. But wonder as such is not yet *biocentric* wonder; and biocentric wonder, though very much worth fostering, will be less widely available and more difficult to foster than wonder as such, since it requires that people overcome their anthropocentric bias. Our best chances would arguably be with young children (whose propensity to wonder at living beings is mentioned repeatedly by Bendik-Keymer), but since they would still grow up in a thoroughly anthropocentric social world it would be a challenge to maintain and cultivate their biocentric wonder.[47]

Nevertheless, Bendik-Keymer's argument does show that, insofar as people are able to experience an ethically charged wonder that recognizes the inherent value of others, such wonder has political importance, too. Wonder can be part of the foundation for recognition, and recognition is not just an ethical value and obligation, but also a central political principle.[48]

Wonder and Political Responsibility

Half of wonder's political importance lies in creating distance from 'politics', the other half in foregrounding 'the political' as a dimension of human living together (with each other and other beings). In the 'distant', in a sense 'detached', perspective of wonder the particular order of our society is presented as just one contingent instance of human living together. The shift of perspective occasioned by wonder therefore also shifts our attention from politics to the

[46] Ibid., 350.

[47] Kopnina, Sitka-Sage, Blenkinsop, and Piersol offer telling examples of the stubbornness with which anthropocentric 'common sense' persists despite nature-based early childhood education in Helen Kopnina, Michael Sitka-Sage, Sean Blenkinsop, and Laura Piersol, 'Moving beyond Innocence: Educating Children in a Post-Nature World', in *Research Handbook on Childhoodnature*, eds. Amy Cutter-Mackenzie, Karen Malone, Elisabeth Barratt Hacking (Cham: Springer, 2018), https://doi.org/10.1007/978-3-319-51949-4_40-1.

[48] See, for instance, Axel Honneth, *The Struggle for Recognition: The Moral Grammar of Social Conflicts* (Cambridge MA: The MIT Press, 1992) and, for an overview of recognition theory, Mattias Iser, 'Recognition', *The Stanford Encyclopedia of Philosophy* (Summer 2019 edition), ed. Edward N. Zalta. https://plato.stanford.edu/archives/sum2019/entries/recognition/.

political, to the fact that human living together is unthinkable without some kind of order which will inevitably entail a political dimension – but that any realized order is just one possibility among many, and that as such it will do violence that it is important to acknowledge, even if we are convinced that the current order is the least violent possible at this particular historical junction.

Yet the distance created by wonder need not at all lead to political detachment; in fact, wonder's responsiveness to the world can, especially if attended to and cultivated, also 'responsibilize' the person who wonders. Psychologically, this can be true to the point of logical inconsistency, as in the case of existentialists like Sartre, whose wonder at the world took the form of nausea at the absurdity of existence, but who nevertheless – and actually *because* of the groundlessness of existence – upheld the strongest possible sense of personal responsibility.[49] And with an 'other-acknowledging' wonder that communicates a sense of the inherent value of other beings we can avoid that inconsistency. Yet the existentialist perspective is informative, because when wonder destroys the 'naturalness' of the existing political order and of accepted schemes of thought, the person who wonders is thrown back on her own resources – she is forced to make up her own mind. As an educator it is important to be aware of this, since a student's response to such a situation may vary from complete disengagement to spirited engagement. Responsible education requires that students are not driven to despair, but are supported in sustaining the tension between the demand to keep an open mind and the need to make up one's mind, between undecidability (in the sense that any decision is underdetermined) and decision.

Wonder and Political Education

I hope to have established that wonder, rather than being inherently anti-political, is a type of experience with political potential and importance. If that is the case it may be something worth cultivating in political education. Political education, as I understand it, should do more than make students literate in the political system of their society, but foster an understanding of the political, and wonder can support that effort. Through its connection with the imagination and the emotions it can both stimulate the search for political alternatives and

[49] Hence an existentialist education is one 'which grips a child by his moral coat collars and lifts him up to see over the crowd to the task of taking *personal responsibility* for being human'; Van Cleve Morris, *Existentialism in Education* (New York, Evanston, and London: Harper & Row, Publishers, 1966), 116.

motivate political action. It is a critical-constructive mode of consciousness that can lead to philosophical inquiry and critical thinking.

One possible objection is that we do not *need* wonder to stimulate critical thinking; critical thinking is perfectly possible without wonder (especially deep wonder), so why not skip wonder and move straight on to the promotion of critical thinking instead? My reply is that it is certainly true that critical thinking is possible without wonder, but that such thinking will lack an important quality that enriches critical thinking inspired by wonder. Without wonder at the extraordinary phenomenon of human societies – and at such things as borders, trade agreements, currencies, elections, propaganda, belief in propaganda, war, justifications for war and so on and so forth – and the change of outlook this awareness effects, critical thinking is bound to take itself and therefore its object (what it is thinking) too seriously, in a sense I will explain. Egan saw romantic understanding, in which awe and wonder play an important role, as a stage on the road to ironic understanding, in which all absolute certainties are dissolved, and which is characterized by reflexiveness about our own understanding, beliefs, and opinions.[50] Part of the value of irony is that it disallows that we take ourselves too seriously, and that it relativizes our concerns and the world as we see it. The problem with remaining in an 'ironic' stance, however (though I do not think this applies to Egan's understanding of it) is that it easily becomes a stance from which we are no longer able to take anything seriously anymore. A responsive and responsible relation with the world requires that we pass through an 'ironic' stage to rediscover seriousness on a deeper level. Seriousness is an attitude in which we recognize that the world is real, not our projection or construction, that the beings living on it are real, and that what we do has real consequences for which we are responsible; and at the same time we do not get so caught up in our dealings with the world that we forget that our perspective on it is still just that.[51] Now, the problem with critical thinking, I suggest, is that, left to its own devices – i.e. uninspired by wonder – it is less likely to make the transition to ironic understanding, and even less to move on from there to rediscovered seriousness. It is too tied to its object of critique to reach the detachment needed for the former, too intellectual to manage the latter.

[50] He mentioned awe in connection with ironic understanding in Kieran Egan, *Romantic Understanding: The Development of Rationality and Imagination, Ages 8–15* (New York and London: Routledge, 1990), 169; the concept of ironic understanding is developed in Kieran Egan, *The Educated Mind: How Cognitive Tools Shape Our Understanding* (Chicago and London: The University of Chicago Press, 1997.

[51] This notion of seriousness is inspired by Paul Goodman, *Growing up Absurd: Problems of Youth in the Organized Society* (New York: New York Review Books, 2012).

A related (second) possible objection is that wonder – deep or contemplative wonder – cannot be critical, that we need *inquisitive* wonder for that. But this objection relies on a misunderstanding of that distinction. Although deep wonder is not a state that is at the same time an investigative mode, it is not a passive state, and it does not immobilize us for the future. Whereas inquisitive wonder, like curiosity, seeks knowledge, explanations, so a particular type of understanding, deep wonder seeks meaning. It puts us in a space from which we may begin to answer another type of question (wonder is, after all, the 'beginning' of philosophy), namely meaning questions, and from which creative constructions of meaning can arise. Deep wonder is a mode of consciousness in which we are attuned to the ineffable mystery of existence, in which we sometimes even observe everyday life from a cosmic or a microscopic perspective – a perspective, at any rate, in which all opinions dissolve. But that distancing, that dissolution of opinions, is a valuable educational moment.

And a third possible objection is that wonder not just effects a change of perspective and a deepening of understanding but also *depends* on prior understanding and one's prior perspective, and that a political education that affords too great a role to wonder is therefore likely to become *politicized* education. This response is understandable. The examples I would be inclined to give would certainly be inspired by my own views. For instance, I might observe in class that when we read in the newspaper that the CEO of some corporation earns twenty times as much as a 'floor worker' in the same company we probably don't even blink. It is too familiar a fact of contemporary life in capitalist societies for most of us to even notice. Furthermore, many students would probably try to justify it by appealing to the laws of supply and demand, or by linking higher pay with higher education or greater responsibility. Many of them would assent to the statement: 'It is justifiable and acceptable that people with certain jobs are paid more than people with other jobs'. I might then offer them the following statement: 'It is justifiable and acceptable that people with certain jobs enjoy greater freedom in their lives than people with other jobs'. I am confident that many more students would disagree with this statement than with the former. And yet it merely spells out an important consequence of the first statement. Now, this is the type of example I, with my anti-capitalist leanings, would come up with in order to begin to stir up wonder. But is this problematic? I would argue that it only becomes problematic if students are *systematically* made to question things from one particular perspective. That examples are used to make students question the status quo is not in itself problematic, for it is exactly the taken-for-grantedness of the status quo that needs to be overcome. But success is not measured by the extent to which students come to oppose the status quo, but only by the extent to which they no longer take it for granted; they may well come to the conclusion that it deserves to be supported. Wonder is thus not necessarily opposed to the status quo, but only to its 'naturalness', and it can lead to a renewed and more authentic appreciation for it, as well as to a search for alternatives.

Conclusion

The problem with power is that it tends to fall into the hands of those who want it. My guess is that more often than not, these are not the hands of people particularly prone to wonder. So in this restricted sense, wonder might be said to be antipolitical. But one does not need to 'possess' power in order to change its course, and as soon as we acknowledge that, we can see that wonder is not in itself antipolitical at all, but a potential source of inspiration for political thinking and action. It is clearly not a political emotion (like anger or indignation can be); it does not stir people to action or lead to answers to political questions in any immediate sense. It keeps a certain distance from 'politics'. But it is exactly in its 'apolitical' nature (in this specific sense) that wonder's political importance lies, and its value in political education.[52]

As I have argued – and tried to show in other ways – in this chapter, wonder is essentially world-oriented and world-interested; it creates distance from politics and draws attention to the political, and thereby puts us in a space from which we may criticize existing arrangements as well as our own views and consider alternative possibilities; it helps us imagine alternatives; it can function as a cognitive–affective basis for recognition; and it can be a 'responsibilizing' mode of consciousness. It is not necessarily opposed to the status quo, but only to an attitude that takes the status quo for granted; and for the same reason it is not necessarily affiliated with any particular political perspective, but only with certain qualities that political perspectives may have (for instance, being undogmatic, critical, or attentive).

[52] This shows again the intrinsic connection between wonder and education; they are interested in the world for its own sake, and this makes them potentially subversive. A very similar view is defended by Hodgson, Vlieghe, and Zamojski, 'Education and the Love for the World'.

6

Concluding Chapter: Implications for Policy and Practice

This is a dangerous chapter – for me, as a philosopher. The risk of sliding seamlessly from philosophical reasoning about the educational importance of wonder (and vice versa) into handing out practical advice from the proverbial armchair is something to be constantly aware of, a temptation to be resisted. This is not at all to say that nothing of practical relevance follows from the foregoing chapters, but rather that this cannot take the form of concrete prescriptions. I am not in a position to dole out pedagogical or didactical prescriptions or advice on specific policy measures to be taken. About the former others have written more and with more authority than I could.[1] Given the state of education in countries like the UK, the Netherlands, and many others – given the preoccupation of these educational systems with measurement and performativity[2] – the argument of this book obviously implies that more should be done to foster children's sense of wonder, to support educators' sense of wonder about the world, and to facilitate educators' wonder towards their students. The current educational system in countries in the grip of PISA (the Program of International Student Assessment) exerts pressure on teachers to pin students down too much and too early to

[1] For instance many authors in Egan, Cant, and Judson, *Wonder-Full Education*, and Yannis Hadzigeorgiou (various works cited before); see also Andrew Gilbert, 'Using the Notion of "Wonder" to Develop Positive Conceptions of Science with Future Primary Teachers', *Science Education International* 24, no. 1 (2013), and Andrew Gilbert and Christie C. Byers, 'Wonder as a Tool to Engage Preservice Elementary Teachers in Science Learning and Teaching', *Science Teacher Education* (2017), https://onlinelibrary.wiley.com/doi/pdf/10.1002/sce.21300.

[2] Trotman, 'Wow! What if? So What?: Education and the Imagination of Wonder: Fascination, Possibilities and Opportunities Missed', in *Wonder-full Education: The Centrality of Wonder in Teaching and Learning Across the Curriculum*, eds. Kieran Egan, Annabella Cant, and Gillian Judson (New York: Routledge, 2014), 32, who refers to Stephen J. Ball, 'Performativity, Privatisation, Professionals, and the State', in *Exploring Professionalism*, ed. Bryan Cunningham (London: Institute of Education, 2008). Trotman also observes for the UK context that 'the official curriculum for many young people has become one from which they are increasingly disenfranchised', and that this partly explains the high prevalence of truancy in the UK.

their test scores, and to forget that to know a student's test scores is not to know the student, or even what she is capable of. Trotman closes his discussion of educational policy in the UK with the following statement: 'It would seem that a curriculum that enables the conditions for wonder to flourish and which is meaningfully connected to the lifeworlds of young people is now more necessary than ever'.[3] It is these conditions that I want to focus on first, and from these implications for educational practice will follow implications for educational policy. But before that let me sketch a handful of pictures of 'wonder-full' and 'wonderless' education (from imagined school contexts); they help both to give a sense of what conditions are and are not favourable or hospitable to wonder *and* to show that there is not just one way to make education wonder-full, underlining the fact that educators need to find their own way of doing so, and that what may be good advice for one teacher might be bad advice for another.

Some Pictures of Wonder-full and Wonderless Education

Many different types of education and many different teaching styles can make for 'wonder-full' education – partly for different reasons, and partly due to shared characteristics – (and the same goes for its opposite). The purpose of the present section is merely to hint at this diversity through a few examples and (ideal–typical) sketches.

Wonderful Education

The Old-fashioned History Teacher

If you were lucky, you had one of these at some point in your school career: a grandfatherly or grandmotherly teacher whose way to teach history was by telling stories – exciting, colourful, vivid, suspenseful stories told by a master storyteller. From a single flat picture in an uninspiring history book such a teacher can conjure a four-dimensional world that you as a student are transported to. The factual veracity of the story matters less here than another kind of truth: the visceral realization that this world – or something like it – *really* existed once, that people actually walked around in such clothes as pictured in the book,

[3] Ibid., 33.

paid with such coins, fought and killed with such weapons. Children hooked by stories like this are likely to be filled with a deep sense of wonder, a kind of disbelieving belief bordering on awe. They are all sitting quietly at their desks, but they are not passive – in their minds they are elsewhere, travelling, taking it all in, making connections.

The 'Modern' Teacher (or: 'Progressive' Education)

Very different from the classroom setting in the above example is one where students sit together in clusters rather than at individual desks, walk around the classroom looking for stuff they can use for the project they are working on, or just to take a look at what others are doing, while the teacher surveys it all, shows interest in what her students are doing, and gives a hand or offers advice as needed. The projects are self-chosen by the students, and those that had similar ideas are working together. They have been given the chance to work on something that really fascinates them, and the teacher affirms their choice of project. Part of every school day is reserved for this: following one's own interests, exploring, messing about. The teacher facilitates this, points out interesting possibilities and asks questions not to test children's knowledge but to stimulate their thinking and imagination (what Miyazaki calls 'unknown questions').[4]

The Excursion into 'the Great Outdoors'

Dave Trotman describes an again entirely different but equally wonder-full educational setting: a 'trip to an outdoor education Centre in the heart of the English countryside', where some thirty 7- to 10-year-olds make a woodland walk led by Jake, a young tutor. At some point a girl, Jaspal, lets out an 'ear-piercing squeal of excitement'.[5]

> An intrigued crowd of children and adults were then drawn to Jake's call of 'Look everybody! Look what Jaspal's found!'
>
> Holding out a trembling hand, Jaspal presented a clod of earth out of which appeared a very large, wriggling worm. Jaspal, now with eyes the size of saucers, was transfixed. My colleagues and I, on the other hand, were now watchful

[4] Kiyotaka Miyazaki, 'From "Unknown Questions" Begins a Wonderful Education: Kyozai-Kaishaku and the Dialogic Classroom', in *Wonder-full Education: The Centrality of Wonder in Teaching and Learning across the Curriculum*, eds. Kieran Egan, Annabella Cant and Gillian Judson (New York: Routledge, 2014).

[5] Trotman, 'Wow! What if? So What?' 23.

of heading-off the inevitable responses of 'Big deal' and moans of general disappointment from the other kids. The exchange that followed between Jake, Jaspal, the children, the watchful teachers and a wriggly worm was, however, pure educational theatre.

It was an event in which Jake shared, with incredible skilfulness, the excitement of the discovery and at the same time had drawn all the observers into Jaspal's moment of wonder. I still remember it as a significant point in time when an eight-year-old girl makes, what was for her, the most astonishing discovery; a discovery in which the tactile, the environmental, the aesthetic, and emotional all collide in one magical moment.

Wonderless Education

Sticking to the Lesson Plan, or: Missed Opportunities

Laura Piersol offers a great example of a missed opportunity to allow wonder into the classroom:

> I was in a grade three classroom and some excited students interrupted the teacher to tell her that there was a 'humongous' beetle on the floor. The teacher asked one of the students to take it outside and continued with her lesson. In ignoring such discoveries we are suggesting to children that the very act of 'wondering' is a waste of time and that the objects that they marvel at are actually insignificant.[6]

Piersol observes that 'students in our current education system are taught to be more like dogmatic puppies than humble wonderers'. 'Instead of guiding students to dismantle existing assumptions and gain the courage to consider "strange" new ideas, we lead them to concrete answers and present most subjects as static entities in which there is little left that is unknown'.[7] A perfect illustration of this is offered by Lynne Wolbert:

> My son had to bring a stuffed animal to school that is a pet. He chose to bring a sheep. At the end of that day, the sheep came back home with him. The teacher had told him he was wrong; sheep aren't pets, but rabbits for example are. To my mind, this was an act of foreclosure. My son's fresh encounter with the concept 'pets', for which he had not internalised generally accepted frames yet, was closed off prematurely, by not going along with him in his exploration and imagination

6 Piersol, 'Our Hearts Leap up', 17.
7 Ibid., 11.

of what the world is like. Instead, he was presented with right and wrong answers, thereby leaving him no room to make his own inquiry into the world.[8]

Teaching to the Test

'Teaching to the test' is such a well-known phrase in contemporary debates about education that it even has its own Wikipedia page, which describes it as 'a colloquial term for any method of education whose curriculum is heavily focused on preparing students for a standardized test'. It says further that

> [O]pponents of this practice argue that it forces teachers to limit curriculum to a set range of knowledge or skills in order to increase student performance on the mandated test. This produces an unhealthy focus on excessive repetition of simple, isolated skills ('drill and kill') and limits the teacher's ability to focus on a holistic understanding of the subject matter. (…) Teaching to the test entails instruction devoid of passion and meaning as students are taught information from a stripped-down curriculum.

Needless to say, 'teaching to the test' as understood here leaves little or no room for wonder in the classroom.

No Time for Romance

Alfred North Whitehead distinguished three stages of 'mental growth' (three stages of learning, we might say): the stage of *romance*, in which a topic of interest is discovered and found to harbour all sorts of tantalizing possibilities and potential for exploration, the stage of *precision*, where one's grasp of that topic is enhanced by systematic study, and the stage of *generalization*, a return to romance with fuller knowledge and understanding and wider possibilities of application.[9] Where time is of the essence and there is pressure on teachers to get much done in little time it may be tempting to try to skip or drastically shorten the stage of romance and move straight to the stage of precision. As Whitehead warns, however, 'a stage of precision is barren without a previous

[8] Lynne Wolbert, 'What Should Schools Do to Promote Wonder?' forthcoming in *Oxford Review of Education*.

[9] The three stages are described in Alfred North Whitehead, 'The Rhythm of Education', in *The Aims of Education and Other Essays* (London: Ernest Benn Limited) and Whitehead, 'The Rhythmic Claims'. They are also discussed briefly in Hadzigeorgiou, 'Reclaiming' and Keiichi Takaya, 'Renewing the Sense of Wonder in the Minds of High School and College Students', in *Wonder-full Education: The Centrality of Wonder in Teaching and Learning across the Curriculum*, eds. Kieran Egan, Annabella Cant and Gillian Judson (New York: Routledge, 2014). Kieran Egan (modestly) writes that his own work on romantic understanding 'may be seen merely as an elaboration of these remarks by Whitehead'; Egan, *Romantic Understanding*, 205.

stage of romance'.[10] Education without romance – having to learn things just 'because', without an inkling of why they might be interesting or important – is education without wonder. (And if Whitehead is right, as I think he is, it will also be impoverished in its results.)

Going Through the Motions

The teacher's own wonder is essential to wonderful education. So another example of wonderless education would be when a teacher – weary, perhaps, due to the constant changes demanded by the government, school boards desperately seeking to innovate to attract more (or different) pupils, or some other 'interested' party – has lost all interest in either the subject matter or the children and is merely going through the motions until the release of retirement. It is very sad when it happens, but we have probably all witnessed it.

Implications for Educational Practice

The illustrations above suggest a number of conditions that determine whether an educational climate is more or less hospitable to wonder, conditions that may be clustered, paradoxically, under the headings 'stimuli' and 'absence of stimuli'.

Absence of Stimuli

Wonder is a mode of consciousness one cannot simply enter at will, under any circumstances. Generally speaking, it requires a peaceful external and internal environment – quiet surroundings, time on your side, absence of pressure (to finish something quickly, to get high marks), an atmosphere of safety and trust, freedom to explore and/or to let one's mind wander, and so on. These are conditions that promote receptiveness to whatever chooses to arrest one's attention, and that support sustained attention. There are no distractions; that is, no things that disturb the peace, that violently interrupt one's attention. Conditions like these are favourable to the occurrence of wonder – but at the same time, when conditions are like this, in many cases (in many minds) nothing remarkable will happen. Sometimes wonder arises spontaneously – triggered by some perception or even a seemingly unprovoked thought – but often some kind of stimulus is needed.[11]

[10] Whitehead, 'The Rhythm of Education', 29.
[11] Hadzigeorgiou, 'Wonder, Its Nature and Its Role in the Learning Process'.

Stimuli

Wonder is more likely to occur in a 'rich' material (and, for that matter, spiritual) environment, whether indoors or outdoors. But even then it often needs to be actively evoked, for instance by a teacher providing some new information about a known or unknown thing, or by presenting something familiar in a new light – by creating a contrast between reality and expectations about reality, perhaps, or between two apparent truths that are almost impossible to hold in the mind at the same time (life is precious, the universe does not care). Two examples given by Hadzigeorgiou are explaining to students that 'we are all stardust' (i.e. made up of substances that are remnants of stars that died in explosions)[12] and pointing out 'that some of the water molecules contained in a glass of water today are the same molecules contained in the water that dinosaurs drank more than sixty million years ago'.[13] These are clearly ways to defamiliarize the familiar (in this case our bodies and the water we drink every day).[14] But stimuli can be of an even more subtle, almost 'negative', nature – e.g. recognizing the value of not-knowing (the excitement of not-yet knowing, the space it affords to the imagination, the appropriate humility it inspires)[15] and 'modeling' wonder by allowing one's own wonder to be seen by one's students. And beyond these 'stimuli' lies the *response* of the teacher to each student, a response that needs to be sensitive to (the signs of) the student's wonder and the vulnerability of the student in wonder.[16] In short: fostering and protecting students' wonder requires what Max van Manen has called 'pedagogical tact', a combination of care, sensitivity, and practical wisdom that (ideally) enable a teacher to know and feel what a particular student needs at that particular moment and respond to this in an appropriate way.[17]

12 See Simon Worrall, 'How 40,000 Tons of Cosmic Dust Falling to the Earth Affects You and Me', *National Geographic*, 28 January 2015, https://www.nationalgeographic.com/news/2015/01/150128-big-bang-universe-supernova-astrophysics-health-space-ngbooktalk/.

13 Hadzigeorgiou, 'Wonder, Its Nature and Its Role in the Learning Process'.

14 Kieran Egan, 'Wonder, Awe, and Teaching Techniques', in *Wonder-full Education: The Centrality of Wonder in Teaching and Learning across the Curriculum*, eds. Kieran Egan, Annabella Cant and Gillian Judson (New York: Routledge, 2014), 153, 157.

15 Duckworth, *'The Having of Wonderful Ideas'*, 64–9. N.B. For Duckworth the 'virtues of not knowing' are, by and large, virtues of not-*yet*-knowing. Cf. Piersol, 'Our Hearts Leap up', 12: '[W]e can help our students realize that their knowledge is only a drop in the sea of the unknown'.

16 Hove, 'The Face of Wonder', 437; Wolbert, 'What Should Schools Do'.

17 Max van Manen, *Pedagogical Tact: Knowing What to Do when You Don't Know What to Do* (New York: Routledge, 2016); see also Sander van Perlo, Lynne Wolbert, and Anders Schinkel, 'Het Belang van Pedagogische Tact voor het (H)erkennen van Verwondering bij Leerlingen', forthcoming in *Pedagogiek*; and Wolbert, 'What Should Schools Do'.

General Curricular Implications

Naturally, some types of curriculum are more hospitable to wonder than others, so it is worth drawing out some general curricular implications of the argument in this book.

Some readers may have been surprised to find an absence of references to philosophy for/with children in this book; they may have reasoned that an argument for the importance of wonder in education would almost inevitably also be an argument for assigning a greater role to philosophy (that is, to the activity of philosophizing) in schools. There are two main reasons why I have not discussed this so far. Firstly, the best-known tradition in this field is P4C, developed mostly by Matthew Lipman.[18] This is an educational 'intervention' that aims to teach children to think critically, creatively, and carefully. This is attempted by transforming the classroom into a 'community of inquiry', in which the teacher facilitates dialogic discussions between the children – conversations in which children listen carefully to what the other is trying to say, try to take the other's point of view, argue as best as they can, and strive for conceptual clarity. The emphasis lies squarely on critical thinking skills, on analysis and argumentation. This is by no means necessarily a climate conducive to wonder – though at the same time well-chosen questions may of course evoke wonder and spark philosophical thinking.[19]

Secondly, whether we are talking about P4C or other traditions of philosophy with children, we tend to be dealing with educational activities assigned their own space and time slot in the curriculum – often added onto the standard curriculum.[20] Even if wonder would find a more hospitable home there than tends to be the case elsewhere in the curriculum, it would be a terrible shame if a plea to create more room and opportunities for wonder in the curriculum would boil down to assigning it a place of its own. Furthermore, there is no reason at all why other parts of the curriculum would be less hospitable to wonder than

[18] Matthew Lipman, Ann Margaret Sharp, and Frederick S. Oscanyon, *Philosophy in the Classroom* (Philadelphia: Temple University Press, 1980); Matthew Lipman, 'Philosophy for Children', in *Developing Minds: Programs for Teaching Thinking*, Vol. 2, ed. Arthur L. Costa, 35–8 (Alexandria: Association for Supervision and Curricular Development, 1981); Matthew Lipman, *Thinking in Education* (Cambridge and New York: Cambridge University Press, 2003).

[19] A nice example is the question whether an apple in a fruit bowl is alive; Matthews, *Philosophy & the Young Child*, 6–7. For an example of a conception of Socratic dialogue shaped explicitly to foster a 'community of wonder' (though among adults) see Hansen, 'The Call and Practices of Wonder'.

[20] For an overview of approaches see Michael Pritchard, 'Philosophy for Children', in *The Stanford Encyclopedia of Philosophy* (Winter 2018 edition), ed. Edward N. Zalta, https://plato.stanford.edu/entries/children/.

philosophy with children; *all* subjects, since they all deal with some aspect of a world that is mysterious, puzzling, baffling, extraordinary in many ways, can accommodate wonder and be taught in ways that heighten children's sense of wonder.

Whether this is the case – or the extent to which it is – does depend on general features of the curriculum, that is, of the sum total of experience offered to students in an educational institution. As the vignettes I presented earlier suggested there is no single educational approach one would need to take in order to foster students' sense of wonder. A curriculum's potential to do so lies rather in certain *qualities* that it may embody to a greater or lesser extent. A curriculum can be more or less 'imaginative', for instance; it may do more or less to spark the imagination, support students' own sense-making, and enable students to make a personal and emotional connection with the subject matter.[21] It may emphasize only 'rational' thinking, or rather acknowledge also the value of 'poetic' thinking, an open, responsive type of thinking in which our experience of the world is determined not so much by our preconceptions of it as by that which presences in our experience itself.[22]

In connection with the latter point, a curriculum will also be more wonder-full to the extent that it promotes students' capacity and will to attend to the world in a receptive, careful, and sustained manner. It is not just the external environment that needs to be 'quiet', but the internal environment, too. A common and intuitively plausible concern is that media exposure, or more generally the type of stimuli children are accustomed to, influences children's attention span, with much exposure to fast, high-information media leading to a shorter attention span. So far, the evidence for this remains largely anecdotal. My own sense, too, is that university students today have less patience with longer texts (especially texts, like philosophical articles, that do not offer a quick overview of their contents in the way that empirical publications do) than, say, twenty years ago. It also seems to me that the constant bombardment of information most of us undergo in today's world and the fast pace of contemporary life lead to a certain shallowness of attention – as if we merely skid along the surface of things, without being fully present with them. But 'hard' evidence of any relation between media exposure and attention span or similar cognitive effects seems so far to be lacking, and behind the intuitively plausible idea and the common perception may also lie a

[21] See the references to 'imaginative education' in the previous chapter.

[22] Michael Bonnett, *Children's Thinking: Promoting Understanding in the Primary School* (London: Cassell, 1994), chapter 11.

need 'to manage anxiety over social and technological change' or an attempt 'to reassert the superiority of adult culture (…) over youth culture' or some similar ideological distinction.[23] However this may be, a prolonged attention span is not innate in human beings, nor does it develop entirely without environmental support. And arguably, the type of attention to the world that is required for wonder, or that wonder is an instance of, is the most difficult type to muster, at least for older children and adults. This open, receptive form of attention comes (even) less easily to us than focused, point-directed, active attention;[24] and it may well be that the training we receive in the latter (not least in school), which is after all more useful in the manipulation of our environment, makes it more difficult to summon the former. At any rate the fact that this type of attention is difficult to achieve and sustain (combined with a recognition of the importance of wonder) provides a *prima facie* argument for (introducing elements of) contemplative pedagogy. Some types of contemplative pedagogy stress the importance of (being in touch with) the body and of mindfulness practices, others are contemplative in a more traditional philosophical and spiritual sense, fostering attention to goodness, truth, and beauty.[25] What they have in common, however, is the aim of cultivating a type of attention in which we experience a deep connection with the world, a connection that is not just cognitive, but also emotional and embodied.

Leading on from the above, recognition of the educational importance of wonder provides an argument for a more holistic form of education and a more holistic curriculum than is common today. The standard curriculum is analytical in the sense that '[w]e have fragmented the world into bits and pieces called disciplines and subdisciplines hermetically sealed from other such disciplines', and as a result 'most students graduate without any broad, integrated sense of the unity of things'.[26] It stresses rationality over feeling (things that need not be opposed), and promotes instrumental rationality in particular; the analytical partitioning of the world serves this rationality, it facilitates our control and manipulation of the world, and, as Michael Bonnett has argued, is an expression of the 'metaphysics of mastery' that underlies our perception of the world and

[23] Michael Z. Newman, 'New Media, Young Audiences and Discourses of Attention: From *Sesame Street* to "Snack Culture"', *Media, Culture & Society* 32, no. 4 (2010): 593.

[24] Hence mindfulness and meditation are forms of discipline that it takes years to master.

[25] See, for instance, Jani Pulkki, Bo Dahlin, and Veli-Matti Värri, 'Environmental Education as a Lived-Body Practice? A Contemplative Pedagogy Perspective', *Journal of Philosophy of Education* 51, no. 1 (2017), and Angelo Caranfa, 'Contemplative Instruction and the Gifts of Beauty, Love, and Silence', *Educational Theory* 60, no. 5 (2010).

[26] Orr, *Earth in Mind*, 11.

our everyday understanding of our place in the world.[27] Ron Miller has similarly argued that modern education embodies and transmits a 'reductionistic' worldview, a worldview that is 'materialistic, mechanistic, objectivistic [and] atomistic'; and that the very notion of curriculum 'represents an objectification of human experience, an abbreviation of the life world according to particular ideological imperatives'.[28] In contrast, holistic education would aim to foster experiences of 'things' (rather than 'objects') as wholes, vaguely and fluidly defined, organically related to other things and to oneself in such a way that they cannot be seen as wholly separate;[29] it would thus aim to promote an integrative understanding of things that would at the same time integrate mind and body, thinking and feeling.

Finally, unsurprisingly, there is a strong overlap between holistic education and environmental or ecological education (of a non-anthropocentric kind that rejects the desire for continuous economic growth). The ecological crisis we face – or actually still refuse to face – today calls for, among many other things, holistic, non-anthropocentric ecological education.[30] It has been argued that wonder is central to ecocentric education, and (as we have seen) to environmental ethics in general.[31] But vice versa, if we affirm the educational importance of wonder for the reasons presented in this book, we have reason to try to transform the education offered in our schools in a way that, in effect, will make it at least very similar to holistic ecological education.

Implications for Educational Policy

At the beginning of this chapter I referred briefly to educational policy in the UK and to PISA. PISA is an international comparative research programme

[27] Michael Bonnett, *Retrieving Nature: Educating for a Post-Humanist Age* (Malden, Oxford, and Carlton: Blackwell Publishing, 2004).

[28] Ron Miller, 'Beyond Reductionism: The Emerging Holistic Paradigm in Education', *The Humanistic Psychologist* 28, nos. 1–3 (2000), 383.

[29] Ibid., 65.

[30] Although they do not exactly defend holistic ecological education in the sense described here, Randall Curren and Ellen Metzger do note for the American context that '[s]tandards-based education and accountability through high-stakes testing have dominated educational policy and practice in the United States for some years now. The standardized testing requirements of the No Child Left Behind (NCLB) Act of 2001 led to a narrow focus on reading and mathematics literacy in many schools, creating an unfavorable climate for the integrated, transdisciplinary learning essential to meaningful sustainability education'; Randall Curren and Ellen Metzger, *Living Well Now and in the Future: Why Sustainability Matters* (Cambridge and London: The MIT Press, 2017), 159–60.

[31] Washington, 'Education for Wonder'; Haydn Washington, *A Sense of Wonder towards Nature: Healing the World through Belonging* (London: Routledge, 2018); Moore, 'The Truth of the Barnacles'.

instigated by the OECD (Organisation for Economic Co-operation and Development) in 1997 and first performed in 2000, and every third year since then.[32] It tests 15-year-old students (in 2018 in seventy-nine countries worldwide) on their performance in reading, maths, and science (as well as administering questionnaires on socio-economic status, student attitudes and beliefs, school experiences, and school management and organisation). Trotman comments on the pernicious effects of the emphasis on international comparisons:

> One consequence of [the] pursuit of international comparison is that those aspects of the curriculum that are least amenable to routine testing, by default, come to occupy the least privileged positions in the curriculum. Despite some cursory gestures towards 'awe and wonder' (Ofsted, 2004) and aspects of creative and affective development, ministerial interest in primary school performance rests squarely on test scores of pupil literacy and numeracy.[33]

PISA has had a strong influence on educational policy in many countries; but of course it did not have this effect by itself, but must be seen in a wider European policy context, in particular the Lisbon Strategy formulated in 2000. The Lisbon Strategy stated that the EU was 'to become the most competitive and dynamic knowledge-based economy in the world, capable of sustainable economic growth with more and better jobs and greater social cohesion'.[34] Education, as Gillies explains, was seen as in service of the knowledge economy and international economic competition (in particular with China). Gillies observes that EU education policy since then has been '[r]ooted in human capital theory, which sees education as an investment which later pays economic dividends for both the individual and the state', but that two recent developments have challenged this model, namely the 2015 terrorist attacks in various European countries and the 'shock of Brexit and the rise of populist nationalism across the EU'. These have led to a renewed emphasis on European identity, socialization, and citizenship education. What has *not* changed, however, is the instrumentalist perspective on education: 'Just as education is instrumental for ultimate economic goals, so social stability and community values are seen not as intrinsic goods, but merely

[32] See https://en.wikipedia.org/wiki/Programme_for_International_Student_Assessment.

[33] Trotman, 'Wow! What if? So what?', 31.

[34] European Parliament, *Lisbon European Council 23 and 24 March 2000. Presidency conclusions*, http://www.europarl.europa.eu/summits/lis1_en.htm, cited in Donald Gillies, 'Learning to Make Money: 21st Century EU Education Policy', *On Education. Journal for Research and Debate* 2, no. 6 (2019), https://doi.org/10.17899/on_ed.2019.6.1.

as the optimum basis from which economic growth can be stimulated'.[35] And indeed, in line with European policy as described by Gillies, in its latest 'state of education' report the Dutch Inspectorate of Education explicitly defines the core tasks of the Dutch school system as 'allocation, socialization, qualification, and selection with equal opportunities' – the only addition (albeit an important one in itself) being equality of opportunity. These tasks are framed in the context of the demands of the future labour market and students' and their parents' desire for certainty about the (economic) value of school diplomas; and it is observed that a lack of consensus about the stated aims is problematic, because, 'as underlined by the OECD' a lack of consensus about educational aims can lead to a 'weakening of the system'.[36] No reference is made to education as valuable in itself or for the art of living; no reference is made to the world, the subject matter of education, the 'holy ground' between teacher and student, as worth attending to in its own right; no reference is made, either, to what is without a doubt *the* problem that should concern us today, namely the global ecological crisis – climate change and its many attendant problems, species extinctions, decreasing biodiversity, loss of fertile topsoil, et cetera. It will be clear, therefore, that from the perspective advanced in this book, educational policy in Europe and all countries with similar educational policies needs to change, and change quite dramatically.

As I said at the start of this chapter I am not in a position to suggest specific policy measures, to say which steps ought to be taken by whom and when, in order to move the education system in the right direction. But I can articulate a number of general policy implications that I believe follow from an acknowledgement of the educational importance of wonder, in combination with a recognition of the urgency of change imposed upon us by the ecological crisis.

It is clear that education policy in Europe, the United States and other countries is caught up in an instrumentalist, reductionist outlook on the world. Of course, preparing children for the labour market or more broadly for the ability to function well and independently in society is a legitimate goal; so is the aim at social stability (at least to the extent that a society is just). But to pursue these goals exclusively, and for that matter instrumentally, in service of the ultimate good of economic growth and global economic competition, is indefensible. It is a 'thoughtless' (in the Arendtian sense) running in pursuit of

35 Gillies, 'Learning to Make Money'.

36 Inspectie van het Onderwijs, *De Staat van het Onderwijs 2019* (Utrecht: Inspectie van het Onderwijs, 2019), 6.

unexamined goals, which, when questioned by others, are defended instinctively as 'necessary' or 'inevitable' (TINA). Those caught up in this discourse and this belief system tend to argue that the economy is the *conditio sine qua non* for everything else; the obvious error is that in fact the economy occupies an important but intermediary position, and that it is *ecology* that is the precondition for everything else. Economists outside of the mainstream have long recognized this; in *For the Common Good*, economist Herman Daly and process theologian John Cobb write: 'We human beings are being led to a *dead* end – all too literally. We are living by an ideology of death and accordingly we are destroying our own humanity and killing the planet.'[37] If this sounds dramatic, that is because the situation *is* dramatic. We urgently need to change the way we live; and educational change will simply have to be a part of that.[38]

We need to wake up, step back, and look at ourselves and what we are doing in wonder – and then we can turn our gaze outward. We urgently need to break the narcissistic trance that keeps us spellbound, that locks us in human self-absorption, that almost constant state in which all we are ever concerned with – all we can see or hear – is our human world. Paradoxically, we need to do this for our own sake, too, not only for the sake of the non-human life with which we share this planet. For our own sake as much as any other beings', we need to pierce the illusion of inevitability – all these supposed economic or political necessities are self-created necessities, and can therefore be uncreated.

Educational policy that takes the world seriously and that takes wonder seriously will have to begin by taking education itself seriously – instead of seeing it merely as an instrument of economic power. This is often expressed as education for education's sake, but this is only defensible on a world-oriented understanding of education. And unless one's audience or conversation partners are fully aware that education is understood in this way, 'education for education's sake' is bound to be misunderstood as an elitist hobby.[39] What matters is the world, is existence, is life in all its manifestations; this is what wonder-inspired education would constantly remind us of. So what this asks for is a fundamental reorientation, in which the world in all its abundance, rather than some

[37] Herman E. Daly and John B. Cobb, Jr., *For the Common Good: Redirecting the Economy toward Community, the Environment, and a Sustainable Future* (Boston: Beacon Press, 1994), 21.

[38] To appreciate the urgency of the situation see the wealth of scientific evidence collected in Naomi Klein, *This Changes Everything* (n.p.: Penguin Books, 2015) and Wallace-Wells, *The Uninhabitable Earth*.

[39] Hodgson, Vlieghe, and Zamojski, 'Education and the Love for the World' do defend a world-oriented conception of 'education for education's sake', but as said the latter phrase may still be (strategically) unfortunate.

extrinsic goal(s) education is supposed to serve, becomes the orient. This also means a reorientation of educational assessment towards the intrinsic quality of education: its ability to open up the world to children and open children up to the world. Only in such a climate, rather than today's pressure cooker, can wonder thrive and can all children thrive.

To make such a move requires courage and trust – trust that world-oriented rather than economic growth-oriented education will still 'produce' citizens capable of functioning well in our society and will not plunge our societies in economic or social crisis. But why would it? Why would a deeper, more integrative and holistic understanding of our world – of our social and economic order and its dependence on the ecosystems of our planet – make people incapable of maintaining our society? They may well wish to change it, but that is hardly something to be opposed to. And why would an enhanced sense of wonder threaten our social order? Again, it may inspire efforts to change it – wonder can certainly be 'subversive' – but is any society that is no longer willing to change not doomed? Alfred North Whitehead once wrote:

> The foundation of all understanding of sociological theory – that is to say, of all understanding of human life – is that no static maintenance of perfection is possible. This axiom is rooted in the nature of things. Advance or Decadence are the only choices offered to mankind. The pure conservative is fighting against the essence of the universe.[40]

Despite all talk of innovation and progress it seems to me we are an insecure, anxious society; as a society we lack the spirit of adventure that today lies on the side of those who seek alternative, sustainable, modes of living.

In short, educational policy needs to be reoriented towards the promotion of education that opens up the world in all its dimensions; that is inspired by and in turn inspires a sense of wonder and a spirit of adventure; that is not assessed in terms of its contribution to economic growth but in terms of the degree to which it has opened up the world to each particular child – which is also the degree to which it has discovered the unique abilities of that child; that is assessed, too, in terms of the extent to which it has succeeded in conveying a sense of the world as an interdependent 'whole' rather than a collection of separate or even spare parts. Naturally, all this could only succeed in the context of broader societal changes in the same spirit.

[40] Whitehead, *Adventures of Ideas*, 273.

Conclusion

I have argued that if we acknowledge the educational importance of wonder – and, in tandem with this, the reality of the ecological crisis we are facing – we need to be attentive to the creation and maintenance of wonder-supporting conditions in education, transform the curriculum to make it truly world-oriented, and replace educational policy based on an instrumentalist, economistic ideology with world-oriented educational policy. '[C]ursed be the dullard who destroys wonder,' said Whitehead.[41] Cursed, indeed.

How likely is it that we will see such a reorientation occur in educational policy? That the necessary changes will begin top-down? How hopeful am I in this regard? To be honest, not very. It seems to me extremely unlikely, given the lack of meaningful action we have seen on climate change so far, for instance, that we will see such a shift in policy in the near future. But if there is one thing wonder tells us, it is that *everything* is unlikely. There is thus a connection between wonder and hope. I admit I find it difficult to be hopeful, but I hold fast to my wonder and hope that this will give me hope.

And of course for us as individuals there is no need to wait for change. Every single one of us – not least any educator – can act out of a world-affirming wonder, out of a sense 'that there is something of value to pass on'.[42] We can act *as if* there is hope, and as a result there may well *be* hope, and cause for hope. All change must begin somewhere, in some experience. Educators thus have the potential to make a difference. We tend to remember few of our teachers, but among the ones we do remember are almost always those who lit or fanned the flame of wonder in us, who nourished our sense that the world is a remarkable place.

[41] Whitehead, 'Rhythmic Claims', 50–1.

[42] Hodgson, Vlieghe, and Zamojski, 'Education and the Love for the World'.

Bibliography

Arendt, Hannah. 'The Crisis in Education'. In Hannah Arendt, *Between Past and Future*, 170–93. New York: Penguin Books, 2006.

Arendt, Hannah. *The Human Condition*, Chicago: University of Chicago Press, 1958.

Arendt, Hannah. 'Martin Heidegger at Eighty'. In *Heidegger and Modern Philosophy*, edited by Michael Murray, 293–303. New Haven: Yale University Press, 1978.

Argyle, Michael. *Psychology and Religion: An Introduction*, London and New York: Routledge, 2005.

Ashworth, Peter, and Man Cheung Chung. 'Conclusion: Phenomenology and Psychological Science'. In *Phenomenology and Psychological Science: Historical and Philosophical Perspectives*, edited by Peter Ashworth and Man Cheung Chung, 197–206. New York: Springer, 2006.

Ball, Stephen J. 'Performativity, Privatisation, Professionals, and the State'. In *Exploring Professionalism*, edited by Bryan Cunningham, 52–68. London: Institute of Education, 2008.

Barrow, Robin. '"Or What's a Heaven For?" The Importance of Aims in Education'. In *The Aims of Education*, edited by Roger Marples, 14–22. London and New York: Routledge, 1999.

Batchelor, Stephen. *After Buddhism: Rethinking the Dharma for a Secular Age*, New Haven and London: Yale University Press, 2015.

Batson, C. Daniel, Patricia Schoenrade, and W. Larry Ventis. *Religion and the Individual*, New York: Oxford University Press, 1993.

Baumeister, Roy. *Meanings of Life*, New York: Guilford Press, 1991.

Beer, John. *Wordsworth and the Human Heart*, Houndmills: Macmillan, 1978.

Bendik-Keymer, Jeremy. 'The Reasonableness of Wonder', *Journal of Human Development and Capabilities* 18, no. 3 (2017): 337–55.

Bergson, Henri. *Creative Evolution*, Mineola: Dover Publications, 1998.

Bergson, Henri. *Introduction to Metaphysics*, New York: Philosophical Library, 1961.

Bergson, Henri. *L'Évolution Créatrice*, Édition Électronique (ePub, PDF) v.: 1.0, Les Echos de Maquis, 2013. https://philosophie.cegeptr.qc.ca/wp-content/documents/L%C3%A9volution-cr%C3%A9atrice.pdf

Berlyne, Daniel E. 'A Theory of Human Curiosity', *British Journal of Psychology* 45, no. 3 (1954): 180–91.

Biesta, Gert. *The Beautiful Risk of Education*, London and New York: Routledge, 2016.

Biesta, Gert. 'De School als Toegang tot de Wereld: Een Pedagogische Kijk op Goed Onderwijs'. In *Wat is Goed Onderwijs: Bijdragen uit de Pedagogiek*, edited by Ruud Klarus and Wim Wardekker, 15–35. Den Haag: Boom Lemma, 2011.

Biesta, Gert. *Good Education in an Age of Measurement*, Boulder, CO: Paradigm Publishers, 2010.

Biesta, Gert. 'Good Education in an Age of Measurement: On the Need to Reconnect with the Question of Purpose in Education', *Educational Assessment, Evaluation, and Accountability* 21, no. 1 (2009): 33–46.

Bonner, Edward T., and Harris L. Friedman. 'A Conceptual Clarification of the Experience of Awe: An Interpretative Phenomenological Analysis', *The Humanist Psychologist* 39 (2011): 222–35.

Bonnett, Alastair. *Off the Map: Lost Spaces, Invisible Cities, Forgotten Islands, Feral Places, and What They Tell Us about the World*, London: Aurum Press, 2015.

Bonnett, Michael. *Children's Thinking: Promoting Understanding in the Primary School*, London: Cassell, 1994.

Bonnett, Michael. *Retrieving Nature: Educating for a Post-Humanist Age*, Malden, Oxford, and Carlton: Blackwell Publishing, 2004.

Brennan, Jason. *Against Democracy*, Princeton and Oxford: Princeton University Press, 2017.

Brennan, Tom. *Political Education and Democracy*, Cambridge and New York: Cambridge University Press, 1981.

Brighouse, Harry. *On Education*, Abingdon and New York: Routledge, 2006.

Brümmer, Vincent. *Theology & Philosophical Inquiry: An Introduction*, London and Basingstoke: The Macmillan Press Ltd, 1981.

Buber, Martin. *I and Thou*, London and New York: Continuum, 2004.

Buber, Martin. *Reden über Erziehung*, Heidelberg: Verlag Lambert Schneider, 1962.

Burke, Edmund. *A Philosophical Enquiry into the Origin of Our Ideas of the Sublime and Beautiful*, London: Routledge & Kegan Paul, 1958.

Bynum, Caroline Walker, 'Presidential Address: Wonder', *American Historical Review* 102, no. 1 (1997): 1–26.

Cahill, Kevin M. *The Fate of Wonder: Wittgenstein's Critique of Metaphysics and Modernity*, New York: Columbia University Press, 2011.

Caranfa, Angelo. 'Contemplative Instruction and the Gifts of Beauty, Love, and Silence', *Educational Theory* 60, no. 5 (2010): 561–85.

Carson, Rachel. *The Edge of the Sea*, Boston: Houghton Mifflin, 1955.

Carson, Rachel. *The Sense of Wonder*, New York: HarperCollins, 1998.

Cusanus, Nicholas. *Of Learned Ignorance*, translated by Germain Heron. Eugene: Wipf & Stock Publishers, 2007.

Cuypers, Stefaan. 'R. S. Peters' "The Justification of Education" Revisited', *Ethics and Education* 7, no. 1 (2012): 3–17.

Daly, Herman E., and John B. Cobb, Jr. *For the Common Good: Redirecting the Economy toward Community, the Environment, and a Sustainable Future*, Boston: Beacon Press, 1994.

Darwin, Charles. *Beagle Diary*, edited by Richard Darwin Keynes. Cambridge: Cambridge University Press, 2001. http://darwin-online.org.uk/content/frameset?itemID=F1925&viewtype=text&pageseq=1

Daston, Lorraine, and Katharine Park. *Wonders and the Order of Nature, 1150–1750*, New York: Zone Books, 1998.

Davis, Andrew, and John White. 'Accountability and School Inspection: In Defence of Audited Self-Review', *Journal of Philosophy of Education* 35, no. 4 (2001): 667–81.

Degenhardt, Mike A.B. 'R.S. Peters: Liberal Traditionalist'. In *The SAGE Handbook of Philosophy of Education*, edited by Richard Bailey, Robin Barrow, David Carr, and Christine McCarthy. London: Sage, 2010. http://dx.doi.org/10.4135/9781446200872.n9.

De Groot, Isolde and Wiel Veugelers. 'Why We Need to Question the Democratic Engagement of Adolescents in Europe', *Journal of Social Science Education* 14, no. 4 (2015): 27–38.

Dennett, Daniel. *Consciousness Explained*, Boston: Little, Brown, and Company, 1991.

Dennett, Daniel. *From Bacteria to Bach and Back: The Evolution of Minds*, n.p.: Penguin Books, 2018.

De Pascuale, Juan. 'A Wonder Full Life', *Notre Dame Magazine*, Spring 2003. https://magazine.nd.edu/stories/a-wonder-full-life/

De Ruyter, Doret J. *De Betekenis van Educatie: De Bijdrage aan Menselijk Floreren in een Diverse Samenleving*, Utrecht: Universiteit voor Humanistiek, 2019.

De Ruyter, Doret J. 'Ideals, Education, and Happy Flourishing', *Educational Theory* 57, no. 1 (2007): 23–35.

De Ruyter, Doret J. 'Pottering in the Garden? On Human Flourishing and Education', *British Journal of Educational Studies* 52, no. 4 (2004): 377–89.

De Waal, Frans. *Chimpanzee Politics: Power and Sex among Apes*, revised ed., Baltimore: Johns Hopkins University Press, 1998.

Dewey, John. *Democracy and Education*, New York: The Free Press, 1997.

Di Paolantonio, Mario. 'Wonder, Guarding against Thoughtlessness in Education', *Studies in Philosophy and Education* 38 (2019): 213–28.

Drerup, Johannes. 'A Theory of Moral Education', *Educational Theory* 68, no. 4–5 (2018): 577–83.

Dreyfus, Hubert L. *Being-in-the-World: A Commentary on Heidegger's Being and Time, Division I*, Cambridge, MA and London: The MIT Press, 1991.

Duckworth, Eleanor. *'The Having of Wonderful Ideas' and Other Essays on Teaching and Learning*, 2nd ed. New York: Teachers College Press, 1996.

Egan, Kieran. *The Educated Mind: How Cognitive Tools Shape Our Understanding*, Chicago and London: The University of Chicago Press, 1997.

Egan, Kieran. *Imagination in Teaching and Learning – Ages 8 to 15*, London: Routledge, 2001.

Egan, Kieran. *Romantic Understanding: The Development of Rationality and Imagination, Ages 8–15*, New York and London: Routledge, 1990.

Egan, Kieran. 'Wonder, Awe, and Teaching Techniques'. In *Wonder-full Education: The Centrality of Wonder in Teaching and Learning across the Curriculum*, edited by Kieran Egan, Annabella Cant and Gillian Judson, 149–61. New York: Routledge, 2014.

Egan, Kieran and Gillian Judson. *Imagination and the Engaged Learner: Cognitive Tools for the Classroom*, New York: Teachers' College Press, 2016.

Egan, Kieran, Annabella Cant, and Gillian Judson, eds. *Wonder-full Education: The Centrality of Wonder in Teaching and Learning across the Curriculum*, New York: Routledge, 2014.

European Parliament. *Lisbon European Council 23 and 24 March 2000. Presidency Conclusions.* http://www.europarl.europa.eu/summits/lis1_en.htm

Evans, Howell M. 'Medicine, the Body and an Invitation to Wonder', *Medical Humanities* 42, no. 2 (2016): 97–102.

Evans, Howell M. 'Wonder and the Clinical Encounter', *Theoretical Medicine and Bioethics* 33 (2012): 123–36.

Evans, Howell M. 'Wonder and the Patient', *Journal of Medical Humanities* 36 (2015): 47–58.

Fann, K. T. *Wittgenstein's Conception of Philosophy*, Oxford: Basil Blackwell, 1969.

Fisher, Philip. *Wonder, the Rainbow, and the Aesthetics of Rare Experiences*, Cambridge and London: Harvard University Press, 1998.

Frijda, Nico. *The Emotions*, Cambridge and New York: Cambridge University Press/ Paris: Édition de la Maison des Sciences de l'Homme, 1986.

Fuller, Robert C. *Wonder: From Emotion to Spirituality*, Chapel Hill: The University of North Carolina Press, 2006.

Gaita, Raimond. *Good and Evil: An Absolute Conception*, 2nd ed., Abingdon: Routledge, 2006.

Gaston, Sean. *The Concept of World from Kant to Derrida*, New York: Rowman and Littlefield, 2013.

Gert, Bernard and Joshua Gert. 'The Definition of Morality'. In *The Stanford Encyclopedia of Philosophy* (Spring 2016 edition), edited by E. N. Zalta, 2016. http://plato.stanford.edu/archives/spr2016/entries/morality-definition

Gess, Nicola and Mireille Schnyder, 'Staunen als Grenzphänomen. Eine Einführung'. In *Staunen als Grenzphänomen*, edited by Nicola Gess, Mireille Schnyder, Hugues Marchal, and Johannes Bartuschat, 7–15. Paderborn: Wilhelm Fink, 2017.

Gilbert, Andrew. 'Using the Notion of "Wonder" to Develop Positive Conceptions of Science with Future Primary Teachers', *Science Education International* 24, no. 1 (2013): 6–32.

Gilbert, Andrew and Christie C. Byers, 'Wonder as a Tool to Engage Preservice Elementary Teachers in Science Learning and Teaching', *Science Teacher Education* (2017): 1–22. https://onlinelibrary.wiley.com/doi/pdf/10.1002/sce.21300

Gillies, Donald. 'Learning to Make Money: 21st Century EU Education Policy', *On Education. Journal for Research and Debate* 2, no. 6 (2019). https://doi.org/10.17899/on_ed.2019.6.1

Gilroy, Peter. 'The Aims of Education and the Philosophy of Education'. In *The Aims of Education*, edited by Roger Marples, 23–34. London and New York: Routledge, 1999.

Goodman, Paul. *Growing up Absurd: Problems of Youth in the Organized Society*, New York: New York Review Books, 2012.

Goodwin, Alan. 'Wonder in Science Teaching and Learning: An Update', *School Science Review* 83, no. 302 (2001): 69–73.

Gottlieb, Jacqueline, Pierre-Yves Oudeyer, Manuel Lopes, and Adrien Baranes. 'Information-seeking, Curiosity, and Attention: Computational and Neural Mechanisms', *Trends in Cognitive Sciences* 17, no. 11 (2013): 585–93.

Götz, Margarete. *Die Grundschule in der Zeit des Nationalsozialismus: Eine Untersuchung der inneren Ausgestaltung der vier unteren Jahrgänge der Volksschule auf der Grundlage amtlicher Maßnahmen*. Bad Heilbrunn: Verlag Julius Klinkhardt, 1997.

Green, Thomas. *The Activities of Teaching*, New York: McGraw-Hill Book Company, 1971.

Greene, Maxine. *Landscapes of Learning*, New York: Teachers College Press, 1978.

Hadzigeorgiou, Yannis. 'Fostering a Sense of Wonder in the Science Classroom', *Research in Science Education* 42 (2012): 985–1005.

Hadzigeorgiou, Yannis. 'Reclaiming the Value of Wonder in Science Education'. In *Wonder-full Education: The Centrality of Wonder in Teaching and Learning across the Curriculum*, edited by Kieran Egan, Annabella Cant, and Gillian Judson, 40–65. New York: Routledge, 2014.

Hadzigeorgiou, Yannis. 'Wonder, Its Nature and Its Role in the Learning Process'. In *Wonder, Education, and Human Flourishing*, edited by Anders Schinkel. Amsterdam: VU University Press, 2020.

Haji, Ishtiyaque and Stefaan Cuypers, 'Ultimate Educational Aims, Overridingness, and Personal Well-being', *Studies in Philosophy and Education* 30, no. 6 (2011): 543–56.

Hand, Michael. 'Against Autonomy as an Educational Aim', *Oxford Review of Education* 32, no. 4 (2006): 535–50.

Hand, Michael. *A Theory of Moral Education*, Abingdon: Routledge, 2018.

Hand, Michael. 'Wonder and Moral Education: A Reply to Anders Schinkel', paper presented at the conference Wonder, Education, and Human Flourishing, Amsterdam, the Netherlands, 5–6 April 2019.

Hansen, Finn Thorbjørn. 'The Call and Practices of Wonder: How to Evoke a Socratic Community of Wonder in Professional Settings'. In *The Socratic Handbook: Dialogue Methods for Philosophical Practice*, edited by Michael Noah Weiss, 217–44. Münster: LIT Verlag, 2015.

Hawks, Ellison. *The Earth Shown to the Children*, London and Edinburgh: T.C. & E.C. Jack, 1914.

Heidegger, Martin. *The Basic Problems of Phenomenology*, translated by Albert Hofstadter. Oxford: Blackwell, 1988.

Heidegger, Martin. 'Letter on Humanism'. In *Martin Heidegger: Basic Writings; Revised and Expanded Edition*, edited by David Farrell Krell, translated by Frank A. Capuzzi and J. Glenn Gray, 217–65. London: Routledge, 1993.

Heidegger, Martin. *Sein und Zeit*, Tübingen: Max Niemeyer Verlag, 1984.

Hepburn, Ronald W. 'The Inaugural Address: Wonder', *The Aristotelian Society, Supplementary Volume* LIV (1980): 1–23.

Heske, Franz. *German Forestry*, New Haven: Yale University Press, 1938.

Hodgson, Naomi, Joris Vlieghe, and Piotr Zamojski. 'Education and the Love for the World: Articulating a Post-critical Educational Philosophy', *Foro de Educación* 16, no. 24 (2018): 7–20.

Hoffman, Martin L. *Empathy and Moral Development*, Cambridge: Cambridge University Press, 2000.

Honneth, Axel. *The Struggle for Recognition: The Moral Grammar of Social Conflicts*, Cambridge MA: The MIT Press, 1992.

Horowitz, Alexandra. *On Looking: Eleven Walks with Expert Eyes*, New York: Scribner, 2013.

Hove, Philo. 'The Face of Wonder', *Journal of Curriculum Studies* 28, no. 4 (1996): 437–62.

Hurka, Thomas. *Perfectionism*, Oxford: Oxford University Press, 1993.

Irigaray, Luce. *An Ethics of Sexual Difference*, translated by Carolyn Burke and Gillian C. Gill. Ithaca: Cornell University Press, 1993.

Iser, Mattias. 'Recognition', *The Stanford Encyclopedia of Philosophy* (Summer 2019 edition), edited by Edward N. Zalta. https://plato.stanford.edu/archives/sum2019/entries/recognition/.

James, William. *Some Problems of Philosophy: A Beginning of an Introduction to Philosophy*, New York: Longmans, Green, and Co., 1916.

James, William. *The Varieties of Religious Experience: A Study in Human Nature*, New York, London, and Bombay: Longmans, Green, and Co., 1902.

Jirout, Jamie and David Klahr. 'Children's Scientific Curiosity: In Search of an Operational Definition of an Elusive Concept', *Developmental Review* 32, no. 2 (2012): 125–60.

Judson, Gillian. *Engaging Imagination in Ecological Education: Practical Strategies for Teaching*, Vancouver: Pacific Educational Press, 2015.

Judson, Gillian. *Imaginative Ecological Education*, PhD diss., Simon Fraser University, 2008.

Judson, Gillian. *A Walking Curriculum: Walking, Wonder, & Sense of Place (K-12)*, n.p.: 2018.

Kant, Immanuel. *Critique of the Power of Judgment*, edited by Paul Guyer, translated by Paul Guyer and Eric Matthews. Cambridge: Cambridge University Press, 2000.

Kashdan, Todd B. and Paul J. Silvia. 'Curiosity and Interest: The Benefits of Thriving on Novelty and Challenge'. In *The Oxford Handbook of Positive Psychology*, 2nd ed., edited by Shane J. Lopez and C. R. Snyder, 367–75. Oxford: Oxford University Press: 2009.

Keltner, Dacher and Jonathan Haidt. 'Approaching Awe, a Moral, Spiritual, and Aesthetic Emotion', *Cognition and Emotion* 17, no. 2 (2003): 297–314.

Kingsnorth, Paul. *Confessions of a Recovering Environmentalist*, London: Faber & Faber, 2017.

Kohn, Alfie. *The Case against Standardized Testing: Raising the Scores, Ruining the Schools*, Portsmouth, NH: Heinemann, 2000.

Kolbert, Elizabeth. *The Sixth Extinction: An Unnatural History*, London: Bloomsbury, 2015.

Kopnina, Helen, Michael Sitka-Sage, Sean Blenkinsop, and Laura Piersol. 'Moving beyond Innocence: Educating Children in a Post-Nature World'. In *Research Handbook on Childhoodnature*, edited by Amy Cutter-Mackenzie, Karen Malone, and Elisabeth Barratt Hacking. Cham: Springer, 2018. https://doi.org/10.1007/978-3-319-51949-4_40-1

Kreitler, Schulamith, Edward Ziegler, and Hans Kreitler. 'The Nature of Curiosity in Children', *Journal of School Psychology* 13, no. 3 (1975): 185–200.

Kristjánsson, Kristján. 'Awe: An Aristotelian Analysis of a Non-Aristotelian Virtuous Emotion', *Philosophia* 45 (2017): 125–42.

Kristjánsson, Kristján. 'Epiphanic Moral Conversions: Going beyond Kohlberg and Aristotle'. In *Self-Transcendence and Virtue: Perspectives from Philosophy, Psychology, and Theology*, edited by Jennifer A. Frey and Candace Vogler, 15–38. London: Routledge, 2019.

Kristjánsson, Kristján. *Flourishing as the Aim of Education: A Neo-Aristotelian View*, London and New York: Routledge, 2020.

La Caze, Marguerite. 'The Encounter between Wonder and Generosity', *Hypatia* 17, no. 3 (2002): 1–19.

Lamont, Peter. 'A Particular Kind of Wonder: The Experience of Magic Past and Present', *Review of General Psychology* 21, no. 1 (2017): 1–8.

Lee, Robert G. and Sabine Wilke. 'Forest as *Volk: Ewiger Wald* and the Religion of Nature in the Third Reich', *Journal of Social and Ecological Boundaries* 1, no. 1 (2005): 21–46.

Le Fanu, James. *Why Us? How Science Rediscovered the Mystery of Ourselves*, London: Harper Press, 2010.

Leopold, Aldo. *A Sand County Almanac*, New York: Ballantine, 1966.

Levinson, Natasha. 'The Paradox of Natality: Teaching in the midst of Belatedness'. In *Hannah Arendt and Education: Renewing Our Common World*, edited by Mordechai Gordon, 11–36. Boulder, CO and Oxford: Westview Press, 2001.

Llewelyn, John. 'On the Saying that Philosophy Begins in *Thaumazein*'. In *Post-Structuralist Classics*, edited by Andrew Benjamin, 173–91. London: Routledge, 1988.

Lipman, Matthew. 'Philosophy for Children'. In *Developing Minds: Programs for Teaching Thinking*, Vol. 2, edited by Arthur L. Costa, 35–8. Alexandria: Association for Supervision and Curricular Development, 1981.

Lipman, Matthew. *Thinking in Education*, Cambridge and New York: Cambridge University Press, 2003.

Lipman, Matthew, Ann Margaret Sharp, and Frederick S. Oscanyon. *Philosophy in the Classroom*, Philadelphia: Temple University Press, 1980.

Litman, Jordan A. 'Curiosity and the Pleasures of Learning: Wanting and Liking New Information', *Cognition and Emotion* 19, no. 6 (2005): 793–814.

Lloyd, Genevieve. *Reclaiming Wonder: After the Sublime*, Edinburgh: Edinburgh University Press, 2018.

Lloyd, Genevieve. 'Wonder and Education: Some Lessons from Spinoza'. In *Wonder, Education, and Human Flourishing*, edited by Anders Schinkel. Amsterdam: VU University Press, 2020.

Loewenstein, George. 'The Psychology of Curiosity: A Review and Reinterpretation', *Psychological Bulletin* 116, no. 1 (1994): 75–98.

Low, Douglas. 'Merleau-Ponty's Criticism of Heidegger', *Philosophy Today* 53 (Fall 2009): 273–93.

Macfarlane, Robert. *Landmarks*, London: Penguin Books, 2016.

Macfarlane, Robert. *Mountains of the Mind: A History of a Fascination*, London: Granta Books, 2008.

Malpas, Jeff. 'Beginning in Wonder', n.d. https://www.academia.edu/3982911/Beginning_in_Wonder

Marcel, Gabriel. *Being and Having*, translated by Katherine Farrer. Boston: Beacon Press, 1951.

Masschelein, Jan and Maarten Simons. *In Defence of the School*, Leuven: E-ducation, Culture & Society Publishers, 2013.

Matthews, Gareth B. 'Philosophy and Children's Literature'. In *Philosophy for Children*, Special Issue of *Metaphilosophy*, edited by Terrell Ward Bynum and Matthew Lipman, 7–16. Oxford: Basil Blackwell, 1976.

Matthews, Gareth B. *Philosophy & the Young Child*, Cambridge, MA and London: Harvard University Press, 1980.

Martens, Ekkehard. *Vom Staunen oder Die Rückkehr der Neugier*, Leipzig: Reclam, 2003.

Merleau-Ponty, Maurice. *The Primacy of Perception and Other Essays on Phenomenological Psychology, the Philosophy of Art, History and Politics*, edited and introduced by James M. Edie. N.p.: Northwestern University Press, 1964.

Merleau-Ponty, Maurice. *The Visible and the Invisible*, edited by Claude Lefort, translated by Alphonso Lingis. Evanston: Northwestern University Press, 1968.

Merry, Michael. 'Can Schools Teach Citizenship?' *Discourse: Studies in the Cultural Politics of Education* (2018). https://doi.org/10.1080/01596306.2018.1488242

Miller, Ron. 'Beyond Reductionism: The Emerging Holistic Paradigm in Education', *The Humanistic Psychologist* 28, nos. 1–3 (2000): 382–93.

Miyazaki, Kiyotaka. 'From "Unknown Questions" Begins a Wonderful Education: Kyozai-Kaishaku and the Dialogic Classroom'. In *Wonder-full Education: The Centrality of Wonder in Teaching and Learning across the Curriculum*, edited by Kieran Egan, Annabella Cant and Gillian Judson, 110–21. New York: Routledge, 2014.

Moore, Kathleen D. 'The Truth of the Barnacles: Rachel Carson and the Moral Significance of Wonder', *Environmental Ethics* 27, no. 3 (2005): 265–77.

Mouffe, Chantal. *On the Political*, London and New York: Routledge, 2005.

Mounce, H. O. *Wittgenstein's Tractatus: An Introduction*, Oxford: Basil Blackwell, 1981.

Muir, John. *The Story of My Boyhood and Youth*, Boston: Houghton Mifflin, 1913.

Murdoch, Iris. *The Sovereignty of Good*, London: Routledge & Kegan Paul, 1980.

Nagel, Thomas. 'What Is It Like to Be a Bat?' In Thomas Nagel, *Mortal Questions*, 165–80. Cambridge: Cambridge University Press, 1979.

Newman, Michael Z. 'New Media, Young Audiences and Discourses of Attention: From *Sesame Street* to "Snack Culture"', *Media, Culture & Society* 32, no. 4 (2010): 581–96.

Nicolson, Marjorie H. *Mountain Gloom and Mountain Glory: The Development of the Aesthetics of the Infinite*, Ithaca: Cornell University Press, 1959.

Noddings, Nel. *Educating Moral People*, New York: Teachers College Press, 2002.

Nussbaum, Martha C. 'Animal Rights: The Need for a Theoretical Basis', *Harvard Law Review* 114, no. 5 (2001): 1506–49.

Nussbaum, Martha C. *Upheavals of Thought: The Intelligence of Emotions*, Cambridge: Cambridge University Press, 2001.

Oatley, Keith, Dacher Keltner, and Jennifer M. Jenkins. *Understanding Emotions*, 2nd ed., Malden: Blackwell Publishing, 2006.

Opdal, Paul M. 'Curiosity, Wonder and Education Seen as Perspective Development', *Studies in Philosophy and Education* 20 (2001): 331–44.

Orr, David W. *Earth in Mind: On Education, the Environment, and the Human Prospect*, Washington/Covelo/London: Island Press, 2004.

Parsons, Howard. 'A Philosophy of Wonder', *Philosophy and Phenomenological Research* 30, no. 1 (1969): 84–101.

Pedersen, Jan B. W. *Balanced Wonder: Experiential Sources of Imagination, Virtues and Human Flourishing*, Lanham: Lexington Books, 2019.

Peters, Richard S. 'Democratic Values and Educational Aims'. In *Essays on Educators*, edited by Richard S. Peters, 32–50. London: George Allen & Unwin, 1981.

Peters, Richard S. *Ethics & Education*, London: George Allen and Unwin Ltd., 1970.

Peters, Richard S. 'Farewell to Aims?' *The London Educational Review* 2 (1973): 1–4.

Peters, Richard S. 'The Justification of Education'. In *Education and the Education of Teachers*, edited by Richard S. Peters, 86–118. London: Routledge & Kegan Paul, 1977.

Peters, Richard S. 'Philosophy of Education'. In *Educational Theory and Its Foundation Disciplines*, edited by Paul H. Hirst, 30–61. London: Routledge & Kegan Paul, 1983.

Pieper, Josef. *Leisure: The Basis of Culture*, New York: Mentor Omega/Random House, 1963.

Piersol, Laura. "Our Hearts Leap Up: Awakening Wonder within the Classroom". In *Wonder-full Education: The Centrality of Wonder in Teaching and Learning across the Curriculum*, edited by Kieran Egan, Annabella Cant, and Gillian Judson, 3–21. New York: Routledge, 2014.

Pois, Robert A. *National Socialism and the Religion of Nature*, New York: St Martin's Press, 1986.

Pritchard, Michael. 'Philosophy for Children'. In *The Stanford Encyclopedia of Philosophy* (Winter 2018 edition), edited by Edward N. Zalta. https://plato.stanford.edu/entries/children/

Proffitt, Anabel. 'The Importance of Wonder in Educational Ministry', *Religious Education* 93, no. 1 (1998): 10213

Pulkki, Jani, Bo Dahlin, and Veli-Matti Värri. 'Environmental Education as a Lived-Body Practice? A Contemplative Pedagogy Perspective', *Journal of Philosophy of Education* 51, no. 1 (2017): 214–29.

Quinn, Dennis. *Iris Exiled: A Synoptic History of Wonder*, Lanham: University Press of America, 2002.

Radkau, Joachim and Frank Uekötter, eds. *Naturschutz und Nationalsozialismus*, Frankfurt: Campus Verlag, 2003.

Reiss, Michael and John White. *An Aims-Based Curriculum: The Significance of Human Flourishing for Schools*, London: Institute of Education Press, 2013.

Rodger, Alex. 'The Spiritual in Values Education', *Journal of Moral Education* 29, no. 4 (2000): 463–75.

Rorty, Amelie. 'Educating the Practical Imagination: A Prolegomenon'. In *The Oxford Handbook of Philosophy of Education*, edited by Harvey Siegel. Oxford: Oxford University Press, 2018. DOI: 10.1093/oxfordhb/9780195312881.003.0012

Rubenstein, Mary-Jane. 'Heidegger's Caves: On Dwelling in Wonder'. In *Practices of Wonder: Cross-Disciplinary Perspectives*, edited by Sophia Vasalou, 144–65. Cambridge: James Clarke & Co., 2015.

Rubenstein, Mary-Jane. *Strange Wonder: The Closure of Metaphysics and the Opening of Awe*, New York: Columbia University Press, 2011.

Rudwick, Martin J. S. *The Meaning of Fossils: Episodes in the History of Paleontology*, Chicago and London: The University of Chicago Press, 1985.

Sagberg, Sturla. 'Wonder and the Question of Truth in Religious Education', *Sewanee Theological Review* 48, no. 4 (2005): 409–35.

Schinkel, Anders. *Conscience and Conscientious Objections*, Amsterdam: Pallas Publications, 2007.

Schinkel, Anders. 'Education and Ultimate Meaning', *Oxford Review of Education* 41, no. 6 (2015): 711–29.

Schinkel, Anders. 'Education as Mediation between Child and World', *Studies in Philosophy and Education* (online first, October 2019). https://doi.org/10.1007/s11217-019-09687-8

Schinkel, Anders. 'The Educational Importance of Deep Wonder', *Journal of Philosophy of Education* 51, no. 2 (2017): 538–53.

Schinkel, Anders. 'On the Justification of Compulsory Schooling'. In *Philosophical Perspectives on Compulsory Education*, edited by Marianna Papastephanou, 75–91. Dordrecht: Springer, 2014.

Schinkel, Anders. 'Wonder and Moral Education', *Educational Theory* 68, no. 1 (2018): 31–48.

Schinkel, Anders. 'Wonder as a Morally Formative Experience', unpublished manuscript.

Schinkel, Anders. 'Wonder, Mystery, and Meaning', *Philosophical Papers* (online first, November 2018): 1–28. https://doi.org/10.1080/05568641.2018.1462667

Schinkel, Willem. *Imagined Societies: A Critique of Immigrant Integration in Western Europe*, Cambridge: Cambridge University Press, 2017.

Schmitt, Frederick F. and Reza Lahroodi. 'The Epistemic Value of Curiosity', *Educational Theory* 58, no. 2 (2008): 125–48.

Schweitzer, Albert. *Die Ehrfurcht vor dem Leben: Grundtexte aus fünf Jahrzehnten*, München: Verlag C. H. Beck, 2003.

Shepherd, Nan. *The Living Mountain*, Introduction by Robert Macfarlane, Afterword by Jeannette Winterson. N.p.: Canongate, 2019.

Shiota, Michelle N., Dacher Keltner, and Amanda Mossman. 'The Nature of Awe: Elicitors, Appraisals, and Effects on Self-Concept'. *Cognition and Emotion* 21, no. 5 (2007): 944–63.

Sinclair, Nathalie, and Anne Watson. 'Wonder, the Rainbow and the Aesthetics of Rare Experiences', *For the Learning of Mathematics* 21, no. 3 (2001): 39–42.

Smith, David Woodruff. 'Phenomenology'. In *The Stanford Encyclopedia of Philosophy*, edited by Edward N. Zalta, 2018. https://plato.stanford.edu/archives/sum2018/entries/phenomenology

Sprigge, Timothy. 'Final Causes', *Proceedings of the Aristotelian Society*, Suppl. Vol. 45 (1971): 149–70.

Sprigge, Timothy. *The Importance of Subjectivity: Selected Essays in Metaphysics and Ethics*, edited by Leemon B. McHenry. Oxford: Oxford University Press, 2011.

Srisuknimit, Veerasak. 'Oral Bacteria May Be Responsible for Alzheimer's Disease', *Science in the News* blog, 7 February 2019. http://sitn.hms.harvard.edu/flash/2019/oral-bacteria-may-responsible-alzheimers-disease/

Stannard, Russell. *Science and Wonders: Conversations about Science and Belief*, London and Boston: Faber Books, 1996.

Takaya, Keiichi. 'Renewing the Sense of Wonder in the Minds of High School and College Students'. In *Wonder-full Education: The Centrality of Wonder in Teaching and Learning across the Curriculum*, edited by Kieran Egan, Annabella Cant and Gillian Judson, 97–109. New York: Routledge, 2014.

Taylor, William. 'Values and Accountability'. In *Accountability in Education*, edited by Tony Becher and Stuart Maclure, 26–60. Windsor: NFER-Nelson, 1978.

Thomas, Keith. *Man and the Natural World: Changing Attitudes in England, 1500–1800*, Harmondsworth: Penguin Books, 1987.

Tobia, Kevin P. 'Wonder and Value', *Res Philosophica* 92, no. 4 (2015): 959–84.

Tokarczuk, Olga. 'The Tender Narrator', Nobel Lecture by the Nobel Laureate in Literature 2018, n.p.: Svenska Akademien/The Nobel Foundation, 2019.

Trotman, Dave. 'Wow! What If? So What?: Education and the Imagination of Wonder: Fascination, Possibilities and Opportunities Missed'. In *Wonder-full Education: The Centrality of Wonder in Teaching and Learning across the Curriculum*, edited by Kieran Egan, Annabella Cant, and Gillian Judson, 22–39. New York: Routledge, 2014.

Ullman, Walter. *Medieval Political Thought*, Harmondsworth: Penguin Books, 1975.

Van Cleve Morris. *Existentialism in Education*, New York, Evanston, and London: Harper & Row, Publishers, 1966.

Van de Goor, Jacky, Anneke M. Sools, Gerben J. Westerhof, and Ernst Bohlmeijer, 'Wonderful Life: Exploring Wonder in Meaningful Moments', *Journal of Humanistic Psychology* (2017). https://doi.org/10.1177%2F0022167817696837

Van Manen, Max. 'But Is It Phenomenology?' *Qualitative Health Research* 27, no. 6 (2017): 775–9.

Van Manen, Max. *Pedagogical Tact: Knowing What to Do when You Don't Know What to Do*, New York: Routledge, 2016.

Van Manen, Max. 'Phenomenology in Its Original Sense', *Qualitative Health Research* 27, no. 6 (2017): 810–25.

Van Manen, Max. 'Phenomenology of Practice', *Phenomenology & Practice* 1, no. 1 (2007): 11–30.

Van Perlo, Sander, Lynne Wolbert, and Anders Schinkel, 'Het Belang van Pedagogische Tact voor het (H)erkennen van Verwondering bij Leerlingen', forthcoming in *Pedagogiek*.

Vasalou, Sophia. *Wonder: A Grammar*, Albany: State University of New York Press, 2015.

Verhoeven, Cornelis. *Inleiding tot de Verwondering*, Bilthoven: Amboboeken, 1971.

Vlieghe, Joris and Piotr Zamojski. *Towards an Ontology of Teaching: Thing-centered Pedagogy, Affirmation, and Love for the World*, Cham: Springer, 2019.

Vogt, Fritz. *Heimatkunde in der Grundschule. Nach den Hand des Lehrers*. Berlin: Osterwieck, 1938.

Wallace-Wells, David. *The Uninhabitable Earth: A Story of the Future*, n.p.: Penguin Books, 2019.

Walzer, Michael. 'Passion and Politics', *Philosophy & Social Criticism* 28, no. 6 (2002): 617–33.

Warnock, Mary. *Imagination*, London and Boston: Faber and Faber, 1976.

Washington, Haydn. 'Education for Wonder', *Education Sciences* 8, no. 3, art. no. 125 (2018). https://doi.org/10.3390/educsci8030125

Washington, Haydn. *A Sense of Wonder towards Nature: Healing the World through Belonging*, London: Routledge, 2018.

Weil, Simone. *Simone Weil: An Anthology*, edited and introduced by Siân Miles. London: Virago Press Limited, 1986.

Wheeler, Michael. 'Martin Heidegger'. In *The Stanford Encyclopedia of Philosophy* (Winter 2018 edition), edited by Edward N. Zalta. https://plato.stanford.edu/archives/win2018/entries/heidegger

White, Alan R. *The Language of Imagination*, Oxford: Blackwell, 1990.

White, John. 'Education and a Meaningful Life', *Oxford Review of Education* 35, no. 4 (2009): 423–35.
White, John. 'What Schools Are for and Why', *Impact* 14 (2007): 1–51.
Whitehead, Alfred North. *Adventures of Ideas*, Cambridge: Cambridge University Press, 1964.
Whitehead, Alfred North. 'The Aims of Education'. In *The Aims of Education and Other Essays*, 1–23. London: Ernest Benn Limited, 1962.
Whitehead, Alfred North. *Modes of Thought*, New York: The Free Press, 1968.
Whitehead, Alfred North. *Process and Reality: An Essay in Cosmology*, New York: The Free Press, 1985.
Whitehead, Alfred North. 'The Rhythmic Claims of Freedom and Discipline'. In *The Aims of Education and Other Essays*, 45–65. London: Ernest Benn Limited, 1962.
Whitehead, Alfred North. *Science and the Modern World*, New York: The Free Press, 1967.
Whitehead, Margaret. 'Meaningful Existence, Embodiment, and Physical Education', *Journal of Philosophy of Education* 24, no. 1 (1990): 1–13.
Willmot, Glenn. *Reading for Wonder: Ecology, Ethics, Enchantment*, Chaim: Palgrave Macmillan, 2018.
Wittgenstein, Ludwig. *Culture and Value* (revised 2nd ed.), edited by G. H. von Wright, translated by Peter Winch. Oxford: Blackwell, 1998.
Wittgenstein, Ludwig. 'A Lecture on Ethics', *Philosophical Review* 74, no. 1 (1965): 3–12.
Wittgenstein, Ludwig. *Philosophical Investigations*, translated by G. E. M. Anscombe. Oxford: Basil Blackwell, 1982.
Wittgenstein, Ludwig. *Philosophische Untersuchungen*. In Ludwig Wittgenstein, *Tractatus logico-philosophicus (Werkausgabe Band 1)*, 225–485. Frankfurt am Main: Suhrkamp, 1993.
Wittgenstein, Ludwig. *Tractatus Logico-Philosophicus*, translated by D. F. Pears and B. F. McGuiness. London: Routledge & Kegan Paul, 1974.
Wittgenstein, Ludwig. *Tractatus Logico-Philosophicus (Werkausgabe, Band 1)*, Frankfurt am Main: Suhrkamp, 1993.
Wittgenstein, Ludwig. *Wittgenstein's Nachlass: The Bergen Electronic Edition. Text and Facsimile Version*, Oxford: Oxford University Press, 2000.
Wolbert, Lynne. 'Flourishing, Fragility and Family Life: Critical Reflections on Human Flourishing as an Aim of Education'. PhD diss., Vrije Universiteit Amsterdam, 2018.
Wolbert, Lynne. 'What Should Schools Do to Promote Wonder?' forthcoming in *Oxford Review of Education*.
Wolin, Sheldon. *Politics and Vision: Continuity and Innovation in Western Political Thought*, expanded ed., Princeton and Oxford: Princeton University Press, 2004.
Wolters, Diena. 'Op het Kippenbedrijf Werd Ik Vegetariër', *Trouw*, 21 June 2019.
Worrall, Simon. 'How 40,000 Tons of Cosmic Dust Falling to the Earth Affects You and Me', *National Geographic*, 28 January 2015. https://www.nationalgeographic.com/news/2015/01/150128-big-bang-universe-supernova-astrophysics-health-space-ngbooktalk/

Young, Iris Marion. 'Asymmetrical Reciprocity: On Moral Respect, Wonder, and Enlarged Thought'. In *Intersecting Voices: Dilemmas of Gender, Political Philosophy, and Policy*, 38–59. Princeton: Princeton University Press, 1997.

Zazkis, Dov, and Rina Zazkis. 'Wondering about Wonder in Mathematics'. In *Wonder-full Education: The Centrality of Wonder in Teaching and Learning across the Curriculum*, edited by Kieran Egan, Annabella Cant, and Gillian Judson, 66–85. New York: Routledge, 2014.

Websites

https://en.wikipedia.org/wiki/Programme_for_International_Student_Assessment
https://en.wikipedia.org/wiki/Teaching_to_the_test
https://ierg.ca/about-us/what-is-imaginative-education/

Index

Lightning Source UK Ltd.
Milton Keynes UK
UKHW022325190223
417299UK00005B/96